MOVING MOUNTAINS

Marie H. Roesgaard

MOVING MOUNTAINS

Japanese Education Reform

Acta Jutlandica LXXIII:1
Humanities Series 71

AARHUS UNIVERSITY PRESS

Copyright: Aarhus University Press, 1998
Printed in England by the Alden Press
ISBN 87 7288 477 0
ISSN 0065 1354 (Acta Jutlandica)
ISSN 0901 0556 (Humanities Series)

AARHUS UNIVERSITY PRESS
Building 170
University of Aarhus
DK-8000 Aarhus C, Denmark
Fax + 45 86 19 84 33

73 Lime Walk,
Headington, Oxford OX3 7AD
Fax (+44) 1865 750 079

Box 511,
Oakville, Conn. 06779
Fax (+ 1) 860 945 9468

ANSI/NISO
Z39.48-1992

Preface

In the time I have spent working on this book, originally a PhD thesis submitted in 1994, I have become indebted to many individuals who have patiently helped and encouraged me in my work. Above all, I want to thank my two academic supervisors, Professor Kirsten Refsing, Hong Kong University, and Dr Stig Thøgersen, University of Aarhus, for their encouragement and insightful criticisms. Dr Roger Goodman of the Nissan Institute in Oxford also provided valuable suggestions and criticisms through his service as examiner of the thesis.

Thanks is also due to the considerable number of people in Japan who have provided information and suggestions pertaining to the thesis. In particular, I should like to thank Professor Amano Ikuo and Professor Fujita Hidenori of the Faculty of Education, Tokyo University, as well as Professor Horio Teruhisa who, at the time, was also at the Faculty of Education, University of Tokyo. Without their kind assistance and encouragement this work would not have been possible.

For the empirical material, I am indebted to all of those who have generously given their time for interviews, as well as the staff and students of the graduate school, Faculty of Education, Tokyo University, who were always ready to suggest material and be of practical assistance.

I would like to acknowledge the financial assistance received from the Danish Research Academy which permitted me to conduct research in Japan and to thank the University of Aarhus and the East Asian Institute in particular for their help and understanding.

Finally, my colleagues at the no-longer existing Centre for East and South East Asia, at the Department of Asian Studies, deserve thanks for their patience and useful suggestions.

Aarhus, April 1998   *Marie H. Roesgaard*

CONTENTS

LIST OF CHARTS

ABBREVIATIONS

ATU   All Japan Teachers' Union, *Zen Nippon Kyooshokuin Kumiai Kyoogikai. (Zenkyoo).*

CCE   Central Council on Education, *Chuuoo Kyooiku Shingikai.*

FLE   Fundamental Law on Education, *Kyooiku Kihon Hoo.*

JCP   Japan Communist Party, *Nihon Kyoosantoo.*

JSP   Japan Socialist Party, *Nihon Shakaitoo.*

JTU   Japan Teachers' Union, *Nihon Kyooshokuin Kumiai. (Nikkyooso).*

LDP   Liberal Deomcratic Party, *Jiyuu Minshuutoo.*

NCER   National Council on Educational Reform, *Rinji Kyooiku Shingikai. (Rinkyooshin).*

NKG   Academic Society for Research on the Educational System, *Nihon Kyooiku Gakkai.*

WDCER   Women's Democratic Council on Educational Reform, *Josei Minkan Kyooiku Shingikai.*

CHAPTER 1

INTRODUCTION
AND THEORETICAL DELIBERATIONS

In any society, regardless of the stage of development, education is a factor of prime concern in the development process. Through education, new ideas, ideals and new knowledge can be transmitted. Rulers can legitimise their system, values can be reinforced and the future supply of a workforce can be ensured if demands are correctly foreseen.

Educational systems are not static, if they were they would hardly be able to meet the demands of our modern world. In any society educational reforms become necessary at different stages. New demands from industry, from the general public or from government shape requests for such reforms.

This is also the case in Japan. A country which for years has been admired — and perhaps feared? — for her spectacular success with industrialisation and modernisation. The Japanese workforce is said to be one of the most well-educated, most people having finished at least upper secondary education. However, Japanese schooling is also known as being strenuous. Much as the average results of Japanese schooling may be admired and envied, the system is also criticised for being too strict, for stealing students' youth, creativity and spontaneity. In recent years the Japanese themselves have increasingly become aware of this loss of creativity and spontaneity, especially in light of the enormous progress in technological development and its demands for new creative ways of thinking.

The idea that reforms should be contemplated is nothing new to the Japanese or their government. Councils on educational reform have abounded ever since the end of the second world war. Under the leadership of Nakasone Yasuhiro (1982-1987), educational reform, along with administrative reform, was made an issue of prime concern. In fact it was one of the main issues in the Nakasone election campaign. Prime Minister Nakasone proceeded to set up in 1984 the National Council on Educational Reform (NCER), asking it to advice him on 'basic strategies for necessary reforms with regard to governmental policies and measures in various aspects, so as to secure such education as will be compatible with the social changes and cultural developments of our country' (Rinkyooshin, 1988, 5).

This council was actually a follow-up to the work of the Central Council on Education (CCE) a permanent advisory council set up in 1952 to advise the

Ministry of Education. NCER continued the line of the CCE working on the implementation of both old and new ideas, primarily basing itself on signals from Prime Minister Nakasone and the Liberal Democratic Party (LDP). What was new about NCER was that it referred directly to the Prime Minister, not the Ministry of Education. This was hoped to give NCER's proposals more impact in relation to other ministries as well as in relation to the Ministry of Education.

NCER between 1984 and 1987 produced four reports analyzing the new educational demands but presented precious little advice for actual action. This was left entirely to the discretion of the government, and in the last resort, to the discretion of the Ministry of Education. Under Nakasone it would seem that the initiative for educational reform rested with the Prime Minister, and indeed Nakasone himself was considered an unusually strong Prime Minister. After the Nakasone era (1982-87) the initiative again came to rest mainly with the Ministry of Education.

One of the reasons for the perceived need for reform in the early 1980s in Japan was apprehension about the Japanese educational system's ability to supply the future manpower for further development. In Japan the level of education is high, illiteracy is said to be virtually non-existent so these new demands no longer concerned basic education. NCER's reports made it clear that desired educational and societal developments in Japan were 'educating more individually creative workers and researchers, an organised system for life-long learning, internationalisation and adaptation to the information society'. These were *ends* for which *means* were to be found primarily through educational reform.[1]

Another reason for the desire to reform the educational system was the dissatisfaction with the system felt by many conservatives. They saw it as having been designed singlehandedly by the Americans and, for that reason, felt it did not suit Japan because it ignored Japanese tradition. The emphasis placed on *rights* as against *duty*, to which it was felt the educational system was inclined, was particularly regretted by many.

On the need for individuality (*kosei*)[2] and creativity (*soozooryoku*)[3] the following remarks were made by NCER in its first report:

1. There are striking similarities with the reform issues discussed by the British conservatives under Margaret Thatcher. See for example Tomlinson 'The Schools' in Kavanagh and Seldon, 1989, *The Thatcher Effect*, Clarendon, Oxford.
2. Kosei was officially translated as 'individuality' but it also means 'individual characteristics'.
3. The official translation of *soozooryoku* was 'creativity' but it is more precisely translated as 'power of imagination'.

One of the most important changes to be made in our educational system is the rejection of standardisation, inflexibility, closedness and ethnocentrism and a new emphasis on respect for the individual and his freedom, autonomy and responsibility, in other words, respect for individuality (*kosei juushi*). The term 'individuality' concerns not only that of the individual but also the individuality of the family, the school, the community, the country etc. These individualities are all linked. (Rinkyooshin, 1988, 12)

Creativity and individuality were seen as prerequisites for Japanese international scientific contribution, but as the report also stated: '... Japan's education so far has tended to be characterised by "cramming" with an emphasis on memorisation' (Rinkyooshin, 1988, 14).

This made it necessary to further emphasise the ability to make use of the acquired information. Hence, emphasis should be placed on 'cultivating, while building on fundamentals, creativity and thinking power — including the ability to think logically, to form abstractions and to be creative — as well as the ability to express oneself' (Rinkyooshin, 1988, 14). Individuality and creativity were key words repeated over and over again by the NCER.

Studying educational reform efforts in Japan means taking into consideration a host of conditions and problems peculiar to this country. But the idea of reform is certainly not alien to other countries. All modernised societies are working on how to adapt their educational systems to the demands of the twenty-first century, and most societies know the problem of how to make schooling an integral part of life rather than making it something that is over and done with at an early stage in life. Life-long learning becomes a more and more important issue now that most modern societies are experiencing the ageing of society and they will soon have difficulties meeting the demands for highly qualified manpower if the situation is not dealt with.

The efforts directed at enhancing life-long learning (*shoogaigakushuu*) were mainly prompted by the above mentioned demographic trend — the fact that Japanese society was ageing — and also by UNESCO efforts in the area. The 1985 UNESCO meeting in Paris concerning adult education no doubt stimulated further the debate on this issue. A favourite expression of NCER as well as the Ministry of Education was 'moving from the 50-year career life style to the 80-year career lifestyle' (Rinkyooshin, 1988, 15). The need for transforming society into something more relevant to the longer life span of the population was emphasised. Another reason for introducing life-long learning was a change in value systems:

Today the Japanese people have come to place more value on improving the quality of life and on spiritual and cultural fulfilment rather than on material desires. (...) In addition, as our society is going to be more information-oriented and more internationalised, it will be essential for people to engage constantly in learning new knowledge and new techniques. Given this sort of impact on education, it will be very important to create a 'life-long learning society' where various learning opportunities are provided for people throughout life, in other words, a society where people are 'learning while working' and where due regard is paid to individual and diverse lifestyles. (Rinkyooshin, 1988, 15)

Further, the existence of a life-long learning system was expected to help modify the competition for entering top-universities by giving people a 'second chance' later in life. Life-long learning, as seen by NCER, was necessitated by societal, social, economic and technological changes and developments.

As for internationalisation (*kokusaika*) and how it should be promoted, it was described by NCER in its first report from 1985 as follows:

If our nation is to survive and develop in the age of internationalisation, it is essential that we design our educational reform from the standpoint of internationalisation. In order to respond to the great expectations regarding Japan from overseas, it is necessary for the Japanese people to contribute actively to the international community, keeping in mind a broad understanding and love of Japanese culture. (...) we must establish the kind of education which will teach the Japanese to be good Japanese, to love their country and be aware of the individuality of Japanese culture while also showing a deep understanding for other cultures and traditions. (Rinkyooshin, 1988, 15-16)

Finally, the adaptation to the information society (*joohooka*) was emphasised as an indispensable part of the educational policies in the 21st century. The educational system was to adapt to new technology while also coping with the spread of information:

Concerning the adaptation to the information society education should strive to develop the educational potential of the new media as well as to cope with the possible negative effects this spread of information might have on people. Also education should utilise results of the new technology in the content and methods of education. (Rinkyooshin, 1988, 16)

In the years immediately following the reports the public debate on edu-cational reform was lively but, to the regret of many, quickly waned, among others Professor Amano Ikuo of Tokyo University, who in 1989 published a volume of essays on educational reform in which he called for a revival of the debate, because without debate the government's reforms were bound to be unsatisfactory, he stated. The concrete results of the NCER proposals in terms of new laws may not be conspicuous but from the viewpoint of the opposition, the situation appears by no means static; further, the changes have been made without any chance for the opposition to participate or exert influence.

As evident from Professor Amano's statement, the public debate on education in 1989 was not exactly concerned with the reforms proposed by the NCER. During the deliberations of NCER their publicised summaries and reports received some attention in the press, but after NCER's end of term the broad public did not seem to feel particularly concerned with them. On July 17, 1985 the Mainichi newspaper, immediately after the first NCER report had been published, featured a survey undertaken by the Prime Minister's office concerning the public's knowledge of NCER. Some 42% had no idea the report had been issued, whilst on the other hand 67% of those acquainted with it had great expectations to NCER's future deliberations.

Two years later, in 1987, letters to the Asahi newspaper on education-related problems concerned mainly bullying, violence in schools, cost of education and university entrance examinations. NCER's themes seemed to have disappeared as far as those letter writers were concerned.

The first of two central propositions in this study suggests that educational policies are not quite as immobile as some may claim. Leonard J. Schoppa has conducted an extensive study of the policy processes in Japanese education in which he implies that the reason nothing, or almost nothing, is happening in Japanese education is that the different actors in the debate counterbalance each other's influence, resulting in immobilization. It is true that if one looks at the laws passed to implement reforms, the picture is almost unchanged, therefore as far as the legal aspect is concerned the *immobilist* case is convincing. In the process of my analysis, however, I hope to add another dimension to this picture. An important method for the Ministry of Education to implement reform is by issuing administrative guidelines. Seen in this light the educational system is in fact undergoing a lot of changes and though Diet policies may be static, the Ministry of Education policies are quite active.

The second proposition of this study is that there is a conflict between rhetoric and political practice. By way of an analysis of the agendas for reform of the different parties in the Japanese educational debate and through the identification of the purposes of such reforms the relation between the rhetoric and the political practice is analyzed. The reports employed words which were popular in international discourse on education but the actual proposals and elaborations moved in other directions as did the policies which were later formulated by the Ministry of Education. The vocabulary of NCER was adapted to international trends and served to ward off criticism both domestically and internationally, but the proposals for actualisation clearly demonstrated that the main concerns of educational reform were centered on national and economic needs rather than on the key words borrowed from the international reform rhetoric. To overcome this problem those popular key words were redefined in the NCER reports to suit a Japanese context.

Using the four NCER reports as a basis, this study aims at identifying the main actors in the reform debate, as well as the main issues, and determining what reforms have actually been implemented. Conflict between rhetoric and political practice is manifest in the material. For example, the material contains a lot of debate on the need to reform the entrance examinations and for 'freeing' education, while the Ministry of Education on the other hand is apparently moving in another direction with the new curriculum guidelines (issued in 1989, effective for elementary school in 1992, middle school in 1993, high school in 1994) which make the curriculum even more demanding. How does the increased burden of school work centring around reading/writing and the natural sciences affect key issues as individuality and creativity?

NCER is referred to as an entity. This is not to say that there were no internal disagreements. It merely signifies that the NCER reports are taken to present a result acceptable to the whole group.

An aspect of this study is the myth of the practice of consensus decisions. In the area of educational reform it certainly is not the normal practice, unless we count the kind of 'consensus' reached between those who agreed from the start, and exclude the opposition — which is what seems to be the general procedure in Japanese educational policy. The Ministry of Education reigns supreme when initiating reform, but what does the opposition have to say? How do they view the NCER reports? The conclusion is that either the consensus model is simply wrong, or it is not applicable to education because education is a particular area. It is difficult to determine precisely the extent to which the consensus-model really works, for example in managerial practices in Japanese firms, but my impression is that though the scope is hugely overestimated particularly in the more popular analyses of Japanese society and management, it would probably be wrong to entirely dismiss its existence as an ideal. The extent of consensus decisions in Japan has not been the aim of this study, so I refer to the critical analyses of consensus in Japan made by such scholars as Mouer & Sugimoto in *Images of Japanese Society*, Peter Dale in *The Myth of Japanese Uniqueness* and Krauss, Rohlen & Steinhoff in *Conflict in Japan*.

Educational matters may indeed present a particularly difficult case since education has the role of character-formation and transmission of culture. Attempts at international harmonisation may work in business relations but education is difficult to harmonise, tied up as it is with perceptions of national identity and culture. It is an area in which ideology is expressed quite strongly and many people feel the need to have an opinion about it. In

Japan we see how business groups not only talk about manpower needs in terms of skills, but also of the need to educate certain types of people and promote certain values. An example illustrating just how difficult it is to harmonise education is the issue of moving the start of the Japanese school year from April to September. This has been on the agenda for years, NCER supported it strongly because it would make international exchange much easier but, for what has been termed 'practical reasons', it has not been realised as so many other practices would have to change also. What really seems to be the greatest obstacle here is tradition.

The two central propositions this study revolves around are: that Japanese educational reform is immobilist only as far as the lack of legal changes is concerned and that there is a mismatch of rhetoric and political practice.

The present discussions in the field of Japanese education centre very much on the growing conservatism and nationalism that seems to be the basis of the changes presently carried out in Japanese education. Looming large in the present debate are specific topics like the fate faced by Japanese children upon returning to the crammed Japanese educational system after long periods overseas, the pressure of entrance examinations, and the position of moral education or textbook authorization. I hope to be able to contribute to these discussions by arguing that the Japanese government is in fact seeking to introduce into education, if not exactly 'pre-war ideals', then at least what can be termed more historically 'conservative Japanese practices'.

Roughly there are two camps in the debate on Japanese education. Those who think things are changing — or will do so — and those who consider that only minor adaptations are possible. My research results have placed me in the first group. Reform of the Japanese educational system as formulated by the LDP dominated government, and with the assistance from groups in the business world has tended towards a more utilitaristic, conservative and patriotic education and a centralised administration of education. With the breakdown of LDP rule this may change, education seems to be left more and more to the Ministry of Education alone, indeed educational reform in the last few years seems to have been of much lower priority than reform of the electorial system or the taxation system.

In order to analyze the rhetoric the *interpretation* of the NCER reports comes into focus. Various actors in the debate interpret the reports differently according to their backgrounds and hence draw very different pictures of the nature of the NCER proposals. This makes it is necessary to know more about how the specific issues of the reports are interpreted by those who implement educational reform, and by those who participate more or less officially in the educational reform debate. To get a clear picture of this, it has been imperative to collect written material on the subject from opposing groups, as well as interviewing key representatives on particular points to support the official reports and to get commentaries on them. Interviews have been used as a means of supplementing the written material produced by the organisations on the subject of NCER's reform proposals.

As background material, and as sources of information on specific issues, secondary literature in Japanese and English has been used. The literature on Japanese education is too vast and extensive to be exhaustively described here but a few main trends can be discerned. As Roger Goodman has analyzed the post-war situation two main themes have emerged[4]: 1) The idea that the Japanese model was culturally founded and therefore could not be borrowed; 2) The idea that the Japanese success was based on thorough and pragmatical application of Western ideas[5]. Since these explanations did not solve or offer a solution to the problem of the ever-widening trade gaps between Western countries and Japan, education was offered as an alternative explanation — not least because the Japanese themselves evidently regarded it as important for their success. From this a body of literature grew on the idea that education was at the root of the Japanese economic success. Examples of such literature are : U.S. Department of Education, 1987, *Japanese Education Today*; Lynn, 1988, *Educational Achievement in Japan: Lessons for the West* or White, 1987, *The Japanese Educational Challenge: A Commitment to Children* to name but a few. What these works have in common is that the Japanese educational system is used rather as a model to castigate Western systems and educational views. Other works question this idea of Japan as a model, like Rohlen, 1983, 'Japan's High Schools' who, comparing with the United States, saw the Japanese system not so much as a model to be copied, the American traditions were too different from the Japanese for that, but as a mirror — as an inspiration, to make efforts to match the Japanese accomplishments (Rohlen, 1983, 325).

The NCER reforms themselves have not really been seen as objects for copying. Leonard J. Schoppa in his book from 1991: *Education Reform in Japan: A Case of Immobilist Policies*, tries to answer the specific question 'to what extent are Japanese leaders able to achieve the policy changes they see as necessary?' Not attempting to draw direct lessons for the West, Schoppa deals with Japanese policy-making in the educational field and concludes that the system is marked by immobilism. Though my findings are somewhat different

4. Goodman, 1992. 'Japan — Pupil Turned Teacher?' in *Oxford Studies in Comparative Education*, vol. 1, Triangle Books, p. 155-73.
5. Mouer and Sugimoto identify no less than six different themes in the general literature on Japan: Interest in the sources of industrialisation, interest in competing with the Japanese, Japanese lessons for the industrialised world, assessing the pluses and minuses of Japanese-style development, the debates on convergence and divergence, internationalisation and Japanese society. (Mouer and Sugimoto, 1986, 2-7)

this work has been extremely useful for its political analysis and the wealth of information on the actors in the educational debate.

Many Japanese sources on the topic of educational reform, and NCER reform in particular, have been used. Horio Teruhisa, who has published in both English and Japanese, and Morita Toshio, share a left-wing persuasion which makes them extremely critical of the government. The history of left-wing politics in Japan has been one of long struggle against the authorities and this has influenced left-wing groups in such a way as to make them often see things only as black (government) or white (opposition). Horio and Morita describe their own views in terms of democracy and human rights, while conflicting views are accused of being nationalistic, authoritarian or harking back to pre-war ideals. Still, for use in an actor-analysis, their works are very useful representing as they do oppositional views and they provide a lot of information on the ongoing educational debate as well as analyses of educational ideology. Horio's book from 1988: *Educational Thought and Ideology in Modern Japan* has its weakness in the somewhat incoherent structure, which is probably due to the fact that it is a translation of a selection of essays, but this is more than made up for in the Japanese material he has produced where his discussion of children's human rights has been particularly useful.

On the history of the Japanese educational system the following have been the main sources: Herbert Passin, 1982, *Society and Education in Japan*; Ronald Dore, 1978, *The Legacy*, Byron Marshall, 1995, *Learning to Be Modern: Japanese Political Discourse on Education*. This information has been supplemented with publications from The Ministry of Education and articles published by the teachers' organisations and the Academic Society for Research on the Educational System (*Nihon Kyooiku Gakkai*) as well as material from the above mentioned Western scholars. Professor Amano Ikuo in numerous books and articles has dealt specifically with the history of Japanese education and naturally this source has been used a lot. Though mainly descriptive in his style he also shows a critical attitude towards the government attempts at reform and is also very concerned with the quality of Japanese university education.

As the concern of this study is the analysis of rhetoric, the fact that the materials from the teacher organisations and scholars like Horio and Morita are so clearly left-wing and that that of the Ministry of Education is so obviously conservative[6] is not a problem. On the contrary, this difference is

---

6. 'Conservative' here is conservatism as a political ideology, not necessarily having anything to do with 'conserving' the existing practices and institutions.

the target of the study, the object is *what is said*, not any notion about an objective truth.

The four NCER reports published between 1984 and 1987 are the central documents and they are supplemented with documents from the Ministry of Education on the reform proposals and their progress. Further, Ministry sponsored publications on the development of desired reforms in Japanese education have been used. Analyses by All-Japan Teachers' Union, Horio Teruhisa, Amano Ikuo and Morita Toshio of NCER's reports and of the changes occurring in the educational system have been used as well. The documentary material has been supplemented with interviews with key representatives from All-Japan Teachers' Union, Japan Teachers' Union, NCER, the Ministry of Education and the Women's Democratic Council on Educational Reform.

1.1 Analysis of the Rhetoric

The process of finding a method which is suitable for analyzing Japan is wrought with problems, particularly for someone with a philological background like myself. Often we distrust all 'Western' methods and become 'method-less' or at least inarticulate as to how we progress. This is as inexpedient as unreflected reliance on Western models.

The question of the relation between rhetoric and political practice is central in this study. Rhetoric is closely linked to ideology. For Jürgen Habermas, ideology is a form of communication systematically distorted by power. The discourse is the medium of domination and the language is bent out of its communicative shape by the power interests impinging upon it. (Eagleton, 1991, 129-30) Such language bent out of its communicative shape I shall term *rhetoric*. Rhetoric is a device by which ideology persuades, it is one of the more obvious signs by which we can identify the communication as being ideology. The interesting point about studying rhetoric is its function as verbalised ideology. But as Eagleton notes, it is not enough just to unscramble the distorted text; we need also to explain the causes of the textual distortion itself. (Eagleton, 1991, 133) In other words, it is not enough to identify the rhetoric of Japanese educational debate, it is also necessary to look at the motivations behind the rhetoric.

The power relations and the ideology of the 'speaker' are central points. The party producing the 'distorted text', the rhetoric, will do so in accordance with its persuasions and its aims, in accordance with the structural build-up of power. Structural norms — which in many cases could also be termed ideological, but certainly not always — are norms such as gender roles, family structure and function, norms and routines which are seen as natural and obvious and therefore are accepted uncritically. In Pierre Bourdieu's terms this structural power is called the *habitus*, a 'cultural unconscious' which explains how people's actions can be regulated and harmonised without being in any sense the result of conscious obedience to rules, without any reference to some conscious intention:

The conditionings associated with a particular class of conditions of existence produce *habitus*, systems of durable, transposable dispositions, structured structures predisposed to function as structuring structures, that is, as principles which generate and organise practices and representations that can be objectively adapted to their outcomes without presupposing a conscious aiming at ends or an express mastery of the operations necessary in order to attain them. (Bourdieu, 1990, 53)

One may say that structural power encompasses the whole structure within which decision making takes place or within which rhetoric works as a persuasive force for ideology. In the actor-analysis of power and control made by Christensen and Daugård Jensen, structural power is not within the scope of any formalised process of decision but is a determining factor for what can be done and said, it means that certain aspects of reality elude consciousness, an idea quite similar to Bourdieu's 'cultural unconscious'. They add this concept of structural power to the model proposed by the sociologist Steven Lukes in his book *Power — A Radical View*, (Macmillan, London, 1974) in which he refers to models developed by Bachrach and Baratz (*Power and Poverty*, Oxford University Press, 1970). Lukes presents the Bachrach and Baratz-model of power with the addition of a filter that controls people's consciousness. But as this model operates with the term 'objective interest' as the initial stage, without further defining how such objective interests come about, Christensen and Daugård Jensen added the concept of structural power, the given. Structural power becomes the box within which action is taken (see chart 1).

On the matter of educational debate in Japan, what a model like Lukes' can give us is a glimpse of how it is that some issues are not perceived as 'issues', and how some issues are raised but never enter the arena of decision.

In my interpretation the Christensen & Daugård Jensen-Lukes' model works as follows: 1) 'Unreflected interests', in order to materialise as realised interests, have to pass through a filter of consciousness control, which is a set of unspoken — unconscious — rules for what can be validly uttered or perceived within the structure. Such rules operate as a mode of what Bourdieu terms 'symbolic violence'. Since symbolic violence is legitimate it generally goes unrecognised *as* violence (Bourdieu, 1992). In the Japanese case an example of this could be the impossibility of questioning the value of education.

Chart 1. Lukes' Model

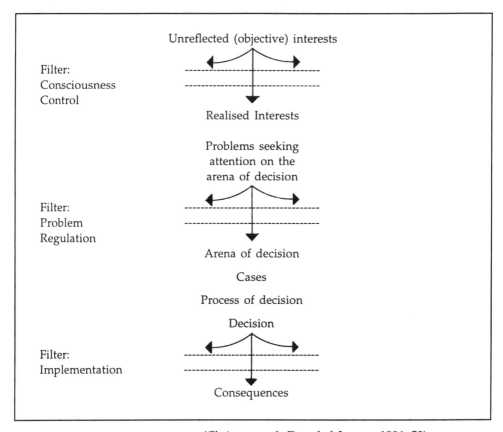

(Christensen & Daugård Jensen, 1986, 53)

2) Once interests are realised they will become problems seeking attention in the arena of decision. Here a Japanese example could be the issue of mother tongue teaching for foreigners in the schools. 3) To be accepted in the arena of decision one has to pass a problem-regulating filter with which the power holders regulate access to setting the agenda. In Japan we will see that the business groups have been able to pass this filter quite easily while the teacher organisations only did so with the greatest of difficulties. 4) Once inside the arena of decision the problem has become a 'case' which via a process of decision becomes a decision. 5) To have any consequences the decision finally will have to pass through a filter of implementation. In Japan the actors on this level are the bureaucracy and the teachers, in some cases also parents and students (Christensen & Daugård Jensen, 1986).

This actor model provides an explanation of how interests are accepted as issues and how issues can be set on the agenda or not, and of the power relations guiding them. In the example of Japan the definition of 'power holders' appears simple since the LDP has been in power for very long and hence has established a close relationship with the bureaucracy. Of course this relationship is presently disturbed by the political changes taking place in Japan, but during the period mainly dealt with in this study the situation has been stable. 'Power holders' are, in this context, exclusively those acting within the political framework, and other potential 'power holders' like those with economic power, are related in terms of their ability to penetrate the filters and enter the arena of decision.

We can view the consciousness control-filter *or* perhaps we should call it the structural filter, as directed by social mores and norms, the problem regulating-filter as directed by the power holders, and the implementation-filter as regulated mainly by bureaucrats and teachers. The actors in this Japanese type of the actor-model thus are: structural norms, power holders/rulers, bureaucrats and teachers.

In this model academics, parents and children are omitted unless they participate in any of the above mentioned groups. Their way of participation goes through getting their interests accepted by the system of decision making. Figuratively speaking, the actor-model lacks an 'opposition arrow' jutting in from the side in the decision making process, by which is meant that, at this stage, there is really no way of influence for opposition groups. The NCER reports went through public hearings and emerged unchanged. The NCER called upon academics for advice but did not follow it. The chance for such groups of being heard is minimal. Even if the group is sufficiently large to have its interests accepted, the outcome is not certain to be in accord with their requests. We can look at an example: Japanese parents feel that entrance examinations are too harsh, the issue enters the arena of decision, a decision is made to create one unified examination, it is implemented, but not necessarily with the effect of alleviating the pressure on children. The point is, that while the groups without direct access to the decision making can perhaps manage to get some issue on the agenda, their inability to participate in the decision making process is likely to mean that the decision will not be the desired response to the problem. Further, a desired decision can be modified by the implementation filter. But it is also through this implementation filter that parents, and particularly teachers, have a chance of influencing the educational policies in Japan.

The actor-model with is restrictiveness towards oppositional claims in the decision making process, is well suited to analyze the case of the Japanese debate on educational reform wherein the opposition when it comes to decision-making is virtually shut out of direct influence, but has the choice of trying to 'go by the rules' and get those in power to accept their interests, or of influencing the decisions at implementation level.

1.2 Educational Ideology in Japan

One major conflict in the Japanese educational debate is whether education should be termed the *right* or the *duty* of the citizen. If considered a duty the state and the government naturally must have influence far beyond the 'advisory and administrative duties' stipulated in the Fundamental Law of Education (Roppoo, 1990, 28).

The extent of government influence exercised in the name of 'administration' is, however, amazing. There are examples of the government implementing a law through a procedural mechanism of revising the Ministry of Education Law or through the application of official 'administrative guidance' after the Diet failed to pass legislation on education. Then, when faced with a fait accompli, the Diet later passed the law in question. This effectively reduces legislation to a matter of convenience. An example was the attempt in 1956 to pass a law on textbooks designed to strengthen the government's control over the contents of education. Intense criticism inside and outside the Diet caused the plan to fail. Yet the aims of the proposal were realised later through an administrative measure (*gyoosei sochi*). Another example is the 1973 'legislation' of the Head Teacher system, which had already effectively been put into operation through a ministerial order in 1957 (Horio, 1988, 164).

At the core of the conflict is that the Fundamental Law of Education, which was designed by the Allied Occupation Authorities, was considered too abstract by many conservatives, and even 'un-Japanese' by some. It was however, fiercely defended by most of the opposition. A further point of disagreement is that any decision passed by the Diet, however much in opposition to the intentions of the Fundamental Law of Education, has been considered to represent the will of the people and in this way legitimized.

After the Second World War attempts were made by the Allied Occupation Authorities to curtail ministerial control over education and to prevent any kind of censorship. This was done by including a paragraph inhibiting 'improper control' of education in the Fundamental Law of Education (FLE), and by formally placing educational authority with the people. After the occupation, when Japan started to adapt the new laws to Japanese conditions, the FLE was reinterpreted. As for 'improper control', as far as the government was concerned this was apparently taken to mainly concern the improper control teachers could exercise in schools and in their day-to-day teaching (Horio, 1988, 121). This re-interpretation brought into focus the question of the political neutrality of the teachers.

Horio Teruhisa in his *Educational Thought and Ideology in Modern Japan* is very critical of government educational policy. The central goal for the government, he maintains, is none other than to achieve precisely that 'improper control' prohibited by the FLE (Horio, 1988, 121). The state claims to be protector and defender of educational fairness, advocating equality of opportunity, or of facilities at least, and simultaneously works towards goals such as securing manpower supplies in close cooperation with industry. Concretely, this emphasis can be seen in the heavy investment in natural sciences and technology at the national universities, while the humanities — not so directly useful to industry — are mostly neglected.

In concrete terms, the government's attempt at achieving what FLE calls 'improper control' was manifested in a wish for a more centralised educational system, for more control over the goals of education, for less autonomy for schools and teachers and for control over the administration of schools. Also the government has put down very strict rules for the curriculum, thus controlling the contents of education.

In Japan, courts have been used to fight state control and to force through state policies. Passive resistance has certainly been used by Japanese teachers to modify the effects of central policies (the implementation filter of the actor model), but the state, not least because of its status as employer, is strong enough to make a significant number of teachers comply with most of its directives, so the path of non-compliance has not been entirely effective. Though taking cases to court in Japan is generally not a favoured mode of action, cases on textbook authorisation and disputes over student conduct have been taken to court, but procedures are very slow and the Supreme Court in particular is inclined to rule in favour of the government, so it is not a very effective measure against state control (Horio, 1988, 213).

Also, the courts can hardly be expected to have much expertise on education, so the problem with this way of settling disagreements is that courts, rather than judging by educational considerations, have a tendency to judge by political considerations. This is manifest in, for example, disputes over the contents of history books in Japan where considerations made by the courts in their rulings were clearly political (Horio, 1988, 214).

Presently, no textbook can be used for teaching unless it is authorised by the Ministry of Education — and the Ministry does not have wide limits for what is evaluated as 'suitable' knowledge for children.[7]

7. Examples of textbook screening are as follows: In one case the Ministry of Education in a Japanese language textbook intended for sixth graders, rejected the use of a poem called 'The River' for the reason that the onomatopoeic words corresponding to the sounds of a river in standard Japanese were slightly different form those found in the poem. In another case the use of the word *kenka* (fight, squabble) was declared not permissible in a Japanese language textbook. To be acceptable, the author was told, rewording like 'they went to the next village to have *sumoo* (wrestling) with the boys there' was necessary (Horio, 1988, 174-75). It seems a little naive on the part of the Ministry to believe that harmony and the essence of 'Japaneseness' is preserved in this

As Horio has seen it, 'the people' were fighting for the spirit of FLE to be recognised through, for instance, the courts, while the government was consciously working against it. Chances for the people winning were slim, not least because a great proportion of the same people did not exactly disagree with the view that education was the *duty* of the citizen and the property of the state (Horio, 1988, 100). Further, as described by Amano, popular enthusiasm for educational reform appeared to be neither great nor consistent. As the critic Higuchi Keiko put it:

As a parent you only encounter education-related problems once. As soon as your two children have passed through the system you forget all about them. (Interview with Higuchi Keiko, June 27, 1991)

In official Japanese educational ideology one can see a very clear example of bourgeois, conservative educational ideology, but though the ideology looks the same as in many other countries, the educational system and tradition differs in many aspects from what we see elsewhere, and there is a different emphasis on reform issues. Japanese education never really felt the impact of the sixties' and early seventies' educational ideology, which put the student and his or her needs more at the centre of the educational effort.

A mood of liberalism swept over the global as well as the Japanese educational debate in the beginning of the 1980s, in particular inspired by the business world and the need to adapt the economy and manpower supplies to anticipated future developments and needs. No overt charges were brought against the Japanese curriculum for being anti-family or anti-patriot, but many clearly felt that it did not support family and nation adequately and certainly the educational system was seen as anti-free enterprise. An example is the issue of the mandatory existence of school districts, free choice existing only in higher education. Liberalisation proposals in Japanese education have, among other things, pointed to an abolishment of the school district system, although with equality in mind, arguments have been made for creating district systems for high schools also. What is emphasised the most at the moment in Japanese government reform plans is the need for central administration, for more state control with the curriculum and teaching methods, particularly the latter as the first has for some time been more or less established, albeit unofficially. Liberalisation and diversification of the system as well as internationalisation are also important issues, as we will see through the example of the NCER reforms.

way, but it certainly is an illuminating example of just how detailed textbook screening can be.

The actor model shows how interests can move through the system of decision making, but also that the rulers are powerful agenda setters. It is also important to note that when the government or its representatives outline agendas, like Nakasone did to the NCER when he gave them their commission, it is of course done with the available solutions in mind. One is not asking for dreams or idealised models. The available solutions have hitherto been copied from other developed countries, resulting in much the same approach to educational reform as in countries with quite different educational traditions. The Occupation reforms are an example of this kind of copying, in which the Japanese were assisted or guided by the occupational forces. The educational problems which were later pinpointed by LDP and after that elaborated by NCER, are not unique to the Japanese educational debate. In many respects they are similar to problems experienced in other countries and the similarity is also clear in the rhetoric, but at the same time dissimilarities, perhaps the result of dissimilar traditions, are evident in the political practices concerning the educational system.

Whether the unstable political situation will for once mean that the immobilism of the legal reform of Japanese education will evaporate and fundamental reforms will be carried out is something only the future can unmask. What is possible to do through a study of the NCER reforms, is to identify present tendencies and the basis any future reforms would have — if not to build on, then at the very least define their own relations to.

1.3 Structure

The structural study is contained in *Chapter 2*, dealing with the Japanese Educational System. Section 2.1 covers the history of Japanese educational reform while Section 2.2 describes the educational system as it looked in the 1980s plus notes on the changes introduced by the new curriculum guidelines to become effective during the first years of the 1990s.

Chapter 3 deals with the debate on reform with Section 3.1 being about the NCER, its function as an actor in the debate and the main NCER issues. *Chapter 3* proceeds with three sections dealing with other actors in the debate, describing their backgrounds and the contents of their proposals. The groups are the Japan Teachers' Union and the All-Japan Teachers' Union in Section 3.2, the Women's Democratic Council on Educational Reform and the Academic Society for Research on the Educational System in Section 3.3, and the industrial group, Kyoto Group, and the Education Council in Section 3.4.

Chapter 4, entitled 'Attitudes to NCER's Proposals' contains descriptions of the four main themes. First comes the NCER version, then follows the oppositional criticism of it, proposals for implementation and actual reforms carried out. Section 4.1 of this *Chapter* deals with the new curriculum guidelines, as they represent not only a change in the system but are also referred to by the opposition in their criticism of the reform efforts concerning the four NCER themes. Section 4.2 is on individuality, Section 4.3 about life-long learning, Section 4.4 internationalisation, and Section 4.5, the information society. Final conclusions are found in *Chapter 5*.

Japanese names have been written with the surname first as is customary in Japan and long vowels are doubled as in *Kyooiku*. Japanese words and titles are written in italics, except in well-known place names like Tokyo.

CHAPTER 2

THE JAPANESE EDUCATIONAL SYSTEM
1868 — 1984

2.1 The History of the Educational System[1]

Until the end of the nineteenth century schooling in Japan was non-compulsory and run by the domains, the *shoogun* (the military ruler of Japan), the temples and private individuals. It was not considered the ruler's obligation to provide education for the masses, rather education was considered to be an individual matter.

Japanese education before the Edo period (1600-1868) was strongly influenced by Buddhism and Confucianism. This was natural as the first educated men and teachers were priests and monks, and great Nara-temples like *Toodaiji* of the *Kegon* sect and *Hooryuuji* of the *Hossoo* sect were among the very first centres for learning.

The first formal school was established according to the *Taihoo* Code of AD 701. This school — the *Daigakuryoo* — was for the children of the aristocracy and was modelled on Chinese principles. The purpose of the *Daigakuryoo* was to educate bureaucrats for government administration and it was the centre of Confucian moral indoctrination.

Education was neglected from the tenth century and until the Edo period because of the many wars between rivalling military clans. It was not until the establishment of a centralised state by Tokugawa Ieyasu, marking the start of the Edo period, that education became more widespread (Passin, 1982).

Until the end of the Muromachi-period (1336-1600) and the start of the Edo period education for commoners was quite sporadic. Then the so-called

---

1. Good reference works on Japanese educational history include Passin, Herbert, 1982. *Society and education in Japan*, Koodansha, Tokyo, on the history from the initiation of formalised national education till the 1960's. This study is brought up to date in Byron K. Marshall's *Learning to be Modern: Japanese Political Discourse on Education*, 1995, Westview Press, Boulder, Colorado. Amano Ikuo in a number of articles and books, for example in 1990, *Education and Examination in Modern Japan*, University of Tokyo Press, also works on Japanese educational history. Horio Teruhisa in his book from 1989, *Educational Thought and Ideology in Modern Japan*, University of Tokyo Press, deals with the history of educational ideology from the Meiji Restoration in 1868 up until the end of the 1980's.

terakoya[2]-school gradually spread all over the country. *Terakoya*-schools were private schools for children of commoners. For children of the aristocracy there were domain schools. Towards the end of the Edo period it is estimated that 40 to 50% of the boys and 10% of the girls received education in the *terakoya*. This meant that before the Meiji Restoration (1868), there was a broad foundation, even among commoners, for mass literacy as well as the discipline of receiving instruction (Passin, 1982, 47, 56; Dore, 1978, 18).[3]

This meant that the notion of the possibility of 'improvement' of one's mind and of one's social status was diffused in the populace; Japan was not the sort of traditional society where 'things are as they are'. Popular education in 1879 was secular and practical and had the potential of improving the individual's life-chances in a material sense. As the notion of individual self-improvement by education was widely diffused, directing this towards the notion of national improvement by education could be more readily accepted than would have been the case in the absence of such a popularly accepted notion (Dore, 1978, 18-19). The variation in education in the Edo period should be emphasised. Schooling was mainly a domain matter and there was no expressed national policy on education. Schools could thus vary according to domain and to social stratum. Nevertheless, commonalities in the experiences of the domain rulers afforded a degree of similarity in the approach to education (Marshall, 1995, 6-15).

During the Edo period the *samurai* had to a great extent become bureaucrats and intellectuals rather than warriors. The traditional *samurai* ideal emphasised defending one's land and lord against any threat and this gradually also came to mean that it was a *samurai*'s duty to broaden his mind and indulge in intellectual pursuits for the benefit of his lord. Education became not only a sign of high social status for the *samurai* just like the two swords they were entitled to carry as a tangible sign of their position in society, but also the chief means of rendering service to their lord.

From the middle of the nineteenth century the shoogunate increasingly employed young *samurai* educated in 'Dutch learning'[4] as advisors in political

---

2. The term *terakoya* stems from *terako* 'temple child' or 'school child' as it gradually came to mean. Originally, *terakoya* was just a place which accepted lodging students. Tera means 'temple' and therefore *terakoya* is often translated as 'temple school' but this is misleading. *Terakoya* education in the Edo period did not have the religious overtones associated with the term 'temple school'. Hence the original Japanese term is preferred here.
3. A thorough history of Edo period education can be found in Dore, Ronald, 1965. *Education in Tokugawa Japan*, University of California Press, Berkeley. See also Marshall, 1995, ch. 1 'Clarifying Loyalty and Filial Piety: 1800-1850s', p. 5-24.
4. In the beginning of the isolationalistic Edo period — the *shoogun* in 1635-39 closed the borders of Japan to foreigners and made travelling abroad illegal for Japanese —

and diplomatic questions. Diplomatic skills were becoming increasingly important because Western powers were encroaching on Japan and it was no longer possible to react according to precedent as had been the policy in earlier days.

The new advisors were educated in the shoogunate's own elite school, the *Shooheikoo*.[5] They were trained to record and understand new and unfamiliar things and to make judgements on that basis, to a much larger extent than the old advisors who were educated in the Confucian classics and in writing poetry rather than in how to understand the West (Sakata, 1985, 74; Marshall, 1995, 11-14). The old system operated with the notion of learning as a finite entity. This notion was gradually modified by the new breed of advisors.

The Meiji-Restoration in 1868 became a sort of mobilisation of the (*samurai-*) talent of the country for the Emperor, but it was not led by him. The source of power was with the young *samurai* who had participated in the Restoration. Though constituting only 2% of the population, a section of the *samurai* managed to stay in power, and their level of education was an important prerequisite for the Restoration and its plans for modernising.

After the Meiji-Restoration this new elite, among other things, began to create a formal, public educational system. In 1871 the first Ministry of Education was established, and in 1872 an educational system of elementary schools, middle schools, and universities was introduced.

Early Meiji-plans had been to retain the dual system of high schools for the samurai and literacy schools for commoners, but instead a unified, universal school system was created in 1872. The unified school system created by the 1872 ordinance helped break down the feudal boundaries of social class and ancestral regional affiliation that had divided people, but nevertheless encouraged acceptance of the existing order (Dore, 1978, 23; Amano, 1984, 9-10).[6]

The reason for the ruling class choosing unification over elitism is to be sought in their perception of the purpose of education. First of all, instead of creating subversive disaffection like it did in England, universal education in Japan promoted loyal obedience, particularly due to the ethics courses. The ruling class in Japan was intellectually united — unlike the British middle and

Western influence was limited to the 'Dutch studies'. As the only connection with the West were the Dutch at Deshima, 'Dutch learning' became synonymous with Western learning. Dutch learning especially concentrated on medicine and military technology and was undertaken by *samurai* sponsored by the domains.

5. Whether or not the institute for training in Western learning — The *Bansho Shirabesho* — was indeed a part of the *Shooheikoo* itself is not agreed upon in my sources. Sakata claims it was, Marshall (1995, 20) treats them as two different facilities.

6. See also Marshall, 1995, 32-50 for a comprehensive description of the events concerning the promulgation of the *Gakusei* in 1872.

upper classes — and saw an advantage in the diffusion of their Confucian orthodoxy through education (Dore, 1978, 25).

This was by no means the last time elitism and preferences for mass education were to clash. As a very common issue of the Japanese educational debate it has remained a sensitive issue to this day. By the late 19th century the state had become responsible for education and also had the power to set the agenda for education. This has continued to be discussed in terms of state authority over education versus popular authority over education.

In 1885 the cabinet system had come into being and Mori Arinori[7] was appointed Minister of Education. He created a unified educational network using the Prussian model. In 1886, realising the important role education could play in modernising the country, he issued orders for elementary schools, middle schools, the Imperial University (until 1897 there was only Tokyo Imperial University), and normal schools (teacher training schools).

Compulsory education was three to four years and elementary schools were to train loyal subjects in basic skills, middle schools to prepare students for university and finally, universities were to educate capable leaders. The state's requirements were emphasised throughout the system, most notably embodied in the Imperial Rescript on Education from 1890 which demanded 'loyalty to the Emperor and love of country'. In this way, the use of popular education to create loyal and obedient citizens became a predominant motive in the government's educational policy (Dore, 1978, 25; Amano, 1984, 10-11; Marshall, 1995, ch. 2 & 3).

With these precautions having been taken, the diffusion of education in society did not pose any threat to the established political power-holders. For instance, on Mori's initiative, the talent mobilisation aspect was later toned down and 'obligation to the state' was emphasised instead (Marshall, 1995, 57). From an early stage nation-building interests influenced Japanese education.

Teacher education reinforced the loyal-citizen ideology of the Imperial Rescript and the 1882 Regulations for Primary School Instructors (*Shoogakkoo Kyooin Kokoroe*) emphasised their role as servants of the Emperor and expected submissiveness and servility towards superiors.

---

7. Mori Arinori (1889-1947). Mori had had much contact with the West, particularly England. He was supported in his efforts to reform Japanese Education by Motoda Eifu, the Imperial Confucian advisor, and he was known as a nationalist. Nevertheless, he was assassinated by a fanatic nationalist, ostensibly for violating the Shintoo sanctuary at Ise — he lifted the curtain before the altar with his walking cane to look inside — thereby showing disrespect for the descent of the divine Emperor. His Western inspiration for educational reform led to the suspicion among fanatic nationalists that he was a Christian, which is probably why he was assassinated (Morikawa, 1989, 39-65).

A set of regulations given to all graduates of First Normal School in Aichi Prefecture in 1883 declared:

Participate in proper societies for the study of the arts and sciences, but never join groups whose meetings breed doubts. If you come into contact with seditious or dangerous writings, report this immediately to and discuss them with your school's principal. (Horio, 1988, 254-55)

The task of modernising the country was approached in much the same way as a war. The citizens were to be educated for the good of the country, to be soldiers fighting for their country's welfare. The goal appears to have been both modernisation and the creation of a unified national consciousness among the people.

2.1.1 Reforms before the Second World War

The conviction that education was primarily for the good of the state seemed to be dominant in early Meiji educational politics. Mori Arinori, the Minister of Education appointed in 1885, in a speech to Saitama Normal School in February the same year, expressed the goal of education in this way:

Our country must move from its third class position to second class, and from second class to first; and ultimately to the leading position among all countries of the world. The best way to do this is [by laying] the foundations of elementary education. (Passin, 1982, 68)

Mori's nationalist views were evident in his opposition in 1885 to a proposal by the statesman, who was to be chief architect of the Constitution of 1889, Itoo Hirobumi, that the Emperor should enforce laws only with the approval of the new legislative body, the Imperial Diet. Whereas Itoo wanted a more democratic procedure Mori wanted recognition of the Emperor's ultimate authority over the Diet (Morikawa, 1989, 58).[8]

Another proponent of the view that education was to benefit the state was Fukuzawa Yukichi. He was in some respects more liberal than the government, and later he gained fame as the founder of one of the more prestigious private universities, the *Keioo* University, as well as for his opinions on education and the modernisation of Japan. In his 'Encouragement

---

8. Mori's position is causing considerable discussion in which the characteristics considered most important vary to a great extent. He is described by Morikawa and Horio as a thoroughbred nationalist, but by Marshall as an ardent and untraditional moderniser. Now, both may be true of course, but the impression of the person differs considerably.

for Learning' (*Gakumon no Susume*) he was much in line with Mori: 'Every citizen must take the responsibility for the nation upon himself, regardless of personal status or prestige' (Fukuzawa, 1969, 17).

Saying so, Fukuzawa was in accord with the leadership. The Meiji-leaders aimed at a) providing a compulsory elementary education of four years for all boys and girls, b) at a great expansion in the number of middle schools and c) at a network of national universities (Passin, 1982, 73; Marshall, 1995, 40).

Initially, people like Fukuzawa Yukichi and influential persons in the government like Mori Arinori seemed to agree on what the educational needs of Japan and the Japanese were; i. e. learning about technology, autonomy, and self esteem, from the strong Western countries, but this agreement did not go as far as explaining *how* this objective was to be realised.

Fukuzawa and Mori disagreed when it came to the methods. Mori felt that education should be administered by the state, that is enlightenment from above, whereas Fukuzawa propagated liberal values such as building a society on free access to information, — enlightenment from below (Horio, 1988, 29; Marshall, 1995, 579). Thus, his initial agreement with Mori did not entail his acceptance that the state was the prime *beneficiary* of education. Rather, he saw the obligation of the individual towards the state as the obligation of a free person towards a society of other free persons.

Fukuzawa, and the progressive movement with him, felt that a people kept in ignorance would be dangerously easy to seduce, and would have difficulties handling the kind of political influence it would get through, for instance, universal suffrage. Thus the people should have access to education based on modern scientific principles (Horio, 1988, 34, 39).

Mori on the other hand, wanted — and established — a centralised system of education, emphasising the separation of education and scholarship from politics. Education was not to be politically tinged and the administration apparently saw itself as the closest one could come to an unbiased institution to be trusted with separating the two and defining them. In any case, it became the administration's — and therefore also the government's — business to 'preserve political neutrality'[9] (Horio, 1988, 40).

A change seems to have taken place in the perception of the role of education in society during the years after the early Meiji 1872 ordinance created the unified school system. It seems that whereas education was not linked with politics, or at least not with 'undesirable' policies in the early years, Mori and Fukuzawa were well aware of the latent political powers it

---

9. This term has later been used to 'manipulate', as the opposition would put it, with education. (Thurston, 1973, 94-95) The official demand for political neutrality has functioned as an excuse for sanctions against teachers who were politically active.

could awake in the population. Education apparently had come to be considered potentially more 'dangerous' and therefore an object of stricter control.

The conservative camp, with Mori at its head, further propagated the view that scholarship and education really did not have anything to do with one another. Scholarship was for the nation's elite and education was a necessary activity for the training of the nation's masses (Horio, 1988, 48).

This marks a return to the idea of a dual or elitist system as was also initially contemplated by the early Meiji reformers, but eventually given up in favour of the unified system.

The exact words Mori and his followers used for scholarship and education were *gakumon* for scholarship and *kyooiku* for education. *Kyooiku* — separated from *gakumon* and in Mori's terminology — meant intellectual, moral and physical training received under the guidance of one's teacher. This implied that the people did not 'need' abstract thinking, nor a realisation that there was no one correct opinion to be held, that is, pluralism as found in scholarship. In this way 'education' became a more mechanical way of learning, much like animals could be 'trained' to perform particular skills. 'Scholarship' would go further and — ideally, and still in Mori's terms — involve the process of individual development with the individual essentially responsible for his own development (Morikawa, 1989, 61). Mass training rather than mass education — in the sense of scholarship — would enable the rulers to act more freely with no anticipation of interference from the ruled.

The reaction against what was in many government circles viewed as excessive Westernisation further propelled the tendency towards central control and reduced the impact of the progressive camp (the camp headed by people like Fukuzawa). The perceived loss of Japanese values was especially regretted. A movement for Western technology and Eastern philosophy (*Wakon yoosai*) gained strength in a society which was also experiencing radical new ideas like Marxism, civil rights and unionism for the first time. For education, *wakon yoosai* meant aiming at maintaining basic Japanese values while also mobilising the talent of the nation through a centralised, meritocratic, 'modern' educational system (Schoppa, 1991, 23; Passin, 1982, 149).

At this early stage of the formal educational system, the roots of the views of the two opponents in the modern educational debate are clear. The conservative camp, with the welfare of the nation as its concern and aiming at educating well-behaved citizens, saw as first and foremost the obligations of the people towards the state. The progressive camp, concerned with the development of the individual and a healthy democracy — which would in the end also ensure more direct political influence for their camp — emphasised the people's right to education and the state's obligation to provide it equally for everybody. But opinions were divided, even within the government. In fact, the decade after 1868 had tended towards liberalism. Minister of Education, Tanaka Fujimaro, in May 1875 had argued that teachers and localities should be allowed a fair measure of autonomy and that scholars and educators should never be forced to follow official orders. Thus, he raised the issue of educational autonomy versus bureaucratic 'interventionism', an issue which has been prominent in the Japanese educational debate ever since and linked to the authority debate (Passin, 1982, 72; Horio, 1991, 253).

The end of the liberal mood was marked by an Imperial tour of Japan. What the Emperor had seen in the schools apparently alarmed him, because he had his Confucian lecturer, Motoda Eifu,[10] draft a statement called *Kyoogaku Taishi* (The Great Principles of Education). This was issued in 1879 as an Imperial rescript and came to be the centre of the controversy between the progressive movement and the conservative movement (Passin, 1982, 83, 227; Marshall, 1995, 53).

During the 1880s attention became more and more focused on moral issues. Japanese morality and values, Japanese social loyalties and practices became basic to the new system of education (Rohlen, 1983, 53; Passin, 1982, 84). The intention was to provide a stable foundation for education in a society that was shaken by new influences.

Education was seen as one of the people's three *duties* towards the state.[11] It was something to be done for the good of the state and not for the good of the individual (in which case it would have to be characterised as a *right*) (Horio, 1991, 245; Morris-Suzuki, 1984, 18; Amano & Aso, 1972, 8, 36).

The Imperial Rescript on Education, which was issued in 1890, is a clear indication of the perception of education as a duty of the individual towards the state. The Rescript was part of the movement for Japanese values and patriotism, at the centre of which was reverence for the Emperor. In it were Confucian concepts such as 'filial piety' as well as Japanese nationalist concepts such as 'offer yourselves courageously to the state'. In 1889, copies of the Imperial Portrait had been distributed to the schools for their care and reverence. The Imperial Rescript on Education in 1890 joined the Imperial Portrait as one of the two sacred objects to be maintained reverently by the schools. It became common practice to let the pupils memorise the Rescript

10. Also known as Motoda Nagazane (1818 — 1891). Neo-confucian. Entered the Imperial Household agency in 1871 as tutor (*jidoku*) to Emperor Meiji. In 1886 he became a court adviser and member of the Privy Council in 1888. In 1882 he published an Imperially sponsored morals textbook called *Yoogaku Kooyoo* (Essentials for the education of Youth). (Dai Nihon Hyakka Jiten, 1967)
11. The two other duties were tax payment and military service.

and recite it on formal occasions[12] (Rohlen, 1983, 64; Horio, 1988, 70; Wolferen, 1989, 342; Marshall, 1995, 58-61).

The Elementary School Regulations of 1890 stated that the objectives of education were moral training, the development of a distinctive national polity and the cultivation of skills and knowledge — in that order. In 1891 the Explanation of School Matters (*Gakuji Setsumeisho*) stated that the first objective of education was to be the cultivation of 'the spirit of reverence for the Emperor and patriotism' (*sonnoo aikoku*) (Passin, 1982, 151; Horio, 1988, 70; Rohlen, 1983, 53-4). Clearly the prime objective of education was not learning, but the training of loyal subjects and the strengthening of national morality.

Until the end of the Second World War the Imperial Rescript on Education remained the basic statement of official educational aims.

The Rescript formulated the moral base to mandate the switch in people's loyalties from traditional family and clan loyalty to Emperor and nation loyalty. This idea of the divinity of the Emperor was a partial revival of pre-feudal concepts. As Marshall notes, the references to the 'ordinary morality of the Japanese that has been transmitted from earliest times' probably served to satisfy the progressive camp as it was read as rejecting classical Chinese values like those held by Motoda Eifu (Marshall, 1995, 59). During the feudal period, primary loyalty was owed to one's personal overlord. The principle of unquestioning loyalty was retained by the Imperial Rescript but this loyalty was transferred to the Emperor. Family and state ethics were considered to reinforce each other. Filial piety was the prototype for loyalty to superiors, to the state and eventually to the Emperor.

There had been some discussions in educational circles stating that the Japanese did not have anything like Christianity in Europe to provide them with a moral foundation. The Meiji-leaders, with Motoda Eifu and other Confucians as their guides, decided to fill this void by making the Emperor the foundation of a new national morality. They employed the ancient myths of a single line of Emperors descending from the Sun-goddess Amaterasu to achieve a sense of divine causality, and they also incorporated the idea of the 'essential national polity', thus creating an Emperor-State. Education was an important medium for dispersing this ideology (Horio, 1988, 68; Passin, 1982, 153).

The Meiji-leaders did not have a particular model of education that they were trying to copy, but they did have some guiding principles. Nationalism was one. The objective was to regain the Japanese national prestige which had suffered from the forceful opening of the country. Second, they wanted to select only part of what Western civilisation had to offer — the *wakon yoosai*

---

12. Donald Thurston (1973), quotes a detailed description of the ceremony of Emperor worshipping in Japanese schools before the Second World War.

concept. Third, they saw the state as the ideal guide for the masses, in control of schools and education; fourth, they saw no role for the people in decision-making processes concerning education. Finally, there was evolutionary pragmatism as a guiding principle, the idea that a weak country would be overcome by a strong country and hence Japan had to become stronger, an idea shared by Fukuzawa and the political leader Itoo Hirobumi among others (Amano & Aso, 1972, 8-13; Amano, 1988b, 50).

Mirroring the conviction that scholarship was for the few, education was divided into two tracks, the ordinary elementary track and the elite track. The ultimate elite course was: *Seishi* Primary School in *Hongoo* ward — Tokyo First Middle School — First Higher School — Tokyo Imperial University (Passin, 1982, 106). In 1886 there was one middle school in each prefecture and seven higher middle schools in the country, the latter being closely associated with the imperial universities as preparatory schools.

Though it was a system where, in principle, ability was the means of selection, it cannot be said to have been truly egalitarian. The fact that seventeen years of schooling were necessary *before* entering university had a discouraging effect on most people. Not only was there the expense of feeding an extra mouth for such a long time and paying tuition fees, there was also a loss of income as the student started to make his own money at a much later age than was usually the case. Therefore, in reality, ability *and* wealth were the real criteria of selection (Amano & Aso, 1972, 23-26; Amano, 1988b, 52-53; Passin, 1982, 107).

The ten-year period after the inauguration of the cabinet system was a period of unstable educational policies, because there were nine changes in minister of education. In 1895 a memorial was submitted to the House of Peers by forty influential people requesting the establishment of the Higher Council for Education (*Kootoo Kyooiku Kaigi*). This council was to assist the government by discussing important matters of education. Up until then the intention had been a long term policy, but with the ever changing ministers of education, a lot of arbitrary changes had been made. The memorial was also submitted to the House of Representatives, and both houses approved of it. Initially, the government refused to accept it, claiming that such an organ was unnecessary, but finally it decided to set up the Higher Council for Education by the end of 1896. This was the start of the council system which has continued up to today's Central Educational Council (*Chuuoo Kyooiku Shingikai*) (Amano, 1988b, 56).

In the years from 1897 to 1906, in answer to growing demands for vocational and higher education created by industrial development, an organised structure of girls' 'high schools',[13] vocational schools, professional

---

13. Special girls' schools providing middle school training.

schools and universities was created. The direct connection between education and social structure became established; now education clearly was a means of creating social strata, a placement mechanism.[14] At the same time it was also a means of possible social mobility for those who had the talent — even though this was to some extent illusory if there was no money to go with the ability. The social structure gradually became based on a direct relationship between educational background and employment, instead of the traditional model where social status was usually inherited (Passin, 1982, 104-5; Marshall, 1995, 69-70, 74, 95-98).

The special school (*senmon gakkoo*) in this period presented a particular problem. These schools had long been placed at a lower stratum in the higher education system but now, as they improved qualitatively, demanded that their status be raised. The movement for raising the status of special schools gained strength when *Waseda* University was founded in 1912 on the basis of Tokyo *Senmon Gakkoo*. This inspired other major private special schools to use the term 'university' in their name too. Legally, they were special schools until 1918 when the University Ordinance (*Daigakurei*) was passed, granting the title '*daigaku*' (university) to special schools deemed worthy of it from a qualitative point of view (Amano, 1988b, 63, 66; Amano, 1990, 5; Marshall, 1995, 98).

The University Ordinance had been suggested by the Extraordinary Commission on Education (*Rinji Kyooiku Kaigi*, ECE) which had been set up by the government in 1917 to establish general educational expansion for the purpose of 'training faithful and loyal people filled with the spirit of service to the country' (Amano & Aso, 1972, 44; Marshall, 1995, 93).

The commission worked for only two years but its reports became the foundation for educational expansion in the following decade, particularly the influence of the council was felt in higher education as the University Ordinance exemplifies.

Until the 1920s no major legal changes occurred in the educational system, but there were frequent demands for democratisation, equality of opportunity and more institutions of higher education (Amano, 1988b, 67). By the end of the 1920s almost everyone received six years of compulsory education and the level of secondary schooling measured favourably internationally. Japan had about the same percentage of enrolment as the United States — 2.3% — or more than twice as high as that of France or Britain (Marshall, 1995, 116-17).

The First World War meant an economic boom for Japan and industry's

14. Regine Mathias, in her article 'From farm to urban middle class' in Goodman and Refsing (eds.), 1992, *Ideology and Practice in Modern Japan*, provides an example of upward social mobility in the first half of the century. She describes a family of rural background and its advance into the proprietary urban middle class.

share of the GNP steadily became larger than the agricultural share. This fact naturally had an effect on industry's relationship with education. Until then, education had ranked above industry. As an activity of the mind it was traditionally accorded more status than the kind of menial work carried out in industry. Education gave little attention to the needs of industry. Industry would have to take the graduates as they were if it had any use for them. But with industry's greater influence on the national economy, education was gradually reduced to a lower rank and instead became the supplier of manpower. It was no longer just an intellectual pastime, or a basic commodity to be passed on to the people, but an activity with the definite goal of turning out productive members of society. Manpower needs began to directly influence education in various ways. An example of this is the white collar workers who became middle managers, public servants, and the like. The fact that white collar workers were educated in middle schools, meant that in 1921-24 middle school experienced a boom. A more obvious example was the growth in vocationally oriented schools.

From 1917 to 1919 the above mentioned Extraordinary Commission on Education (ECE) was in session and it proposed changes at all levels. Middle school was to offer more electives in order to help further the students' employment careers. More courses related to the students' work-life were suggested. ECE also suggested more moral education, an improved administrative structure, decreasing the number of regulations on schools, more cooperation with industry when determining the contents of the training, and the encouragement of retraining. It recommended the establishment of more higher education institutions to ease the pressure on existing ones, and to achieve this, private universities and single department colleges were to be allowed.

The result was that the high schools (formerly higher middle schools) were separated from the universities and thus they were no longer just preparatory schools. In 1918 several private universities were allowed to grant academic degrees and there was a sharp rise in the percentage of people with a university degree. Between 1910 and 1930 the number of universities swelled from 3 to 46 and already by 1920 Japan had reached a level comparable to European standards (Amano & Aso, 1972, 44-49; Amano, 1984, 11-12; Marshall, 1995, 98, 107, 117).

Government control of education became unstable in the twenties. There were political changes, and the period was characterised by the advocacy of new ideas like socialism, communism, liberalism and democracy. In education adherents of child-centred pedagogy, and teachers' and students' movements rose to oppose the nationalistic education inherited from the Meiji reformers, and unions were formed. Economically, business and industry produced an ever-larger share of the GNP, national income rose and the 'new middle class' emerged, consisting largely of white collar workers, teachers, etc. Changes in social structure made way for educational changes, but the changes in education were not drastic. The nationalistic system was kept alive and the changes were carried out inside that framework (Amano & Aso, 1972, 49; Marshall, 1995, 101-16).

The many new trends of thought entering Japan were supportive of the idea of educational reform, but they also posed a threat to the system of state. The government wanted to preserve the nationalistic system and changes were to be within the bounds of the existing system. Therefore the government countered the new currents of thought with political repression and the promotion of the Japanese Spirit (*Nihon seishin*). The new ideas were a threat to the established order of society and could not be tolerated. Unions were especially seen as detrimental to national interests (Schirokauer, 1978, 514; Marshall, 1995, 110-12).

With the depression and economic crisis in the thirties, the government began to fear subversive activities in society inspired by the many new ideas coming from the West. Japanese authorities used intervention in Asia (Manchuria primarily) as a measure to re-unite the people in agreement on national goals. To maintain the state, anti-Western nationalist propaganda was spread. As the Second World War drew nearer the schools became increasingly nationalistic and militaristic in content and education became extremely centralised under government control.

One of the strategies for making the schools more militaristic in content was the training teachers received in normal schools. The use of army methods was by no means alien in teacher education. Mori Arinori as early as in his Saitama speech mentioned above, declared that obedience, dignity and friendship were important virtues for a teacher as well as in the army. Accordingly, he introduced into the normal school a military type of physical training and mandatory dormitory life (Morikawa, 1989, 60). By the 1930s normal schools had in reality become military institutions. Army officers trained teachers in discipline, the use of weapons, marching and military leadership. Since 1927 teachers had been required to serve at least five months in the military before actually starting teaching at a school in order to understand the 'military spirit' (Duke, 1973, 19; Schoppa, 1991, 30).[12]

In 1935 the Education Reform Council was established as an advisory body for the Minister of Education. The main reason for establishing it was

12. Regine Mathias, op. cit., picturing the career of one Takemura Shizue, describes the normal school around 1920 as '[a] rigid system ... often compared to service in the army by former students' (Mathias, 1992, 104). I have not been able to determine, however, whether the compulsory military training of later days was required for female students as well as male students at normal schools.

that Western culture had been absorbed along with the desired technology, and this was increasingly seen a threat to the established order and the goals of promoting patriotism and morality. In 1936 the Education Reform Council proclaimed that the trinity in educational reform was to be: 'Shintoism, government and education' (Amano & Aso, 1972, 58; Marshall, 1995, 133).

The pre-war model of education provided a tradition which later proved difficult to shake off. This is the tradition of central control over education, and to this day the ruling parties are not willing to surrender it, despite their willingness to condemn pre-war excesses by the authorities (Schoppa, 1991, 29).

The history of educational reform in Japan until the Second World War gives evidence of a government ideology of education basing itself on elitism and the state's authority over education. Elitism in education is here a relic of feudal education which separated the classes, albeit in its new guise the elite are supposed to consist of the most able. The question of state authority over education is most probably an extrapolation of the Confucian ideal of the benevolent father/ruler onto the state, which is expected in its benevolence to provide for the people. This idea of a state or a ruler who knows what is best for the people, by virtue of being the ruler, is of course not peculiar to Confucianism. We know examples of this notion from the absolute monarchies in Europe and the communist governments in Eastern Europe.

With an ideal benevolent state this might have created a tolerable educational system, but in unison with the agenda of bringing Japan into the first ranks of the world community and the ensuing nationalism, it proved fatal to pre-war Japanese education. Education became a tool for nationalist propaganda and any opposition to this was easily quenched in the name of the interests of the country.

2.1.2 Wartime reforms

In 1937, when Japan was at war with China, the Education Council (*Kyooiku Shingikai*, hereafter EC) was established to provide guidance for the Prime Minister. Increasingly, the aim of the schools became elementary education and basic training in the moral principles of the Japanese Empire. Loyalty towards the Emperor and the state was the one central theme. Business as well as government were interested in educational reform and the main objectives of EC's proposals were to alleviate the pressure of the examinations on the students, to make the system less elitist, to make the curriculum more relevant to the daily lives of people and to shorten the total time spent on education (Amano & Aso, 1972, 57; Amano, 1984, 12).

The orientation towards industrial needs had influenced educational objectives. Shorter education would provide industry with younger workers and temporarily boost the workforce numbers. Evenly distributed education with a curriculum of relevance to daily life — or work — would make these workers better suited for jobs in industry.

EC in 1938 proposed an extension of compulsory education to eight years plus, after elementary education, five years in a part-time compulsory youth school (*seinen gakkoo*). This school would provide vocational and military training. Normal school, which educated teachers, was to have greater capacity and be lifted to the level of professional schools. At the secondary level, middle schools, girls' high schools (in effect middle school level) and vocational schools were to be united in one group as 'secondary schools', (*chuutoo gakkoo*). In this way it was emphasised that those schools were actually on the same level. During the first two years students could change between the different types of schools, as the schools became equal in status. The term of education was four years and the system was put into effect from 1943. Higher education did not experience reform apart from the institutional acceptance of women's universities (Amano, 1988b, 73; Marshall, 1995, 139-41).

In 1943 the full scale mobilisation of students was carried out and the educational system gradually came to a halt because children were either evacuated or working in factories, teachers were at war or working in production. By the end of the war hardly any schools were functioning and most students had not received teaching for a long period.

The wartime reforms emphasised science and technology. It was a nationalistic system but due to the mentioned emphasis, Amano and Aso as well as Marshall detect progressive traits such as increased vocational education, even though the system suffered much during the last part of the war and was in reality not functioning by the end of the war (Amano & Aso, 1972, 57-59; Amano, 1988b, 74; Marshall, 1995, 141-42).

Despite the desire to create a less elitist system, wartime efforts can hardly be said to have dispensed with the traditional ideas such as state authority over education. What *was* new was that industrial needs were now openly accepted as factors to be reckoned with in education, and this trend was carried over into the postwar system.

2.1.3 Postwar reforms

After the Second World War the Allied Occupation Authorities (mainly American) found an educational system geared for a country at war. William J. Sebald, an assistant to General Douglas MacArthur, the head of the Occupation administration, in the publication 'Education in the New Japan' issued by the General Headquarters of the Occupation Administration in 1949, voiced American objections to the pre-war system. He said that it was characterised by 'centralised control, a well-knit bureaucracy', that it had been

used to create an 'obedient and subservient population', that schools had
become 'agencies for indoctrination in militarism and ultranationalism'.
Further, because of the Imperial Rescript on Education the 'importance and
the integrity of the individual were dwarfed into insignificance', he claimed.
The report which was submitted by the U.S. Education Mission to Japan in
1946, had added criticisms concerning the elitism, the tracking and the
undemocratic teachers who were characterised as 'followers rather than
leaders'. In American eyes the system was undemocratic, elitist and
reactionary (Rohlen, 1983, 63-64; Marshall, 1995, 144).

    The occupational reforms targeted nationalism and militarism and aimed
at separating education from politics and religion (*Shintoo*). Though many
reforms were carried out rather quickly there were naturally also a lot of
remnants from the war time system. The abolition of the Imperial Rescript on
Education, for instance, did not happen as promptly as some accounts tempt
us to believe (Beauchamp, 1984; James & Benjamin, 1988; Halpin, 1988),
because they do not mention that time did elapse before the Rescript was
actually abolished. The Rescript was an extremely influential document
regarding the definition of *what* education was all about, and it is important
to note that it continued to be a guiding principle for educational practice for
some years after the end of the war. In fact, though the Occupation started
in August 1945, the Imperial Rescript on Education was not officially repelled
until June 1948, when the Diet decided to withdraw the Rescript on Education
and all other ordinances and rescripts issued by the Emperor or military
persons (Horio, 1991, 272; Marshall, 1995, 155).

    By this time many school officials, dressed in formal mourning clothes,
had already reverently burned their schools' pictures of the Emperor in secret
midnight ceremonies, preparing for the new era (Rohlen, 1983, 64-5). This
clearly shows an awareness that the emperor-cult would have to be
dismantled even if there were several arguments for keeping the Imperial
Rescript. One such argument was that the Rescript was the most simple and
understandable means of communicating educational principles, or any other
legal principles for that matter, to the people. Ashida Hitoshi, who was later
to become Japan's Prime Minister in 1948, made the following remark on the
necessity of a new Imperial Rescript in the First Special Committee of the
Educational Reform Council[13] in September 1946:

Because the Japanese people are incapable of understanding the Constitution, it will
enter their heads better if presented to them in the form of an Imperial Rescript

---

13. This committee was responsible for conducting enquiries on the implementation of a
    new basic educational law to replace the Imperial Rescript. (Horio, 1988, 107)

written in the simplest of languages. Because the Emperor is the most popular figure in Japan, there will be no difficulties whatsoever in utilising the format. (Horio, 1991, 269)

For Ashida, the Prime Minister to be, the Emperor was still a useful symbol of national interests. Amano Teiyuu, later to become Minister of Education, at the same meeting said: 'As the standard of Japanese morality, the Imperial Rescript is indeed a superb thing, and there is absolutely no basis for abandoning it' (Horio, 1991, 268). It would seem that at least part of the Japanese population did not agree at all with the Occupation Authorities' opinion that the Imperial system had failed, and apparently would only dismantle it on the definitive command of the Allied Occupation Authorities.

It would seem also, as Leonard Schoppa remarks in his 'Education Reform in Japan' that though 'the system became more egalitarian, the pre-war model of diversified education has continued to live in the minds of postwar conservatives. 'Gradually the conservatives became more articulate about this, and after the Occupation, they openly began to bemoan the lack of elite institutions to serve the brightest students (Schoppa, 1991, 27).

In 1946 the First U.S. Education Mission visited Japan and the recommendations it made in its report became the basis for the new reforms. The goal of education was changed in accordance with such ideals as individualism and democracy, the curriculum was revised, language was reformed,[14] roman letters were to be taught in school and the administration was to be decentralised. The pre-war multi track system was abolished for a single track system with co-education for boys and girls and new teaching methods. The aim was democracy instead of fascism, freedom instead of control, education for the masses, not just for the elite, diversity as opposed to uniformity, and also decentralisation and internationalisation (Amano & Aso, 1972, 63-64; Amano, 1984, 13; Horio, 1991, 256). Interestingly, many of these issues are still on the agenda of educational reform, diversity and internationalisation in particular.

On March 31, 1947 the Fundamental Law of Education (*Kyooiku Kihon Hoo*, hereafter FLE) was proclaimed. When read today this law may seem totally unexceptional, but at that time it constituted a major breach with the principles that had governed Japanese educational policies until then.

Article 1 stated that the aim of education was the 'full development of personality', to rear a people 'with a sound mind in a healthy body, who would love truth and justice, respect the individual' and who would be 'imbued with an independent spirit' (Roppoo, 1990, 23). Man and the

---

14. In 1946 a list of 1,850 Chinese characters was chosen officially for general use and issued by the Cabinet and the Ministry of Education.

development of personality was to be an end in itself and not a means for constructing an Emperor-state, values like loyalty and patriotism (*chuukun aikoku*) were left out, and human values and the individual included in their place. Ideas and beliefs were no longer considered the monopoly of the state but an inalienable individual right. The FLE represented a tremendous change in ideology. Schools became co-educational, students were to be taught with individualistic principles as a basis, and the physical condition and the health of the pupils also became a matter for the school to take care of. The American principles of education are evident.

On the new ideological basis of revering the individual, the former structure with ordinary and elite education was given up. The 6-3-3-4 system was introduced in which elementary school was six years and was called *shoogakkoo*. Then there was a three year middle school called *chuugakkoo*, a three year high school called *kootoo gakkoo*, and a four year university called *daigaku*. Additionally there were kindergartens, five-year technical colleges, two-year junior colleges (*tanki daigaku*), schools for the handicapped, special training schools and miscellaneous schools. Compulsory education was extended to nine years, that is to include elementary school and middle school. As time went on, however, and popular demand for education grew, compulsory education in reality became twelve years, including high school, and since 1975 more than 90% of an age cohort have attended higher secondary education, (95.8% in 1995), (Shimizu, 1996, 9).

Due to wartime losses and the extension of compulsory education, school facilities were inadequate. Many new schools had to be built, particularly at the compulsory level and this meant sacrifices for the local authorities who were in charge. But public interest in education was great and so was support for the new democratic system. By 1947, 99% of the relevant age cohort attended middle school (Amano & Aso, 1972, 67; Monbushoo, 1992, 11).

The democratisation efforts of the Occupation Authorities concerned not only the particulars about educational administration and content but also the establishment of unions including teacher unions. There were several, and they had a leftist orientation in common. In fact, many of them were so communist that after the first rounds of reform, the Allied Occupation Authorities found that the unions were perhaps too leftist to be acceptable or to be desirable in the creation of a stable state (James & Benjamin, 1988, 42; Marshall, 1995, 151-54). The communist revolution in China and the war in Korea gave the Occupation Authorities quite another view on leftist movements and suddenly they were not as readily associated with a healthy democracy as before.

The political situation just after the war was naturally influenced by the presence of the Occupation Authorities. Japanese politicians were acting cautiously trying to adjust to the new democratic system. Many were purged for activities during the war but there *was* a Japanese political leadership working with the Occupation authorities, though the 'working together' may in many cases have been more like the Japanese government rubber stamping the laws formulated by the Occupation Authorities. It may be interpreted along the lines propounded by the Japanese historian Ogawa: it was a case of 'American rule of Japan under the guise of democracy' (Marshall, 1995, 150).

The overall mood of democratisation and the desire to do away with a militarist past was felt in the schools as well, where a purge of militarists had been carried out just after the end of the war.

Later, in 1949, probably provoked by anxiety over the leftist movements in other parts of Asia as well as by growing support for the discharge of proven communists from schools in the United States, the Occupation Authorities conducted the 'Red Purge' and thus marked the policy change from broad liberal-mindedness towards every ideology except militarism, to a more restrictive democracy where too-leftist an orientation could not be tolerated (Marshall, 1995, 160-61). This purge was also conducted in the state administration and it made room for the return of many of those earlier removed for militarist sympathies and thus helped establish an administration that tended to be very conservative in its outlook.

This policy change has come to be known as the 'reverse course' and in effect demonstrated to the Japanese that one could bend even democratic principles in the face of what was considered by the authorities as subversive forces. It also, in its prosecution of the left, radicalised this movement and further alienated the conservatives in government from their leftist opposition (Schoppa, 1991, 39).

The Allied Occupation Authorities, in an attempt to ensure free, democratic education in Japan, had tried to make the role of the Ministry of Education purely that of providing guidance and coordination. One of the measures to ensure more democratic practices was locally elected school boards in control of the choice of textbooks and formulation of the curriculum for their schools. Also the teachers were to have more control over the schools and they were to be allowed to choose between a number of approved textbooks. In 1947 teachers' unions began to be formed (Amano & Aso, 1972, 68; Thurston, 1973, 52), among them Japan Teachers' Union (*Nihon Kyooshokuin Kumiai*, hereafter JTU), which was formed in 1947 as an amalgamation of two smaller unions, and which was in favour of local control of education rather than ministerial control. It also opposed moral and political education in the schools and favoured egalitarian rather than elite education, and opposed the extensive system of examinations (see also 3.2).

Initially, the Occupation Authorities had been quite hostile to the Ministry of Education, but the Ministry was never purged of militarists after the war.

Naturally a purge could not have been conducted without some ruptures in the work of the Ministry, but the main reason for this apparent lapse probably was that before anything could be done, the Cold War changed the American primary goal from democratising Japan to making Japan a secure bastion against communism — the reverse course was plotted (James & Benjamin, 1988, 42; Marshall, 1995, 161). JTU was leftist in orientation and its leadership had relations to communism. Hence, the Allied Occupation Authorities could not become allied with JTU as an alternative to the Ministry (Oota, 1989, 245, 249).

When the Occupation ended in 1952, voices were soon calling for the 'rectification of the adverse effects of the post-war reforms', notably coming from the state administration and from the government. A government board called for education reform stating that 'many undesirable elements' had been incorporated into the Japanese system, signaling what Marshall characterises as a conservative counterattack (Marshall, 1995, 174). The Occupation Authorities had made a point of decentralising in order to move control over education away from the Ministry of Education. The issue of control has been central in Japanese educational debate ever since. The parties of the conflict are the Ministry of Education versus the local and prefectural governments on the one hand and the teachers' unions on the other. Questions such as elitism versus egalitarian access, the Ministry's 'censorship' of textbooks and moral education often cause clashes of opinions (Marshall, 1995, 179-82; James & Benjamin, 1988, 41; Amano, 1984, 13).

One of the first changes the Ministry of Education made after the Occupation was to reassert control over textbooks and curriculum. Textbooks were to be submitted to the Ministry for approval for use with the curriculum (and not all books were/are accepted) as had been the procedure during the Occupation as well. In fact, the procedure of approving with the proviso that recommended changes would be made, was an inheritance from the Occupation Authorities which was perpetuated (Duke, 1978, 256). Officially textbook screening was conducted in order to ensure the same standards throughout the country and guarantee equality of opportunities.

The move was made with very little opposition at the time because the Ministry was in accord with prevailing opinion among parents. Many parents felt that standardisation was in their child's best interest, because it would secure as equal conditions as possible and hence, supposedly, equal opportunity (James & Benjamin, 1988, 42-43).

The Ministry had issued guidelines for the curriculum in 1947 which were at the time not officially mandatory, but functionally they quickly became so. From 1958 the curriculum guidelines (*Gakushuu Shidoo Yooryoo*) were published in the official Government Register and were endowed with legally binding power. In effect it became illegal to teach anything other than what was prescribed in the curriculum guidelines (Amano, 1992, 3; Horio, 1991, 287). Quite aside from the legal aspect, with a national market for education there was an obvious need for comparable standards and it would be very difficult for a school to uphold local variations without running the risk of reducing their graduates' chances of being admitted to one of the prestigious universities.

With the standardised curriculum, moral education was reintroduced. It had been banned by the Occupation Authorities because of its role in spreading nationalist propaganda during the war, but it was felt that something was needed to compensate for the lack of an inherited set of common ethics and morality. In many Western countries this is provided by Christianity and indeed in the 1880s the view that Christianity was the spiritual foundation for Western dominance in technology was wide spread (Thelle, 1991, 84; Marshall, 1995, 175). The efforts after the war to re-establish moral education in the curriculum were based on the assumption that a country required one common set of ethics and morality to survive and to sustain the growth of a viable society.

Another thing that was changed by the Ministry of Education after the Occupation was the election procedure of the school boards. Instead of elected school boards, the Ministry in 1956 introduced boards that were appointed by the prefectural governor and the local mayor with the approval of the prefectural and local assemblies[15] (Oota, 1989, 251; Schoppa, 1991, 41). The change was explained as being caused by the malfunction of the elective system, which was caused by the fact that people did not understand the Western concept of local boards. Also, since the government was the representative of the people it could, and indeed should, act as such and assume the responsibilities which were placed under the authority of the people, it was claimed (Marshall, 1995, 181-83; Horio, 1988, 6, 121, 150).

Another weighty reason for the Ministry of Education to change the school board was the fact that since teachers were allowed to be board members under the old elective system, provided they resign their teaching positions if elected, many JTU candidates had in fact been elected, and in some areas they dominated the boards. This posed a threat to ministerial control over education because opposition groups like JTU actually got much influence on local school governance holding up to a third of the total number of seats in the 1950s. The step taken by the Ministry was thus explained to be caused by a desire to preserve the 'political neutrality' of education by shutting left-wing groups out of influence (Marshall, 1995, 182-83; Oota, 1989, 251).

15. The law also provided that the Ministry of Education would have power of approval over the appointments of prefectural superintendents of schools and, in unison with the prefectural school boards, veto power over local board decisions. (Oota, 1989, 251)

The changes made after the Occupation tended towards centralisation, more aptitude streaming and more adaptation to the needs of industry. Vocational education was strengthened, achievement was made the crucial measure and the relation between education — job — status was emphasised as before the war. Also, as before the war, emphasis was put on more vocational training and hence the 'reverse course' changes made by the Ministry of Education after the occupation gained support from industry (Amano & Aso, 1972, 73; Amano, 1990, 7-9; Marshall, 1995, 198-205).

The issue of moral practice and patriotic education was also a factor that loomed large in the changes after the Occupation. Soon there was to be support for these changes from a quite unexpected side, namely the Americans who had initially abolished such education.

The debate started in 1951 when the then Minister of Education, Amano Teiyuu, drew up a programme called 'An Outline for National Moral Practice' (*Kokumin Jissen Yooryoo*) and planned to distribute it to the schools.[16] He felt that too much emphasis had been placed on the individual at the expense of the State and this served to weaken the very existence of the State. He planned to develop a new criterion for a national morality based upon, and centred around, love and respect (*keiai*) for the Emperor. This programme was severely criticised in the Diet and nicknamed 'Amano's Imperial Rescript', so it was withdrawn, but later, in 1953, Prime Minister Yoshida Shigeru made the following statement on the government's intention to alter the path of educational reform:

In addition to re-examining the reforms enacted at the end of the war, we must work, in the light of the current conditions prevailing in our country, to promote the cultivation of patriotism, which is the keystone of our national independence. (Horio, 1991, 282-3)

One would expect wild protests from the Americans, the authors of the so-called 'Peace Constitution' and formerly so active in rooting out Japanese nationalism, but this was not so. On the contrary, there was support for the move as long as the Japanese patriotism would be subordinate to American global interests. Memoranda were exchanged between the United States and Japan which said:

...Thus the first responsibility of the Japanese government is to make sure that

---

16. A full translation and an analysis of the text can be found in Dore, Ronald P., 1952. 'The Ethics of New Japan' in *Pacific Affairs*, 25, no. 2, June, p. 147-59. Quoted in Marshall, 1995, 175-76.

education and the various media are used to nourish and propagate the spirits of *patriotism* and *self-defense* throughout society. (Horio, 1991, 284)

The then Vice-President of the United States, Richard M. Nixon, declared on an official visit to Japan in 1953, that the Peace Constitution represented a major 'mistake' in America's postwar policy for the reconstruction of Japan (Livingston et al. , 1973, 264). Evidently, the Americans wanted Japan to re-arm and become a bastion against communism. To this end, the cultivation of patriotism among the Japanese was considered helpful.

The following year the relationship between education and state underwent a radical change. The political neutrality of education had been considered an expression of educational autonomy which was guaranteed by the Constitution and the FLE. Those documents proclaimed that the state should not hold doctrines of its own regarding education and that it must always maintain a neutral position. New legislation, however, conceived of the state as the sole protector and defender of educational fairness and impartiality. It became the responsibility of the state to judge precisely what departed from these principles or what violated them (Horio, 1991, 284-86). Supported by such ideas one could use administrative measures to steer education in the desired direction.

There were also attempts to alter the FLE itself, or 're-examine' it as it was put by Minister of Education, Kiyose Ichiroo. He maintained that it was 'simply not good enough to speak about the rights that accrue to individuals as the members of a democratic society'. It was also necessary to 'nurture among our students feelings of loyalty and devotion to the state'. He particularly attacked the curriculum guidelines for being deficient in this respect and insisted that the 'state's responsibility' for the content of education be clarified with no constraining liberalising objectives as laid out in the FLE.

Three laws were proposed, which were designed to alter the FLE sections on educational objectives (article 1), educational autonomy and the limitations on educational administration. The proposals aroused much criticism and in the end only the Law Concerning the Management and Operation of Local Educational Administration was, by a narrow margin, passed. It took the protection of the Special Task Force (*Kidootai*) officers to maintain order during the debate (Horio, 1991, 285-86).

The effect of this law was to re-establish bureaucratic control of education as the most desirable mode of operation. In 1957 the teachers' freedom was restricted by a system for the evaluation of teachers' performance. It was started by the Board of Education in Ehime Prefecture in 1956 in order to reduce a financial deficit. The idea was that principals secretly rate the efficiency of teachers, and only those teachers with high ratings would receive annual pay increases. One year later the Ministry of Education proposed an extension of the system throughout the country, to evaluate 'the loyalty and love of education' of individual teachers as judged by the principal. The rating criteria should be based on things like classroom management, lesson guidance, disposition of school duties, love of education, sincerity, sense of responsibility, impartiality, knowledge, ability, skills and the like. As in Ehime Prefecture, these ratings should remain secret, and they were to be used for promoting only the teachers who supported the government's educational goals (Marshall, 1995, 189; Horio, 1988, 215; Duke, 1973, 141-42). This was all part of the attempt by the Ministry to 'normalise' education, which had in the Ministry's opinion suffered from the excesses of the democratisation experienced during the occupation.

Thus, by 1958 the Ministry had gained control over the school boards, set limitations to teacher activities and set the curriculum guidelines. With this last measure the Ministry was able to obtain what it had strived for when it proposed a Textbook Law the year before — it could authorise (or censor, some would say) textbooks through unilaterally imposed administrative guidelines (Horio, 1991, 287).

This was taken by opposition groups to be exactly the 'improper control' prohibited in the Fundamental Law of Education of 1947, and therefore a breach of this law and the Constitution that ensures freedom of thought and education. Ever since, teacher organisations, intellectuals and a number of grass roots groups have pointed out that this governmental tendency of excessive control is to grossly overinterpret the term 'guidance'.

In the 1960s demand for higher education began to rise steeply and so did the number of public and private universities to cater for this demand. Especially private universities became a sort of 'buffer' adjusting higher education to changes (increases) in demand. This has meant that today (1995) 73.5% of the university students attend private universities (Shimizu, 1996, 34).

One of the catch phrases in conservative educational policy after the Occupation was 'diversification' (*tayooka*) and under this banner the conservatives in the 1960s worked for increases in student numbers at technical and vocational secondary education. Upper secondary education should be 'diversified in response to careful considerations of societal demands' it was said. Education was to conform to the individual's aptitudes. This was the first time since the war that elite education had been called for in such clear terms.

Chart 2: Number of national, public and private universities 1965 — 1995

	National	Public	Private
1965	73	35	209
1975	81	34	305
1985	95	34	331
1995	98	52	415

(Statistics Bureau, 1992, 658; Shimizu, 1996, 34)

In 1961 the five-year technical colleges had been established (*kootoo senmon gakkoo*) but despite the establishment of numerous such schools the total share of vocational upper secondary education at the end of the 1960s remained steady at 39%. The conservatives had not had much success with their diversification plans, and opposition from the Japan Teachers' Union, for example, condemned the concept as discriminatory (Schoppa, 1991, 44).

By the late 1960s university unrest suddenly put educational reform at the top of the political agenda. As a result, the Central Council on Education — a standing government council — produced a proposal for, among other things, increased diversity in secondary curricula, streaming and grade skipping, a probationary year for new teachers and increased central management of universities (Schoppa, 1991, 3-4).

The Tsukuba University Law of 1973 can be seen to be inspired by this. Prior to the passage of this law there had been plans by individual universities for self-reform encouraged by the Ministry of Education. The 1969 plan of the Tokyo University of Education was one of the most radical, among other things operating with an 'open university', a university corporation with outsiders included in the governing board and a new system to replace the faculties. The fact that student revolts virtually incapacitated a number of universities at this time made the need for reform all the more pressing.

The Ministry of Education accepted the plan from the Tokyo University of Education and the new university was to be situated in the projected Tsukuba Science City. The new features in the Tsukuba concept were: a new location, new structures for research and teaching, a more centralised administration and a new form of university governing. The establishment of this new university marked the first time the Ministry of Education was able to make permanent changes in the basic laws pertaining to university governance (Cummings, 1978, 321-5, 327; Halpin, 1988; Roesgaard, 1991).

The next step was to encourage other institutions of higher education to take on the same new principles. However, as the years have gone by, Tsukuba University has turned out not to be so different from other universities in practice. 'Old wine in new bottles' as William Cummings put it (1978), but the governing system with vice-presidents who are administrators, a very powerful president, and finally the Presidential Advisory Board, are certainly new concepts in Japanese higher education. Especially the latter has provided the government with a legitimate channel of influence on much of the decision-making activities at the university (Halpin, 1988, 143, 159; Roesgaard, 1991).

A major change in the popular conception of education from 1950 to the end of the 1960s was that in the 1950s one could, with some right, consider high school as an elite course as 'only' 51% of the middle school students advanced to high school. But by 1965 this share had risen to 71% and by 1975 to 92%. Likewise the universities had moved from admitting only 8% of the high school students in 1955 to 27% in 1975.

The notion of an elite course was only maintained in the ranking of the individual institutions of learning. Whereas elitism formerly was associated with a collective of institutions, universities for example, it was now associated with specific institutions, like Tokyo University. With the increasing numbers of students at each level, all judged in a single-dimensional, hierarchical scale, the system became exam-dominated and standardised. Diversification was seen as an appropriate measure for fostering the qualities needed in the future (Schoppa, 1991, 45; Marshall, 1996, 204).

The reform debate leading up to the 1980s was concentrated on the deplorable standardisation of education, the need for more technical and vocational education and the need for fostering abilities relevant to the future.

In time, education has become, not just a vehicle for upward social mobility, but a *condition* for social placement at all. It has become absolutely vital to have received at least the first twelve years of education to get anywhere in today's Japan, and to secure white-collar employment, university education has become a prerequisite, whereas in the 1920s middle school was enough. The fact that a strict hierarchy among educational institutions has developed, means that it is also of great importance which institution one has attended. These factors have created strong competition for entering the most prestigious institutions. In turn, this competition has influenced teaching at lower levels, often reducing its functions to that of a preparatory course for the next entrance examination. Standardisation of education throughout the country, in order to provide everyone with the same opportunities for success in the examinations, has been the result.

Politically, Japan from the 1950s to the 1970s was chiefly involved with economic matters. And, as if not daring to express strong opinions on foreign policy or defense policy — and perhaps rightly so, in view of the grudges held against Japan in most of the neighbouring Asian countries — the government engrossed itself in securing Japan's maximum economic success. Besides, being protected by the United States, Japan did not have to worry about defending itself, and this helped keep any debate on defence issues largely a national matter. This emphasis on economy has been successful to the extent that Japan's development since the war is now generally considered an economic miracle.

It wasn't until the late 1980's that Japan actively involved herself in the more inflammable policy questions such as, a) involvement in UN operations and the dispatch of troops overseas, b) bettering relations to countries like China and Korea by recognising and apologising for the atrocities committed during the Second World War, and c) negotiations with Russia, whereby economic support has been promised for the return of the Kuril Islands to Japan, to name but a few.

For education the tone of reform has also been economic in that a great deal of attention was given to industry's manpower needs. But in the case of education, government ideology has been more pronounced than in other areas, it has been a very politicised area. The reintroduction of moral education and the emphasis on traditional values and family values bears evidence to a strongly conservative conviction. The 'reverse course' in education is by no means a phenomenon of the past.

2.2 The Present System

The present system of education in Japan can be characterised as basically the Occupation reforms modified by the revisions made by the government since 1952. The 6-3-3-4 system has been retained and in principle the unified system of education as well. Hierarchy is pronounced, particularly between institutions of higher education, which gives the system an air of elitist meritocracy.

The immense importance of education for social and occupational placement has created a system in which transition between two levels of schooling is accorded enormous importance, and it is a very stressful experience for those participating in the competition for entrance at the most prestigious schools or universities.[17] Competition is a prevalent characteristic of the Japanese educational system and examples of competitive practices can be found right down to kindergarten age. The cramming business is blooming on account of this, providing remedial and extra tutoring.

---

17. For a history of the examination system in Japan see Amano Ikuo, 1990b, *Education and Examination in Modern Japan*, University of Tokyo Press, Tokyo.

From the age of three, when the child enters kindergarten or a daycare centre, its daily activities become regulated by a curriculum. The role school plays in children's lives can be likened to the role work plays for adults in the sense that it is the most important activity for the individual during the daytime. Especially when they are young, the Japanese spend considerably more time on schooling than do their contemporaries in the United States and Northern Europe.

When a child starts schooling the event has the characteristics of an initiation, it is a major event defining the social role of the child. As a youngster, school is what relates the individual to society, the place to meet and make friends, and at the university it is common for girls to expect to be able to find their future husbands. School is a place of socialising as well as learning.

The Japanese system of education is also characterised by its success in securing a high general level of learning for the mass of people. Most people today complete at least twelve years of schooling and the natural sciences and mathematics are particularly emphasised.

In the following, a description of the system of education in the late 1980's is given along with an outline of the contemplated changes.

2.2.1 Pre-school Education

Before entering school at the age of six, children and parents (mostly mothers) are involved in several activities of importance for the child's education. In the home the mother is expected to provide a nurturing, warm, attentive environment and intellectual stimulation. In the interest of a strong lasting relationship Japanese mothers seem very indulgent, not posing strong demands, not exerting authority and avoiding confrontations. In the end this is to make the child form relationships with adults that will make it want to do what the parent or teacher expects.

Mother and child engage in educational activities such as learning to count, doing simple arithmetic, reading the *kana* syllabary and concentrating on following directions in activities. A number of publications help mothers structure these activities and the emphasis is on doing things *together*, not on keeping the child occupied while the mother is busy doing other things (Benjamin, 1991, 256-57).

Generally the public welfare system in Japan is poorly developed, but this is not so at pre-school level. While the popular opinion is that mothers ideally should stay home with their children until they reach the age of three, it is also expected that a child after reaching this age attends an institution. By doing this, the child is expected to make friends and experience group life in preparation for school (Hendry, 1986, 32).

This necessitates a sufficient number of pre-school institutions for this purpose. Also, the fact that nuclear families living separated from their senior generations are becoming more common has meant an increase in the demand for pre-school facilities[18] (Hendry, 1986, 31; Tobin, 1992, 54).

Formal pre-school education in Japan is taken care of in kindergarten (*Yoochien*) and daycare centres (*Hoikuen*). The first are regulated by the School Education Law of 1947 and thus fall under the Ministry of Education (*Monbushoo*) and the latter is regulated by the Child Welfare Law and is placed under the jurisdiction of the Ministry of Health (*Kooseishoo*). Some 91% of all five year-olds attended pre-school in 1987. Of those, 27.5% were in daycare centres and 63.6% were in kindergarten. But there was much regional variation. In Nagano Prefecture, for example, 65% were in daycare centres and 25.2% in kindergarten. At the other end of the scale we find Okinawa with 6.2% in daycare centres and 93.6% in kindergarten (Monbushoo, 1987, 113). In 1995 pre-school attendance had risen to 93.3%. The rise took place in the daycare centres (Shimizu, 1996, 2).

Obviously, the Ministry of Education prefers kindergartens, which are under its own jurisdiction and they are referred to as 'organs of schooling' (*gakkoo kyooiku kikai*). Due to differences in allocation of funds in the prefectures, the spread of kindergartens has been delayed in some areas, but every effort is being made to change this (Monbushoo, 1987, 113).

Daycare centres are usually for working mothers and are considered to be less academic than kindergartens, but there is only a slight difference as there is a lot of overlapping. Daycare centres accept children from six months old to six years and are usually not as well equipped as kindergartens. The last year at daycare centres and kindergartens is, however, usually similar in curriculum. Because they are open only for a few hours every day, kinder- gartens only accept three- to six-year-olds with non-working mothers.

Field studies of pre-school in Japan, such as that conducted by Joy Hendry and described in her book *Becoming Japanese* (1986), Joseph Tobin in Tobin et al. *Preschool in Three Cultures* (1989) and Lois Peak, *Learning to Go to School in Japan* (1991), point out that the difference between the two types of institutions is in practice insignificant. The purpose of both is to supplement home education, develop the minds and health of the children and introduce them to group life.

The purpose of the pre-school curriculum is described in the curriculum guidelines for kindergarten issued by the Ministry of Education in 1990:

18. Other means of response to the demand from nuclear families caused by the absense of grandparents or their decreased influence on children's upbringing (*shitsuke*), are videos for toddlers offering training in good manners and toilet habits. (Noguchi, 1996, 12-13)

1. It is a fundamental requirement of kindergarten (*Yoochien*) education that emphasis be placed on environment. In the course of kindergarten education, the following three matters are most important:

    (1) To create an appropriate environment for children.
    (2) To attain the aim of education in its widest sense mainly by instruction through play.
    (3) To provide guidance in accordance with each individual child's developmental characteristics.

2. The objectives of kindergarten education are as follows:

    (1) To encourage basic living habits and attitudes for a healthy, safe and happy life, and to nurture the foundations for a healthy mind and body.
    (2) To encourage love and trust for people and to cultivate an attitude of independence, cooperation and morality.
    (3) To encourage interest in one's surrounding nature and society and to cultivate sensibilities and a capacity for appreciating one's surroundings.
    (4) To encourage interest in language use in daily life, and to develop attitudes in talking and listening to others with pleasure and to cultivate a language sense.
    (5) To encourage a rich mind, and enrich creativity through various experiences.

    The minimum number of school weeks for kindergarten education is 39 weeks every year, and the standard number of classroom hours per day is four, in consideration of the developmental level of mind and body of the children. (Monbushoo, 1989a, 58)

Increasingly, pre-school is offering school education because the effect of the strong competition for entering the best educational institutions has filtered down to pre-school level.[19] Some pre-schools even have entrance examinations

---

19. In view of the educational pursuits undertaken in the home, some consider the kindergarten more of a social preparation than an intellectual preparation and state that children are sent to kindergarten to learn about 'group life'. (Taniuchi 1985 in Benjamin 1991, 257; Hendry, 1986, 61) However, this will not necessarily be the case in the daycare centre, which is primarily for working mothers — attendance is caused by necessity. The amount of educational activities often undertaken in kindergarten, suggests that its role is more than just socialising, but quite often the teaching of academic subjects as such takes place outside kindergarten. In 1978, 2.4% of the children attending kindergarten also took study related classes outside kindergarten (Hendry, 1986, 68). Tobin in his study of pre-school in Japan further noted some disagreement as to how much emphasis should be placed on group life versus individuality in pre-school. However, all his informants agreed that the American

to select the best candidates. 'Examinations' may be interviews with the three-year olds or assessment of the mothers (Hendry, 1986, 63). Often the pre-schools using this procedure are those connected with the so-called 'escalator-schools'.

An escalator-school is a private school with all levels from kindergarten to university. In a system like this advancement to the next level is made considerably more easy than in unconnected schools, because the children are always prepared for exactly the exam they will encounter at the next level and because they may be promoted on the basis of recommendation by their teachers. Escalators starting at pre-school level will provide a child with a good start and, to a large extent, spare it the painful experience of entrance competition. On the other hand, as compulsory education in Japan is mostly public and attendance is decided on the basis of school districts, the competition for entering the right institution is not strong at this level. Except in extreme cases the choice of kindergartens is more likely to be based on convenience and price, than on the effort to get ahead in the schools rating game (Benjamin, 1991, 257).

Most pre-schoolers learn to read and write the *kana*-system and they learn to sit at desks, to have duties and use workbooks, either at home or in kindergarten. Those who attend kindergarten also learn to behave in a group. It would be extremely difficult for a parent not to send his child to pre-school when most of the children in the neighbourhood go. He would be afraid that he was not giving his child the best possible opportunities — besides, with all the other children away at kindergarten, the child would feel lonely and left out (U.S. Department of Education 1987, 79; Peak 1991, 194).

The kindergarten curriculum includes such subjects as music, language, health, social studies and nature. Music and language in practice means the singing and telling of seasonally related songs and stories; health is concerned with teaching the children to dress appropriately and to be aware of the dangers connected with extreme temperature swings. Social studies record local responses to seasonal variations in farming, fishing etc., and in general, it passes on popular myths and superstitions as well as moral values. Nature is observed through registration of its seasonal changes as related to the other subjects and in the samples of plants, aquarium fish etc. in the class rooms (Hendry, 1986, 141-42).

2.2.2 Elementary School

Elementary school (*shoogakkoo*) is for six to twelve year olds and its purpose

example they were shown put too little emphasis on promoting group life. (Tobin, 1992, 55) is to 'take care of the development of body and mind and to teach the basics'. (Roppoo, 1990, 38) The objectives as stated in the curriculum guidelines from 1989, which were enforced in 1992, are listed here:

1. To encourage generous minds and the ability through educational activities to live an active, productive life, in accordance with the characteristics of the developmental stage of infants, pupils and students; and appropriate to each subject matter.

2. To place importance on basic and essential knowledge necessary for good citizenship, to enrich education to encourage distinctive personalities, and to strive for consistency in the content of all subject matter at all school levels from kindergarten to upper secondary school.

3. To place importance on fostering the ability to act independently to cope with the changes in society, developing a foundation of creativity, and to endeavour to strengthen the child's will to learn independency.

4. To place importance on developing an attitude of respect for the culture and tradition of Japan, and to give children a deeper understanding of the culture and history of the world, and thus to cultivate qualities as Japanese citizens living in an international society. (Monbushoo, 1989a, 60)

The subjects are Japanese Language, Social Studies, Arithmetic, Science, Music, Art and Handicraft, Home Making and Physical Education (see charts). First and second grade have what is called Life Environment Studies instead of Social Studies and Science from April 1992. In addition, there is Moral Education and time for special activities. Special activities include class room assemblies, pupil's councils, club activities, ceremonial events, study-related events, physical education-related events, guidance on school lunch etc. One school hour is 45 minutes and a first grader has 850 hours per year rising to 1,015 in sixth grade (Monbushoo, 1989b, 19). Class size has been set down from 45 to 40 with the new curriculum guidelines and the enrolment rate is 99.99%.

Chart 3: Prescribed subjects and number of school hours in elementary school

Grades/Subjects	1	2	3	4	5	6
Japanese Language	272 306	280 315	280	280	210	210
Social Studies	68 (-)	70 (-)	105	105	105	105
Arithmetic	136	175	175	175	175	175
Science	68 (-)	70 (-)	105	105	105	105
Life Environment Studies	102	105	-	-	-	-
Music	68	70	70	70	70	70
Art & Handicraft	68	70	70	70	70	70
Homemaking	-	-	-	-	70	70
Physical Education	102	105	105	105	105	105
Moral Education	34	35	35	35	35	35
Special Activities	34	35	35	70	70	70
Total	850	910	980	1015	1015	1015

One school hour is a class period of 45 minutes. 'Second numbers' are the number of school hours according to the new curriculum guidelines enforced in April 1992. (Monbushoo 1989a, 61)

Elementary schools are set up by the municipalities who are also responsible for their financing. The curriculum guidelines, which were initially only *guidelines* have now become a standard not to be deviated from. Despite municipal responsibility for elementary schools they teach exactly the same everywhere in Japan, only physical conditions may vary, though those are also remarkably alike right down to the buildings (Cummings, 1980, 105).

The description of a common elementary school would be: A three-storied, rectangular, concrete structure without central heating or air conditioning. Room stoves are used in cold weather. Classrooms are rectangular with windows on one side and a doorway on the other that opens to a hallway running the length of the building. In the class room the desks are usually arranged in rows and it is decorated with the children's drawings or samples of their writing and there may be an aquarium or the like. The school usually has well equipped science, art and music rooms. Also most schools have gymnasia, libraries and playgrounds. Over 75% of the public schools have a swimming pool. Public elementary schools usually do not have uniforms, but use a school badge or a cap to identify the child as belonging to that particular school.[20]

A relative lack of differentiation by income level and occupation in the Japanese neighbourhoods means less variations between schools than in neighbourhood schools in the United States or most European countries (Benjamin, 1991, 258).

Leadership positions at elementary schools are occupied by the principal and the head teacher. Close to 100% of the holders of these posts are men even though 60% of the elementary school teachers are women. The strong male dominance in the leadership is bound to affect the children's views on the roles of the sexes. The principal is responsible for all school activities, he represents the school with local authorities and the Parent-Teacher Association, and through regular addresses to the student body he symbolises the school's authority and expectations.

The head teacher directs the daily life of the school. He coordinates the regular school activities, special projects etc. Teaching only three hours per week his responsibilities are mainly administrative. His salary is not much higher than the regular teacher's but instead he has the respect of his peers and takes a step on the career ladder to becoming a principal.

Regular teachers usually teach 22-23 hours per week. In addition they spend time planning and working together outside class but still staying on the school grounds. Often they are responsible for a club activity such as being coach for the baseball team. They are assigned to a class for whom they are usually responsible for two years. Teachers are formally able to teach at any level, and frequently they do, but first graders usually get the more experienced and talented teachers since this level is considered particularly important for establishing future work habits in the child (U.S. Department of Education, 1987, 25).

An average school day begins at 8:30 and lasts until 3:50 in the afternoon. During the day there would be six class periods and a one-hour lunch break.

The ideal home for an elementary school pupil is supportive and stressless. The child is not expected to do chores, participate in religious schooling or activities or in any way be anything else than a successful student (Benjamin, 1991, 258). Problems in elementary school range from complaints that the curriculum — especially with the new curriculum guidelines — is too demanding, to newspaper stories of bullied and distressed

---

20. The description is based on my own observations and on Cummings 1980, *Education and Equality in Japan* and on Conduit 1996, *Educating Andy*.

children. The curriculum is cumulative and in quick succession presents the children with new concepts and a mass of new material. Though the children come well prepared in the first grade some of them quickly get problems keeping up with the school work. Those are the *ochikobore*, the 'leftovers'. According to one of the teacher organisations the number of *ochikobore* grows roughly proportionally with the grades, that is, ten percent in the first grade, twenty in the second, thirty in the third and so on (Kawai, 1991).

It would be wrong, of course, to blame only the curriculum. Differences in ability,[21] family environment and personality are factors accounting for differences in academic performance. Instruction is not individualised to take care of *ochikobore* although some teachers do offer assistance out of class. Remedial education is almost exclusively found in the private sector. This means either hiring a private tutor or sending the child to a *juku*, a cram school, in this way making the school day even longer for the child and requiring an extra amount of money on the family budget.

Educational success is immensely important as entrance to one of the elite universities is tied up with the chance of landing a high prestige job. Therefore entrance examinations play a big role in children's lives. This poses a problem for both parents and children. It is generally agreed that it is not good for children to have no free time and get caught up in competition at a tender age, but even so, all parents are eager to give their children every advantage, so the *juku* business flourishes (Weisman, 1992; Rohlen, 1983, 106). The social pressure to conform and aim for high positions is strong. To be content with a mediocre performance is admitting defeat.

As far as schooling in the basics is concerned, there is no doubt that the Japanese elementary school is working well. The low rate of illiteracy is the result of schooling at a compulsory level, and observations of elementary school pupils indicate that they are happy, composed and satisfied with their lives (White, 1987, ch. 7; Conduit, 1996). They are secure in their peer group and well looked after by the teachers and at least some of them reach a level of achievement that is remarkable by world standards. But this rosy picture is not true for everyone, and competition in particular, and the pressure to

---

21. The word 'ability' poses some problems. Often one will find statements that the Japanese believe that all children have equal abilities (U.S. Dept. of Ed. 1987; Mainichi, 1985b). Statements like 'if parents believe in their children there is no such thing as baka (stupid)' can be heard. This would explain why instruction is so undifferentiated, but this idea of innate equal ability is more of an ideal than it is believed to be a fact. A Monbushoo director told me 'that is what we say, but it is not true of course' (interview with Satoo Jiroo, June 6 1991), and the very fact that cram schools provide remedial education supports the view that the often mentioned idea of equal ability is not considered a deep rooted truth, not even by the Japanese. Therefore I will use the word 'ability' assuming that there is such a thing as innate differences in ability.

perform well, can make elementary school a disappointing experience for some.

2.2.3 Middle School

Middle school (*chuugakkoo*) is for children aged 12 to 15 who have completed elementary school. Its legal definition of purpose is 'to build upon what has been learnt in elementary school and provide further basic education with due consideration for the developmental stage of mind and body' (Roppoo 1990, 43).

The objectives of middle school are the same as in elementary school. Subjects are divided into required subjects and electives. Required subjects are: Japanese Language, Social Studies, Mathematics, Science, Music, Fine Arts, Health and Physical Education, Industrial Arts and Home Making. With Moral Education, special activities and elective subjects, there is a total of 1,050 hours per year. One class period is 50 minutes.

The atmosphere may be described as more serious than in elementary school due to the oncoming entrance examination to high school. Educational goals and procedures focus on factual knowledge and further development of basic skills.

Middle school buildings and grounds are usually separate from elementary school but are often similar in shape and facilities (U.S. Department of Education 1987, 33). The classrooms are almost without decorations to help the children focus on learning and building their character. They are crowded with desks usually arranged in rows facing the blackboard. Like in elementary school the rooms for special classes such as music or natural sciences are well equipped.

Administration is like that of elementary school but only one third of the teachers are women. Each class is assigned an advisor — a *tannin* — who functions as home room teacher and counsellor. The home room teacher is responsible for academic *and* social guidance and also counsels on personal and behavioral problems (U.S. Department of Education, 1987, 34). School in Japan is almost as much involved in the private life of the children as in their school life. It is not uncommon for schools to set regulations, *koozoku*, for behaviour not only while at school, but also during vacations and free time (interview with Higuchi Keiko, June 27, 1991).

Instruction is based on lectures, and textbooks are strictly adhered to. The emphasis is on memorisation and drill to remember large quantities of factual material, and there is always only one correct answer. The textbooks are authorised by the Ministry of Education and teacher-centred instruction is the rule. Other methods like laboratory work, field trips and student projects are also sometimes used.

Chart 4: Prescribed subjects and number of school hours in middle school

Grade/Subject	1	2	3
Japanese	175	140	140
Social Studies	140	140	105 70-105
Mathematics	105	140	140
Science	105	105	140 105-140
Music	70	70 35-70	35
Fine Arts	70	70 35-70	35
Health & Physical Education	105	105	105 105-140
Industrial Arts & Homemaking	70	70	105 70-105
Moral Education	35	35	35
Special Activities	70 35-70	70 35-70	70 35-70
Elective Subjects	105 105-140	105 105-210	140 140-280
Total	1050	1050	1050

One school hour is a class period of 50 minutes. 'Second numbers' are the number of school hours according to the new curriculum guidelines enforced in April 1993. (Monbushoo, 1989a, 61)

In middle school as well as in elementary schools slow learners experience difficulties with the curriculum (*Mainichi*, March, November, 1985b). Again remedial education is mostly to be found in the private sector and in case it is needed, it can constitute a heavy financial burden on the family.

There is some school violence in Japan, a fact that is much debated in the mass media, but by no means to the degree experienced in some Western countries, notably the United States. Still, it is considered a serious deviation from social norms and therefore receives extensive news coverage (*Asahi*, June, 1987b).

A problem just as serious is *ijime*, bullying/intimidation. The problem seems to be most serious at middle school level and again the media covers it extensively (*Mainichi*, April, Sept., Oct., Nov., 1985b; *Asahi*, Feb., April, June, Sept., Dec., 1987b). Bullied students are often said to share certain characteristics which set them apart from other students, and teachers are being exhorted to be more sensitive to this 'problem behaviour' (U.S. Department of Education, 1987, 37; Ayuki, 1995). Contrary to what might be expected, the problem is often considered to be caused by the victim displaying victim-behaviour, not the bully.

Bullying becomes all the more serious when one takes into consideration the fact that Japanese children are usually not used to being excluded from the group. Exclusion is frightening because it is so rare (Tobin et al. , 1989, 43). Where in the United States and in Europe punishment would often consist of grounding, in Japan the more usual threat would be not allowing the child into the building — exclusion from the group rather than confinement within it.

Middle school is the last stage of compulsory schooling and gradually the child learns to compete and accept it as a necessary part of schooling. Teachers become more stern and the ratio of male — and supposedly 'stern' — teachers rises. Boys are often required to shave their heads (*boozu*) upon entering middle school to show the extent of their commitment. Girls' hair must not reach the collar, longer hair is to be braided. A host of rules governing the appearance of the students (*koozoku*), are ostensibly to 'make life simple' for the students, because they will not have to worry about appearance. Also, there is a belief that disorder in appearance gives evidence to disorder in life and therefore strict dress codes are enforced (*The East*, 1988, 48; Conduit, 1996).

Grades and tests become essential in middle school because in order to advance to the next level of schooling an entrance examination is necessary. So the first competitive experience that will really matter in children's lives they are likely to have at the age of fifteen when they encounter the high school entrance examination. Entering a good high school means significantly better chances of entering an elite university like Tokyo University, Kyoto University or the private *Keioo* or *Waseda*, to name but a few of the top universities.

Due to recruitment policies of some (prestigious) employers, leading to the employment of graduates from particular universities, the chance of securing a good high ranking job is linked to the university you attend and in the end also to the high school you have attended. This, as the competition filters down, also has an effect on middle school. By the time the students apply for high school — and 95.8% did in 1995 — they are well aware of the rankings in the high school and university hierarchy. Mock tests provided by cram schools and other private education businesses and teacher advice help the student choose the school where he or she is most likely to be accepted. Several entrance examinations may be taken. The best students may be given the advantage of having their entrance to the next level recommended by their teachers, but as this is done according to grades and tests it does not really present a leeway for slower students. Only bright students can skip an obstacle in this manner.

The actual procedure for obtaining admission starts with a conference (*soodan*) with the home room teacher. Here the school to which one should apply is selected according to the student's wishes as well as the home room teacher's guidance and assessment of the student's ability. Then the application with credentials is sent to the selected school. Credentials are records of study, records of special activities, general comments on personality, attendance records, records of health etc. Most of this information is contained in the *naishinshoo*, the personal report made by the school. This report is of immense importance for whether a student is admitted and is frequently blamed for being used as a tool to control the students. The *naishinshoo* has influence on a student's future as it determines admission to high school. The student does not have access to see the *naishinshoo* and thus has no idea what it says. Several court suits have been carried out because of *naishinshoo* but most of the suits are won by the schools (Horio, 1988, 280).

When the application has been sent there are three possible outcomes. One: Entrance on the basis of recommendation (*suisen*). In this case the high school may add an interview, a practical test and an aptitude test. A description of the high school examination system in Chiba prefecture by Berman stated that less than 3% of the high school openings in this prefecture were reserved for students who would be admitted on the basis of recommendation. Chiba prefecture is not unusual in its procedures and can thus be taken to exemplify the situation in the other prefectures as well (Berman in Benjamin, 1991, 258).

The second possible outcome: Entrance examination (*nyuugaku shiken*). Once the examination is passed the school may add an interview and tests as in the case of recommendation (Monbushoo, 1989a, 75). The overwhelming majority of students take the entrance examination as the recommendation system operates with a fixed quota determining how many students can be admitted in this manner.

The third possible outcome — failure — has as its consequence that the student cannot attend a public high school that year. The students who fail usually end up in private high schools as the practise of a year's preparation for the next examination is very rare at this stage in contrast to the situation after high school. (See *roonin* in 2.2.5) About 30% of high school students attend private high schools, some by default, some by choice.[22] Success in the examination is vital and as one can only apply to one particular public high school — but to any number of private ones — and it becomes very important to choose the school where one is most likely to be admitted (Benjamin, 1991, 259).

Some have already at this stage entered the 'elite track' by gaining admittance to a private elite middle school, but at this level it is still most common to be enrolled in public middle schools and the hierarchy is by no means as established as it is on the next level, the high school.

2.2.4 High School

High school (*kookoo*) education is to build upon the foundation laid in middle school and, with due consideration for the developmental stage of mind and body, it is to teach basic skills as well as specialised skills (Roppoo, 43, 1990). The curriculum guidelines give the following regulations for high school education: (New curriculum guidelines enforced in 1994)

1. To respect the independent initiative of individual schools so that they maintain and develop their distinctive education.
2. To ensure that the contents of teaching may be better adapted to differing abilities and aptitudes of individual students.
3. To ensure that students may lead a relaxed and full school life.
4. To ensure that students may gain a better understanding and greater enjoyment of working life through some experience-oriented learning, and to lay emphasis on both moral and physical education, aiming at the full development of students.
    (Monbushoo, 1989a, 62)

High school provides general courses and specialised vocational courses. Regardless of which course is chosen, all students are required to study the following subjects: Japanese Language I, Contemporary Society, Mathematics I, Science I, Health, Physical Education and one of the following: Music I, Fine Arts I, Crafts Production I or Calligraphy I. Girls are to study General Home Economics and students in specialised vocational courses to have not less than 30 credits in Specialised Subjects (see Chart 5).

The majority of high school students choose the General Course, which is the academic course, to enter the competition for university admittance.

---

22. Of course, elite private high schools do not accept as students those who fail the public examinations.

Chart 5: Subject areas, subjects and standard number of credits in high school
Example of curriculum for General Course

Subject Areas	Subjects	1st. year	2nd. year	3rd. year	Total
Japanese Language	Japanese I	5			5
	Japanese II		5	3	5
	Contemporary Japanese			3	3
	Classics				3
Social Studies	Contemporary Society	4			4
	Japanese History		2	2	4
	World History		2	2	4
	Geography		2		2
	Politics & Economy			2	2
Mathe-matics	Mathematics	5			5
	Algebra & Geometry		3	2	5
	Basic Analysis		2	2	4
Science	Science I	4			4
	Science II			2	2
	Chemistry		1½	1	2½
	Biology		1½	1	2½
Physical Education & Health	Physical Education	4	4	3	11
	Health	1	1		2
Art	Music I	2	1	-	
	Fine Arts I	in	in		3
	Calligraphy	all	all		
Foreign Language	English I	5			5
	English II		2	3	5
	English IIb		3		3
	English IIc			4	4
Home Economics	General Home Economics	2*	2*		4*
Additional Credits		2	2	2	6
Subject Total		32	32	32	96
Special Activity	Home-room	1	1	1	3
	Clubs	1	1	1	3
Grand Total		34	34	34	102

One school hour is 50 minutes and 35 school hours per year equals one credit.
(Monbushoo, 1989a, 63)   *Only girls.

In May 1987 the distribution by type of course was as follows: 73.1% choose the General Course, Commerce was second with 10.8%, Technical Course was third with 9%, and then followed agriculture 2.9%, Homemaking 2.6%, Nursing 0.5%, Fishery 0.3% and others 0.8% (Monbushoo, 1989b, 15).

With a little less than 30% attending vocational courses in high school it is obvious that the pressure for entering academic courses at university — rather than entering technical colleges or vocational universities — is immense and thus gives rise to strong competition. The students attend cram schools (*juku*) and *yobikoo* (fulltime university preparation school) to better their chances and again at this level, but only much more so than at middle school level, mock tests and lists of the scores necessary for entrance at specific universities are commonly used tools.

Despite the almost universal enrolment in high schools it has not had the social effect of mixing students from different social strata or geographical areas,[23] but in fact just the opposite. More schools have been constructed, but each enrol a narrow segment of the population. The sorting mechanism of entrance examination creates a strongly stratified system of high schools representing significantly different chances of entrance at elite universities. The student bodies of the individual high schools are academically homogeneous, as the students are placed according to their scores. The significance of joining the 'right' high school can be seen by the following example: Attendance at a well-known high school like Nada in Koobe gives the student a chance of entering Tokyo University of around 1 in 2 whereas the average high school student's chance of admission at Tokyo University is about 1 in 440 (Rohlen, 1983, 19).

In this light the great significance attributed to the hierarchy of educational institutions is not a surprise. But this hierarchy would mean nothing if it was not for the fact that prestigious companies and the ministries hire employees on the basis of *where* the applicant managed to gain entrance, not *what* he or she studied once accepted. The hierarchy of educational institutions all comes down to the question of life-time employment. This is only practised in large companies or ministries and to qualify one must prove oneself to belong to the upper echelons of students, namely those able to pass an entrance examination for an elite university.

The university entrance procedures are different for private and public/national universities. As with high school entrance, a university is

---

23. The reason geographical areas are mentioned here is that the group of outcasts known as *burakumin* usually live in segregated, identifiable areas.

chosen that lies within the perceived range of the student's capabilities and according to the student's own wishes if possible. An application with credentials is sent to the selected university/universities. In the instance of a national or local public university the applicant must first pass the 'Joint First-Stage Achievement Test'. This test was introduced in 1979 and was intended to simplify the examination system at least for the public and national universities by making all applicants take the same test, and to make it easier to compare the students on a national level. But as it turns out, all the universities using this joint test (public and national universities mostly), have added an individual Second-Stage Entrance Examination. So, applicants for national and public universities now have to sit for two examinations with the First-Stage Test functioning as a screening device. The private universities usually have only one entrance examination, but the National Centre for University Entrance Examination is working on an examination to be used by all institutions of higher education (Monbushoo, 1989a, 76-7). In light of the fate the First-Stage Achievement Test suffered, it is improbable that a new common examination would fare significantly better. An interesting aspect of the entrance examination system which clearly indicates the effect it has on the educational system as a whole as well as on the aspirations of the students, is a survey of the reasons university students give for their choice of university.

The survey is quoted in a 1985 publication by the Japanese Academic Society on Education (*Nihon Kyooiku Gakkai*). This survey was first published in a magazine called *Gekkan Kookoosei* (Monthly High School Student) in April 1985 and was conducted at the Kansai Humanities and Science University (*Kansai Bunri Gakuin*).

The students were asked to mark reasons for their choice of university and course and the result is shown in Chart 6.

Now, the figures are from 1985, but in the meantime no major changes have occurred either in the examination procedures or in the recruitment procedures to warrant serious doubt that they are a valid indication of the present situation. The figures clearly show the immense importance of the ranking of students for the choice of university. It is worth noticing that reason a) was not listed by anyone and reason b) only in connection with second or third priorities.

The students apparently were not preoccupied with the quality of teaching or research when they had to decide on a university. The status of a university may have been interpreted by the applicants as a true reflection of its quality.

Chart 6: Reasons for choosing a particular university, 1985. (Percentages)

	First priority	Second priority	Third priority
Total	e) 57. 6	g) 25. 1	b) 23. 0
Humanities	e) 56. 5	g) 23. 5	h) 22. 4
Science	e) 58. 8	b) 29. 6	g) 27. 4
Public univ.	e) 56. 0	b) 29. 3	g) 25. 6
Private univ.	e) 58. 3	g) 24. 6	c) 23. 0
Public univ.			
Humanities	e) 52. 6	g) 26. 4	b) 23. 8
Science	e) 58. 1	g) 32. 8	g) 25. 1
Private univ.			
Humanities	e) 57. 8	h) 24. 7	c) 24. 7
Science	e) 59. 7	g) 30. 7	b) 24. 7

The students were asked to choose between the following answers:

a) Educational policy/content; b) Academic milieu; c) Employment situation; d) Fame; e) Rank and own standing; f) Economic reasons; g) Geographical reasons; h) Atmosphere at the university; i) Just having a shot at it; j) Other. (Hosogane, 1985, 49)

2.2.5 Juku and Yobikoo

Apart from the formal educational system, there is an informal, private system of cram schools in Japan, *juku* and *yobikoo*. *Juku* is the kind of cram school which children who are still attending school join, a) in order to prepare for an entrance examination, b) to better their grades or c) just to keep up with the pace in class. It offers remedial teaching as well as supplementary/preparatory teaching. *Yobikoo* is primarily for high school graduates who during one or several *roonin*[24] years, years out of school when they study intensively for a particular entrance examination, receive teaching at this type of cram school.

The cramming market is very diverse. A cram school may belong to a large franchise chain, owned by a large company, enroling thousands of students at several localities. Other cram schools are small and run at home

---

24. The term *roonin* originally referred to a masterless samuari, but it has now come to mean a student with no university affiliation.

by former teachers or housewives. The Ministry of Education in 1985 found that 27% of the cram schools belonged to a franchise chain and the rest were independent and in 1993 the percentage of franchise establishments had dropped to 19.7%. The bulk of cram schools were still small enterprises (Hisatomi, 1987, 41; Monbushoo, 1993, 46).

The teachers have diverse qualifications ranging from virtually none to university education. A Ministry of Education survey found the following figures for cram school teachers' backgrounds in 1985 and 1993:

Chart 7: Educational background of cram school teachers, 1985 & 1993. (Percentage)

Year	University education	School teachers	Experience	No experience
1985	29. 2	4. 7	18. 2	47. 9
1993	37. 3	0	14. 3	48. 4

(Monbushoo, 1993, 51)

Clearly, the people with no educational background for teaching were the majority. They would be the ones to offer primarily remedial teaching and help with homework, while the examination-related extra teaching would often be undertaken by people with a university education.

The 1993 survey included school teachers in the university education category, but in fact the proportion of university educated teachers has risen beyond that. Perhaps this is a sign of the consolidation of cram schools as places offering stable jobs, or perhaps it could be that more stringent demands are now prevailing for higher teacher qualifications? But, if the latter is the case, it seems that only certain cram schools demand such high qualifications, since the proportion of personnel with no educational background or experience in teaching has also risen.

Each cram school tries to develop distinctive features like giving a lot of tests, using elaborate teaching devices or a psychological approach to attract clients. Larger cram school boast the number of clients who have successfully entered Tokyo or other elite universities.

The business has experienced much growth especially since the sixties and seventies when large private academies with sophisticated teaching methods and equipment began to flourish. A recent survey by the Yano Research Institute quoted in the press, found that nearly 4.4 million students were registered as attending some 50,000 to 60,000 cram schools. This represents 18.6% of the elementary school children and 52.2% of the students in the seventh to ninth grades. The amount of money spent on cramming education has almost doubled in seven years[25] (Weisman, 1992). An interesting set of figures was published by the Ministry of Education on the kind of tutoring received by children in cram school in 1985 and 1993:

Chart 8: Content of cram school training, 1985 & 1993. (Percentage)

		Remedial education	Home work	Exam prep.	Other
Elementary school	— 1985	14.0	33.8	18.8	44.3
	— 1993	12.9	40.3	25.6	33.0
Middle school	— 1985	16.0	54.1	36.6	14.5
	— 1993	14.9	49.4	48.9	6.4
Total	— 1985	15.2	45.8	29.3	26.6
	— 1993	14.1	45.6	39.1	17.6

(Monbushoo, 1993, 7)

Evidently cram schools filled a demand for remedial education as well as homework help, though the percentage for the two categories has declined slightly. The most conspicuous change since 1985 has been in the category of 'other', indicating that cram school attendance has in general become more academically oriented. What has generally been considered the purpose of cram school, namely extra teaching in preparation for examinations, accounted for little more than one third of the cram school attenders in 1993. The somewhat one-sided picture many Western media present of cram schools does not reflect the fact that cram schools do actually fill the need that slow learners have for extra tutoring, which the regular schools cannot give them. One problem is, of course, that cram schools are often costly, thus excluding slow learners with no financial back-up from this option.

Figures from an official survey of household spending on education showed that expenses on supplementary education had increased nine-fold from 1971 to 1984 while the cost of other items such as reference books had increased five-fold and the cost of uniforms had increased four-fold in the same period. The overall cost of education during the period had increased slightly more than three-fold, the amounts being 954,369 yen in 1971 and

---

25. An example of a *juku* user was published in the *Herald Tribune* April 1992: 'N.E. feels relentless pressure to get ahead. Rising at dawn, he works a full day with his regular colleagues and another three hours each evening in special study sessions. He then does a couple of hours of work at home before going to bed at midnight. — This is a heavy burden for an 11-year-old.' (Weisman, 1992)

3,195,829 yen in 1984. (At this time one U.S. dollar was worth approximately 216 yen) (Hisatomi, 1987, 41).

Due to the growing demand for remedial and supplementary education for children to help them advance in the regular school system and pass the examinations, cram schools are becoming almost as demanding as regular schools. Some cram schools are so intense that they require an attendance of more than twenty hours a week, plus most vacation time. Top cram schools, that is, those with the best record of clients admitted to elite universities, have entrance examinations themselves and are rumoured to be even more crucial to success than regular school. General interest is high, and parents cannot ignore the cram schools, for it could mean the difference between success or failure in securing the desired employment position.

Some of the more famous cram schools have developed the following system to prepare for entrance examinations to private middle schools:[26]

In the fourth grade of elementary school, a test is taken to gain admittance to the cram school. Then there is a test every Sunday during the two last years of elementary school to place the students in a hierarchy according to the marks achieved. The marks are used as indicators of the entrance examination a student is capable of passing. Three to four times a week the students attend classes at the cram school, they take a mock test on Saturday in preparation for the Sunday test and they attend a summer course lasting 33 days from 8 a.m. to 7 or 8 p.m. The cost of such a course in 1985 was a staggering one million yen (Hisatomi, 1987, 43-45).

On the question *why* parents send their children to cram school, the answers were:

Chart 9: Why parents send their children to cram schools

	1985	1993
— The child wants to go	52.3%	46.0%
— Parents not able to help with homework	29.1%	33. 3%
— With school alone the child won't advance to desired school	27.2%	26.0%
— Child doesn't study when alone	38.0%	32. 4%

(Monbushoo, 1993, 13)

26. Private, because public middle schools do not have entrance examinations.

We see that the percentage of parents listing exam preparation as the reason for sending the child to cram school roughly coincides with the examination related tutoring in cram school, namely around one-third. The most remarkable change from 1985 is the increased feeling of being unable to assist the child with homework and the drop in the number of people citing the child's wish as a reason for cram school attendance.

The reason some parents are willing to spend amounts of money in the vicinity of one million yen on extra tutoring in elementary school, and for putting their children through such an ordeal, is the prospect of entering one of the famous escalator schools. By entering such a school further advancement to higher levels is made much less demanding than say, in the public system.

Parents are aware of the possible negative effects on the children, the loss of fun and innocence, but usually that worry is overcome by the fear that without extra stimulus from a cram school the child will lose out in the race for the elite universities, the good positions and the high social status. (Rohlen, 1983, 106) As one mother put it: 'I am uncomfortable with not sending him [to cram school]' (*Ikasenai no ga fuman desu*) (Kubo, 1996).

The rise of the private cramming business has had consequences for the children's freedom — there is very little spare time for leisure activities or for relaxing. Amano Ikuo, professor at the Faculty of Education, Tokyo University, publicly calls cram school *harmful* to Japanese education and to children, adding that it is not healthy for children to have so little free time or to be caught up in competition at a tender age (Weisman, 1992).

But the rise of the cram school has also meant a clearer division between income strata and their opportunities. The much praised equality of opportunity in Japanese education[27] has suffered a setback. The cram school and private tutoring cost money, the better the teaching the more it costs as it is driven by the rules of the market place. Parents with high incomes can better afford remedial and supplementary education than not-so-well endowed parents. Money may not provide an educational advantage in the public system itself, but in the event of problems, it provides a better opportunity for having them solved. Average performance need not be a problem if the best supplementary education can be bought, but of course this is not an option if the funds are simply not there.

The effect of such cramming was demonstrated by Professor Hisatomi. Scrutinising an entrance examination from a private middle school in 1987 he found that the first question was difficult but soluble, question 2 was shockingly complicated, questions 3-6 getting progressively more difficult requiring a lot of thought. The children had 55 minutes to answer. Professor

27. See for example Cummings 1980, *Education and Equality in Japan*.

Hisatomi stated that 'no adult could have completed this test within the time limit without special training'. Elementary school teachers called the test 'impossible'. A social sciences test given at middle school level could, in Professor Hisatomi's opinion, easily have been set forth as a university entrance examination test (Hisatomi, 1987, 45).

With such demands on the children for gaining entrance to the prestigious middle schools it is obvious that extra tutoring is necessary. However, it is probably also true that the very fact that cram schools can obtain such results with children has contributed to making the entrance examinations progressively more difficult.

The presence of *juku*-cram schools especially, but also *yobikoo*, contribute to the feeling of 'desolation' (*koohai*) of education, which covers a variety of phenomena like: the excessive competition for university entrance and to some degree high school entrance, tired, worn out children who rarely have time to play freely, school phobia, bullying and violence in school. In many cases, the presence of this second structure of educational institution increases the pressure on children and parents and leaves no time for a child to actually be and behave like a child. The situation is described in the following terms by an official from the teachers organisation ATU: 'When I get home late, around nine or ten in the evening, children are on their way home from cram school and the like. Perhaps the parents do it out of love... ?' (Masuda, personal communication, May 16, 1991).

Professor Hisatomi also questioned this practice of cramming, asking whether it did not conflict with the human rights of children as its demands would in some cases leave no time for play (Hisatomi, 1987, 45).

A concrete example of a cram school is the *yobikoo* Yoyogi Seminaaru, the headquarters located in Yoyogi, Tokyo. It is famed for placing many clients in elite universities. More than 20 branch schools of Yoyogi Seminaaru are spread all over Japan, from the Tokyo area over Nagoya to Kobe and Osaka. The school offers both traditional *yobikoo* courses for high school graduates aspiring to university and more *juku*-like courses for high school students. The courses are very specific, for instance course No. 1 is the *Toodai bunka koosu* (The Tokyo University Humanities Course). This is a short course running only ten days during the summer vacation and it offers eight lessons in each of the following subjects: English — translation and understanding, English grammar, mathematics, modern Japanese literature, older Japanese literature. Apparently, this is precisely the knowledge which is important in order to pass the entrance examination for the humanities at Tokyo University. The price for this course is 33,000 yen (approx. $248) plus a 5000 yen admission fee. A mock test costs 3,500 yen. Thus a ten-day preparation for the entrance examination for Tokyo University at Yoyogi Seminaaru costs about 41,500 yen (approx. $312) (Yoyogi, 1991, 16).

Cram schools were definitely an important feature of Japanese education at the time of establishment of the NCER, but the way they were dealt with by official reformers suggested that the critical remarks of Professor Amano did not quite represent the official view on those institutions. In the NCER reports the cram schools were not regretted for being contributing factors to the escalating exam competition, or as being harmful to Japanese education. Rather, they were seen as potential private *alternatives* to the elementary schools, and it was proposed by NCER that cram schools officially be recognised as alternatives to elementary school. In the words of the third NCER report an 'adjustment to cram school and other such private education enterprises' was necessary and private educational enterprises were to 'play a new role' (Rinkyooshin, 1988, 208).

The question of the role of cram schools was connected to another NCER key phrase, namely 'liberalisation' (*jiyuuka*). As a consumer-paid unofficial source of learning, cram schools represented an alternative in which a teacher's or an institution's ability to make the students turn up voluntarily was vital for survival. Evaluation of the teaching was immediate whereas in the public system teachers would automatically have students regardless of the quality of their teaching. Among the most conservative members of NCER the idea that commercialisation and competition for students would ensure that only the 'best' educational institutions would survive gained momentum (Hisatomi, 1987, 39). This would be equivalent to a privatisation of schooling at compulsory level in the interest of 'liberalisation' and presumably with the secondary goal of saving government funds.

It may of course alleviate the pressure on a child if it is required to attend only one of the institutions and not two as is often the case at present, but this proposal did not indicate that cram schools were seen to have anything to do with the problems which Japanese education faced at the time, much less aggravating them. On the contrary, the report ended up suggesting that school choice restrictions be eliminated and, phrasing it more vaguely than in initial statements, that cram schools and special training schools (*senshuu gakkoo*) should play a more important role in the school system (NCER, 1987a, 348, 351; Schoppa, 1991, 224, 335).

Among cram schools many were ready to support ideas such as recognition of their schools by the public system and abolition of school districts. Some even went so far as to claim that elementary schools were unconstitutional because of their inability to differentiate their teaching according to the students' abilities, and therefore recommended that the sixth grade of elementary school was not spent in a public school (Hisatomi, 1987, 45).

The quality of elementary school education was under debate and it was not only the cram schools that were critical. The liberalisation efforts to a great extent rested on the fact that children actually did learn a lot in cram school, leading to the assumption that cram schools were more effective than the regular system of schooling. Other organisations like those of the teachers, were critical of the huge curriculum in elementary school and the lack of time for play.

Whereas people with the former two interests would have welcomed privatisation or liberalisation, the latter were apprehensive that such a change would only aggravate the problems. The cram schools themselves with their public statements bore evidence to their inability to solve the problems of desolation and frustrations in education. Rather, they would intensify them, as was evident from Professor Hisatomi's summarising of a manual for parents published by a cram school:

Children should do their homework during breaks in school and not waste time doing other things, so that they can engage in examination related studies at home. Sports should not be overdone because physical fatigue might influence the quality of studies later that day. On sports days the child should attend only the disciplines it is partaking in itself and spend the rest of the day studying. (Hisatomi, 1987, 46)

When it comes to solving the desolation or frustration problems which lead to violence in schools, the unsuitability of such an examination-oriented cram school is evident. Certainly there were other cram schools with much more humane ideas of proper child-rearing practices who abhorred such Spartan training as described above. But obviously recognition of cram schools would have to cover the whole spectre of what can actually be considered education-related cram schools, and such a recognition would be responsible for introducing much more harsh training in the Japanese educational system than is presently the case.

Cram schools obviously are an important feature of Japanese education, not only as a supplement to the public system, but also as a possible officially recognised alternative or an addition to the public system. The NCER had, so to say, a ready-made model of private education in the cram schools. Cram schools functioned both as an influence on public education and on its contents, as well as a means of political pressure.

2.2.6 University

The university admits high school graduates aged 18 or more. It is moulded upon the American university structure with two years of general education to begin with and two years of specialisation to follow.[28] Legally the purpose of the university is stated as follows:

The university is the central component of the educational system and as such it must not only be an instrument to spread knowledge widely, it must also contribute to the development of special research insights by its employees and, as an institution of higher education, it must develop its intellectual, moral and practical potential. (Roppoo, 1990, 45)

The objectives of the university are left to the individual institution's own discretion, but apart from that the Ministry of Education sets the standards from the requirements for graduation, teacher qualifications, right down to the required floor area of school buildings.

The first two years of general education include Humanities, Natural Sciences and Social Sciences and give 36 credits.[29] The allocation of credits to the particular fields is determined by the individual institutions. Additionally 8 credits for Foreign Languages and 4 credits for Health and Physical Education are required. Specialised education — the last two years of the bachelor course — requires 76 credits making a total of 124 credits necessary for graduation (see Chart 10).

Medicine, dentistry and veterinary medicine are special six year-courses. For other subjects graduate school is elective and divided into two courses: The master's course (two years) and the doctoral course (five years). Graduate school is meant for students who wish to conduct advanced studies in the theoretical and applied sciences and arts (Monbushoo, 1989a, 66-7).

The reason for dividing the two courses of graduate school rather than making the doctoral course an extension of the master's course, is that the master's course is mainly intended for future officials and managers whilst the doctoral course is intended for researcher training (Tsukuba, 1988, 23). With the goals for the two courses so explicitly different, separating them in two appears to be appropriate.

28. There are exceptions to this rule, for instance the University of Tsukuba which was set up by the government in 1973 as an experiment. Here general education is integrated with specialised education and it is possible to convert a small number of credits from general education in order to use them in a favourite subject. (Tsukuba, 1988, 20-5)
29. One credit is granted for 45 hours of study comprised of both teaching and student's preparation. The duration is usually 10 or 15 weeks and the number is calculated like this: One hour for lecture class requiring two hours' preparation, two hours for one seminar class requiring one hour's preparation and three hours for one laboratory class. (Monbushoo, 1989a, 66)

Chart 10: Requirements for graduation from university

	University		Graduate School	
Type of course	Non-medical	medical	Master's	Doctor's*
Years	4	6**	2	5
General Education	36 credits	36 credits		
Foreign Language	8	16 (8)**		
Health & Physical	4	4		
Specialised Education	76	# (134)	30	30
Additional credits required	-	8	-	-
Total	124	64# (182)	30	30
Thesis	Variable requirements	-	Required	Required

*   For medicine and dentistry doctor's course is four years. For veterinary medicine it was shortened from five to four years in 1990.

**   Figures in brackets show the number of credits required in veterinary medicine (course extended form 4 to 6 years in 1984).

\#   In addition to the 64 credits in basic education, medicine and dentistry have 4,200 — 4,800 hours of prescribed professional education.

(Monbushoo, 1989a, 67)

This tendency of specifying the future occupational goal at the point of advancing beyond a bachelor degree is also known in other countries. In Denmark, for instance, in certain fields of the Natural Sciences the system allows for researcher training to start before finishing with a master's degree. Technically, this makes the doctoral student one without a master's degree, which would have been required before in the Danish system.

The majority of the Japanese university students graduate with a bachelor degree. In fact, out of over three million university students in 1995, only around 5% were enrolled in graduate school (Shimizu, 1996, 36).

Social Sciences and Engineering are the most popular courses at the undergraduate level with 40% of the students attending the Social Sciences course and 20% attending Engineering courses. Attendance at the rest of the courses is as follows: Humanities 16%, Education 6%, Medicine and Dentistry 5%, Agriculture 3%, Natural Sciences 4%, Home Economics 2%, others 4%.

However the distribution of students by major field of study varies considerably among national, local public and private universities. In national universities the enrolment rate for Social Science and Humanities is only 24%, while the rate for local public universities is 57% and the rate for private universities is 64% (Shimizu, 1996, 46).

The reasons for this are several. Firstly, the cost of setting up and running the different fields. Setting up a course in Engineering or Natural Science requires more equipment and more funding than a course in the Humanities or Social Science. Hence the private universities, which are mainly financed by tuition fees, are prone to emphasise the less costly subjects, whereas the national universities, which are less dependent on tuition fees, can afford more Natural Science and indeed are encouraged to do so by the Ministry of Education.

This relates to the second reason for the distribution of students according to field. The Ministry of Education actively encourages emphasis on Natural Sciences, and its influence is therefore felt most strongly in the national universities. Some private universities have been established with the explicit purpose of offering subjects in the Humanities field.

Educational expenses paid by parents at the compulsory level are low, between 54,000 and 108,000 yen (1990) (approx. $325 — $650) per student per year.[30] In secondary school this more than doubles to 260,726 yen (for public schools) and for national and public universities the average in 1986 was 388,000 yen ($2,516). Again there are differences between national, public and private universities. The average for a private university is about double the average for national universities and local public universities (Monbushoo, 1994, 100-1).[31]

Needless to say, no matter how this relates to the average income of a family, it provides a powerful incentive to apply for the national universities. Not only are they cheaper. In most cases they are also higher ranking than private universities and thus considered better.

When entering university the students have passed an entrance examination and have participated in the competition for admittance to the prestigious universities or the university of their desire. They have gone through an educational system that has taught them that hard work + ability

30. The expense at elementary level shouldered by parents covers such things as school excursions and outings, specially required sports gear and clothes, school lunches, etc.
31. Figures are (1990): national universities 445,900 yen, local public universities 493,600 yen, private universities 999,500 yen ($1= approx. 133 yen).

= educational attainment = status (James & Benjamin, 1988, 34). However, at university level the virtue of hard work seems to be dispensed with temporarily. Most university students for the first time experience freedom from the pressure to perform, freedom to wear what they like, do what they like when they like (interview with Higuchi Keiko, June 27, 1991). The university undergraduate course is for a great number of the students a four-year holiday before going back to real life in employment somewhere.

This may seem oddly ineffective compared to the rest of the educational system but it certainly has its value when seen as a safety valve letting out excessive pressure. As we have seen, the name of the university and its place in the hierarchy is more important than the course one chooses. University life is characterised by a rich social life organised around clubs reflecting an interest in some leisure-time activity. In many respects university life in Japan is similar to the teenage-life found at high school level in USA and many European countries, with the groupings and socialising and dating.

The better the university one has entered the more relaxed the university years are apt to be. But of course some university students do put a lot of work into their studies. Particularly students at less prestigious universities have an incentive to work for good grades, because the placement officer[32] who controls access to jobs use grades as a sorting device. Since those students do not have the advantage of a prestigious name on the letterhead of their school certificates, their grades come to matter relatively more in the sorting process. Also, at some private universities it is customary for employers to use the seminar courses of certain professors as their main source of job-candidates and hence there is much competition to be accepted at these particular seminars. A small number of students at undergraduate level know that they want to do graduate work and will therefore be harder-working, but only around five percent will ever advance to graduate school (James & Benjamin, 1988, 33).

Talking about reform at this level, the issue of quality versus quantity comes up. As the situation is now, there is a place in the university system for almost every applicant but not necessarily at the university he or she desires. Quantitatively the system is working — if it was not for the hierarchy competition would be unnecessary. But the quality is often questioned. The fact that very few students study earnestly makes it tempting to call it 'waste of time'. Japanese students surpass most of their Western counterparts until university level but apparently this is not utilised in university education.

32. A placement officer is an official at the university, who is a 'go-between' between students/graduates and firms. A university usually has developed stable ties with firms that habitually recruit the graduates of the university in question, and the placement officer assists with the administration of this.

The entire Japanese educational system is focused on the university entrance examinations. Murakami Yasusuke, former professor of Economics at Tokyo University, puts it in unambiguous terms:

Passage through the examination sieve entitles students, especially those in the Humanities, to four years in a university students' leisure resort. One's university years are no more than a painless rite of passage on the way to becoming a company samurai. This is no less true of *Toodai*, the University of Tokyo (and the most prestigious of them all), than of any other school. (Murakami, 1988, 76)

Though this certainly has to do with the structure of the system itself, it can not be blamed solely on an inappropriate structure. Of course more control, more demanding curriculum and graduation exams could be an improvement, but there are other factors contributing to the situation.

From the mid-seventies the aspirations of young people seem to have declined. Gradually, it has become clear that hard work will not always produce the desired outcome. As around 40% (Shimizu, 1996, 38) of the young people presently go on to university, prestige and privilege are no longer at the disposal of every university graduate. Already, a growing number of well-educated university graduates will not receive promotion to managerial positions (Amano, 1988a, 44). The close link that used to exist between university graduation and high status jobs is weakening, and this surely is a discouraging factor for the students. There is also evidence that the way the hierarchy is perceived is changing. The press carries stories of girls in particular who, having been admitted to top-of-the-hierarchy, Tokyo University, have opted for Keioo or Waseda instead (Shuukan Shinchoo, 1994, 56-57).

Working hard while at university will not necessarily put you in a better position for achieving a high status job. As long as employers do not as a general rule look at *what* has been studied and *how well* the student did, working hard at university will not be a very good device for climbing the social ladder or securing the job of one's dreams. Because of the traditional emphasis on the school certificate rather than achievement, the elite universities in particular seem without academic competition. According to the *prestige* of a given university, one's chances for acquiring a high status job can be determined or enhanced at the time of entrance. However, the picture may be somewhat different at *less prestigious* universities as hard work probably is the best recommendation one could obtain from these institutions.

The fact that aspirations are declining may be a recent phenomenon but the emphasis on credentials rather than knowledge is not. In fact, this custom is so deeply rooted in Japanese society that this factor may carry the largest part of the responsibility for the lack of enthusiasm and achievement in Japanese universities. It is significant that the Japanese employers have for a long time not objected to this situation. It would seem that they have been quite happy to mould their new recruits themselves, seeking only proof of the academic *potential* of the recruits as it is found in the fact that they passed a particular entrance examination (Murakami, 1988, 76).

Most students thus graduate with a bachelor's degree and get the rest of their training at the workplace. The fact that only five percent attend graduate school is not an accurate indication of the number of qualified researchers. As many companies conduct their own training in their own laboratories the number of qualified researchers is much higher than the figures for graduate school would indicate.[33] The researchers in the private sector are educated for specific purposes by private enterprise. This means that research in areas not yet profitable is only conducted by the government or if there happens to be a visionary person with influence in a firm that does research. Consequently, the lack of cooperation between industry and universities has the effect that basic research — which is mostly conducted by universities — easily becomes disconnected from and not useful to industry.

The size of the graduate school is indeed considered a problem in Japan. Too few students advance to this level. The cry for creativity is at its highest here where research is to be done. NCER stated that 'if Japan is to contribute to the progress of science in the world, then a drastic improvement and reform of graduate schools will become our urgent task'. They wanted 'researchers who are creative enough to explore unknown fields', and to achieve this 'drastic improvement and reform' of graduate school, NCER proposed that teaching at master's level be more integrated with specialised education at undergraduate level. Also, master's level should be more open to pre- and in-service training of high level professionals. Special emphasis should be put on the researcher training aspect of the doctoral course and also at this level flexibility should be enhanced.

For both courses it was proposed to shorten the length of the course to get younger graduates. Then promising researchers should be rewarded with post-doctoral fellowships (Rinkyooshin, 1988, 110-11).

An issue that has weighed heavily on the reform debate is the individualisation of the universities. The government promised to promote reforms that would help 'individualise, activate and heighten the programmes at the universities' and it would also 'help the universities reform and improve the structures and programmes of their graduate schools'.

Additionally, they wished to promote academic research by encouraging universities and the private sector to conduct cooperative research activities (Monbushoo, 1989b, 53).

33. Firms generally prefer to recruit students with bachelor degrees — a post graduate degree may even be a liability, since such a person is usually not so easy to shape as the less educated recruit.

When the NCER started its deliberations, criticism of the university was centred around the thinly populated graduate school, the severity of the entrance examinations and the ineffectiveness of general education. But there can be no doubt that the most important issue as judged by the public debate was the pressure the entrance examinations were exerting upon the rest of the educational system.

2.2.7 Other Kinds of Post-Secondary Education

After high school some graduates choose to join the labour market while others continue their education. In 1995 nearly 17% of the high school graduates entered advanced courses at special training schools (*senshuu gakkoo*)[34] while slightly over 45% entered university or junior college. (Shimizu, 1996, 38-41).

For those who do not attend either the four-year university or seek employment right after high school, there are a number of institutions providing further education or vocational training. Among them the colleges of technology (*senmon gakkoo*) and the junior colleges (*tanki daigaku* = short-term university) are the institutions that are most often singled out for scrutiny in statistics and surveys, even though this is admittedly a little studied area. Separate from the formal system of education there are a number of vocational training centres run by the Ministry of Labour with the purpose of providing initial training, upgrading of skills etc. (Ishikawa, 1991, 32). The legal foundation for the special school (*kootoo senmongakkoo*) and hence also college of technology, which is classified as a special school, is as follows: '*Kootoo senmon gakkoo* must teach special skills thoroughly and has as its goal to develop the skills necessary for working life' (Roppoo, 1990, 50).

Colleges of technology offer a five-year course with specialised vocational training and can be entered after graduation from middle school or at the age of 15. In this sense roughly two years of the five are actually 'post-secondary'. In 1989 only 2% of those advancing to further education (not including special training schools) went to a college of technology (Ishikawa, 1991, 9). Vocational education is not considered as having the same high status as academic education and therefore is mostly taken on by those who have failed to enter academic tracks at other institutions of education. However, there are of course those who purposely enter vocational education but they seem to be the minority (Gill, 1990). Some 94.1% of the students are men, which makes the technical college even more dominated by men than the junior college is dominated by women (Monbushoo, 1989a, 27).

---

34. Special training schools provide training in industrial skills, nursing, commerce and business etc. for middle and high school graduates (Ishikawa, 1991, 9).

Tanki daigaku or junior college is described in the Law of Education (*Gakkoo Kyooiku Hoo*) in the following way:

A university may ... make its goal the development of scholarly skills along with the teaching of vocational or practical skills necessary for working life. A university like this shall give two or three year courses and be called junior college (*tanki daigaku*). (Roppoo, 1990, 49)

Some 90% of the junior colleges are private. Also, a little more than 90% of the students are women (Benjamin, 1991, 253). Out of the total number of students advancing to university, junior college or college of technology in 1989, 18% went to junior college (Ishikawa, 1991, 9). Numerically we find far more women in the less prestigious junior college than men in technical college. From high school on, the average academic performance of women drops (Lynn, 1988, 15). Their choice after high school is often the less demanding junior college where they can learn skills that prepare them for marriage, and skills that are useful in the 'OL' jobs they usually acquire.[35] Home Economics, Humanities and Child Care are the most popular subjects at junior college. Some junior colleges also offer more directly vocationally oriented training, often in cooperation with a technical high school (Gill, 1990, 25).

Subjects and attendance rates at junior colleges are as follows: Home Economics 23%, Humanities 27%, Education and Teacher Training 19%, Social Science 14%, Medical Science and the Related 6%, Engineering 5%, Fine arts 5%, Agriculture 1%, Others 1% (Shimizu, 1996, 46).

---

35. OL stands for Office Lady, and an OL must be able to type, use a personal computer, make tea and serve it politely, dress well but not too brightly, in short, be decorative and supportive.

CHAPTER 3

THE DEBATE ON REFORM

3.1 NCER and its Function in the Educational Debate

As touched upon briefly in the Introduction, the National Council on Educational Reform (*Rinji Kyooiku Shingikai*, hereafter NCER) was set up by the then Prime Minister, Nakasone Yasuhiro, in 1984 to advise him on 'basic strategies for necessary reforms with regard to governmental policies and measures in various aspects, so as to secure such education as will be compatible with the social changes and cultural developments of our country' (Rinkyooshin, 1988, 5).

Prime Minister Nakasone claimed that the previous reform attempt, that of the Central Council for Education (*Chuukyooshin*, hereafter CCE) in 1971 had fallen a long way short of its goals. The CCE[1] he was talking about had been established in 1967 by the Ministry of Education to examine the school system. It had been asked to produce 'basic guidelines for the development of an integrated educational system suited for contemporary society' (Schoppa, 1991, 3).

Among CCE's recommendations was a proposal that Japan experiment with alternatives to the standardised 6-3-3 system. More concretely CCE proposed pilot projects on lower school-starting age and a unified secondary education. High school should experiment with diversifying by making the curriculum more flexible, allowing streaming and grade-skipping. Also, CCE introduced the idea that new teachers should undergo a full probationary year before being fully employed. Most of these proposals are still regularly aired by the Ministry of Education and its councils, as also by NCER. In addition, CCE suggested the strengthening of school administration, the increase of the ranks of school administrators, raising teachers' salaries and installing a new salary-scale for recognising graduate training of teachers.

Very few of CCE's proposals were implemented and those actually implemented were mainly the ones calling for increased aid at different levels in the school system. In other words, the proposals that were implemented were those that met with the least (or no) opposition from, for example, the

---

1. CCE, *Chuuoo Kyooiku Shingikai*, is really a permanent advisory council for the Minister of Education. It was first set up in 1952, and as it enters new rounds of deliberation, it is often given a new number to identify the round of deliberations.

schools and especially the teachers. In this light Prime Minister Nakasone's claim that the CCE had failed was quite reasonable. He attributed the failure to the fact that the CCE initiative had been dominated by the Ministry of Education. It was argued that since the Ministry of Education was just a single bureaucracy, it did not have sufficient power to enlist the support of other ministries and society at large for anything more than minor improvements. Thus it came to be that an advisory body on education was established directly under the Prime Minister's office (Schoppa, 1991, 3-5, 215).[2]

The idea of creating an advisory body under the Prime Minister's supervision only surfaced after some time. As late as the LDP congress in 1984, when LDP decided to make educational reform a major issue of the party, all, including Nakasone, agreed that the existing Central Council on Education was the proper place for deliberations on educational reform. But only a month later, the idea of a council on education directly under the Prime Minister surfaced publicly at the extraordinary LDP congress in February 1984. Nakasone expressed here his desire to reform three areas: administration, finance and education. The inspiration for a prime ministerial council probably came from Nakasone's experiences with the *Rinchoo* (*Rinji Gyoosei Choosa Kai*, Provisional Commission for Administrative Reform) which was a supra-cabinet council functioning from 1981 to 1983. The fact that Nakasone was able to establish a body like the NCER is a clear indication of his great strength as a leader (Mikami, 1984, 18).

Prime Minister Nakasone's interest in education was only part of a set of reforms he pursued. The parole was 'total clearance of the post-war political accounts' (*sengo seiji no sookessan*) and he advocated administrative reform, tax reform, abolition of limits on defence spending and education reform. The aim was a review of the post-war legacy and Nakasone was concerned because in his opinion 'too many areas of Japanese politics had become taboo due to the nation's experience of militarism and defeat' (Schoppa, 1991, 48, 214).

Nakasone's educational policy was founded upon the publication 'Twelve LDP policies on Educational Reform', more popularly known as the Nishioka-memo, issued in November 1983. It served as the basis of Nakasone's educational policies before and after his election. The main issues were: Revision of the 6-3-3-4 system, revision of entrance examination in high school and university, revision of higher education, moral education, streaming, internationalisation and improved teacher quality.

2. In 1937 the Education Council had served as an advisory group to the cabinet, so the idea of not placing a deliberative body on education under the Ministry of Education was not entirely new, though the practice of placing it directly under the Prime Minister's authority was.

These ideas were later condensed in two papers from the Nakasone cabinet, the 'Five Ground Rules for Educational Reform in the 21st Century' and the 'Memo on Basic Ideas on Educational Reform'. The document containing the five ground rules stated that times had changed and that what had worked well for 'catching up' now had become insufficient. The system had become too standardised and educational reforms were to bring Japan ahead of the rest of the world. The five ground rules which were very similar to the later four main points of the NCER were:

    1)   Internationalisation
    2)   Liberalisation
    3)   Diversification
    4)   The information-oriented society
    5)   Respect for the individual
          (Mikami, 1984, 17-18)

The agenda of reform was set at this point by the LDP and by Prime Minister Nakasone in particular. Later work in the NCER was largely elaborations of these themes and though LDP was certainly inspired by current problems in the educational system, it is also clear that the idea of educational reform originated in purely political and economical considerations within the LDP.

Part of the political considerations of the LDP had to do with the Occupation reforms. Since the 1950's the conservatives had been complaining about the 'Occupation excesses' and Nakasone set out to clear up these excesses. The excesses so sorely deplored by the conservatives were:

    a)   The abolition of the Imperial Rescript, which to the conservatives
          epitomised traditional Japanese morality.
    b)   The abolition of moral education as a separate subject on the
          curriculum.
    c)   The decentralisation of the powers formerly wielded by the
          Ministry of Education.
    d)   The division of the previous five-year secondary schools into two
          three-year schools (middle and high school).
    e)   The lack of officially recognised elite tracks.
          (Schoppa, 1991, 36)

Item b) and c) are perhaps no longer as important as before. Moral education is now a separate subject in elementary and middle school though there may still be some dismay over its content. As for the decentralised powers of the Ministry of Education, the change in the School Board Law in 1956, which meant that boards were to be appointed rather than elected, as well as the massive use of administrative guidelines, dulled the effect of the post-war decentralisation of power. The conservative attitude to education was clearly shaped by experiences during the Occupation but also by their respect for how education was conducted before the war (Schoppa, 1991, 51).

Combined with the above politically determined incentives for reforming education, the Nakasone administration also had more immediate incentives for change. Increasing disorder in the schools (violence, bullying) prompted the call for reform of teacher training and moral education. In February 1983, several particularly violent incidents in the schools focused national attention on school violence and Prime Minister Nakasone spoke of the need for a 'radical solution'.

Maintaining the desire to clear away Occupation excesses, many conservatives felt that violence and bullying were phenomena caused by lack of proper moral education in schools. Students were hearing too much about freedom and not enough about *responsibilities* that go with *rights* in Japanese society. To boost morality, a document like the Imperial Rescript on Education was considered by many conservatives to be just what was needed (Schoppa, 1991, 48-9).

A third inspiration for Nakasone's reform efforts was the need to adapt education to the challenges of the 21st century as stated in the above mentioned paper on the five ground rules for 21st century education. It was argued that the future economy would require creative scientists, fluent foreign language speakers, specialists in extremely complex technology and workers who could use their own initiative and express their views rather than just follow orders. As the examination-based system gave little credit to such abilities it was deemed unsuitable for future needs. Amaya Naohiro, a former senior official of the Ministry of International Trade and Industry and a future member of NCER, warned against repeating the mistake committed during the war of believing that those who were successful in school would also be so in managing battles (Schoppa, 1991, 50-51).

The Prime Minister used the reform of education as one element in his efforts to create for himself a high profile as a person with a lot of initiative, bent on succeeding, even to the point of being considered aggressive. In this respect, he was not exactly a mainstream Japanese politician. This became particularly clear in the defense issue, one of the other elements of Nakasone's high profile. Not satisfied with the mainstream conservative policy of relying on American nuclear defense, he belonged to the minority of the 'new realists' who, arguing that Japan shared philosophical principles with the West, insisted that Japan had to bear more responsibility in the defense area (Reischauer & Craig, 1989, 330). Though he was not too successful in this area he did manage to increase the Japanese defense budget so that in 1987 it exceeded the magical 1% of the GNP which, for many years, had been considered the upper limit of Japanese defense spending.

If Nakasone's defense policy placed him with the military 'hawks' his educational policies placed him in the space between business and the most traditionalist of conservatives. In the NCER reports this was reflected in the emphasis on traditional moral values and manpower needs.

As for the issue of education reform, there were persons other than the Prime Minister in the conservative camp working for educational reform. Business groups regularly published reports on education and had think-tanks and study groups on education.

One of the most influential study groups in connection with the establishment of the NCER was the Kyoto Group for the Study of Global Issues (*Sekai o Kangaeru Kyoto Zakai*, see also 3.4). This group was founded by the industrialist Matsushita Koonosuke to formulate long-range economic, social and educational policies for the 21st century. According to Professor Horio Teruhisa of Tokyo University, it was in fact from this group the impetus for NCER's reforms came, not from the government (Horio, 1988, 364).

A scholarly group, The Study Group on Japanese Education, listed the Nishioka-memo and the publications of the Kyoto Group as the most concrete reform proposals until the start of the NCER deliberations (Kurosaki, 1984, 36).

The Kyoto Group published a report on liberalisation or free competition in education shortly before Nakasone started his education reform campaign in March 1984. The principles of free competition were to be applied to education in the following manner:

The sort of education that can match the needs of the 21st century must be ruled by the principle of fair competition in all areas. A diversified and technologically sophisticated society requires many different types of talented citizens. For that, the school must be a place where students are motivated to learn. An environment must be created which encourages free competition not only among students but also among teachers to become better educators.

Ideally, education should be free and independent of constraints and interference from public authorities. In particular, we would like to see as much de-control as possible — if not the outright abolition of restrictions — in the education system. (Kyoto Group, 1985, 31)

Business thus stated that there was a need for new skills which the old system of education did not provide. The issue of new skills was taken up by the government but on the question of how much influence the central administration should wield, they disagreed. Whereas business called for deregulation of education, government efforts moved in the direction of more central influence on local school boards, teachers, content of education and textbooks.

The strong emphasis on free competition in education voiced by the business world was indeed problematic for the government. Though many blamed the lack of moral standards for the increasing violence in schools, equally strong arguments held the excessive competition for entrance at high school and university responsible. Statistics showed that the increase in violent incidents was a middle school phenomenon in particular, which was explained by the fact that the students at this point were to move from a non-streamed middle school to a highly hierarchical high school. This made the Kyoto Group's call for free competition in all areas of education hard to defend and the competition issue as such was avoided by NCER, perhaps only to be found as an element of the term 'liberalisation'.

On August 21, 1984 the members of NCER were appointed and the specialist members were appointed on December 20, 1984. As will be seen they were mostly people connected to business, to Nakasone, or to the natural sciences. School teachers were under-represented. The regular members were:

Chairman —
Okamoto Michio — Member of the Council for Science and Technology, worked with Nakasone here. Former President of Kyoto University.

Vice Chairman —
Ishikawa Tadao — President, Keioo University. Served on a Nakasone private advisory council on education (PAC), member of three different advisory councils under the Ministry of Education.

Vice Chairman —
Nakayama Sohei — Senior Advisor (former president), The Industrial Bank of Japan, Ltd. Served on Nakasone's PAC on the 'peace problem'.

Amaya Naohiro — President, Japan Economic Foundation. Former official at the Ministry of International Trade and Industry. Member of the Kyoto Group.

Arita Kazuhisa — Vice Chairman of the Association for the Promotion of Social Education Bodies; Chief Executive of Nishi Nippon Koogyoo Gakuen. Former LDP Upper House member.

Dogakinai Naohiro — Professor, Hokkai Gakuen University. Former governor of Hokkaido, failed to win an LDP Upper House seat.

Hosomi Takashi — President, The Overseas Economic Cooperation Fund.

	Member of Nakasone PACs and former official of the Ministry of Finance.
Iijima Sooichi	Former President, Nagoya University. Former CCE member, member of Association of University Presidents and Japan Science Council.
Ishii Takemochi	Professor, University of Tokyo. Advisor to Prime Minister Oohira, later for Nakasone as well, chaired a Nakasone PAC.
Kanasugi Hidenobu	Advisor, Japanese Confederation of Labour (Doomei). Links to the Democratic Socialist Party.
Kimura Harumi	Professor, Chiba Institute of Technology, essayist. Member of the Kyoto Group.
Kobayashi Noboru	General Director, National Children's Hospital. Member of advisory councils of Ministry of Health and Welfare, connected with former P.M. Oohira.
Kooyama Kenichi	Professor, Gakushuuin University. Connected with Oohira.
Minakami Tadashi	Superintendent, Tokyo Metropolitan Board of Education. Long-time local education administrator in Tokyo.
Miura Chizuko	Author — and later replaced with —
Sono Ayako	Author. Connected with Oohira, served on Nakasone PACs.
Miyata Yoshiji	Senior Advisor, Japanese Federation of Iron and Steel Workers' Union (Tekkoo Rooren). Served on Nakasone PAC.
Nakauchi Isao	Chairman, President and Chief Executive Officer, The Daiei Inc. Nakasone supporter, Keidanren[3] member.
Okano Shunichiroo	Secretary General, Japanese Olympic Committee. Former member of CCE.
Saitoo Sei	President, National Theatre of Japan. Former Administrative Vice Minister, Ministry of Education, former CCE member.

---

3. Short for the Federation of Economic Organisations, a major factor in the business world.

Saitoo Toshitsugu	Immediate past-President, Japan Junior Chamber Inc.; Executive Director, Daishoowa Paper Manufacturing Co Ltd. Nakasone's relative.
Seijima Ryuuzoo	Counsellor, C. Itoh & Co., Ltd. Nakasone advisor and PAC member, former CCE member.
Sunobe Ryoozoo	Professor, Kyoorin University. Former Administrative Vice Minister of Ministry of Foreign Affairs.
Tamaru Akiyo	Elementary school Teacher, Chiba Prefecture. Participated in Ministry of Education project on moral education.
Tobari Atsuo	Principal, Toyama Lower Secondary School.
Uchida Kenzoo	Professor, Hoosei University. Former journalist of Kyoodoo Press Service.

(Rinkyooshin, 1988, 319-20; Schoppa, 1991, 220-23)

Among the regular members of NCER were, as we can see, former members of the Kyoto Group, such as Amaya Naohiro, who became chairman of the first NCER subcommittee and Ishii Takemochi, who became chairman of the second NCER subcommittee.

Several of the other NCER members were, or had been, members of different industrial interest groups. Industrial interests were probably those best represented in the NCER (Horio, 1988, 364; Schoppa, 1991, 133). Issues such as liberalisation and the strengthening of moral education originated in proposals from these business related groups. With the possible exception of Kanasugi, Tobari and Uchida, no member was previously unconnected to Nakasone, LDP, the Ministry of Education, or industrial interests.

Against this background, it seems clear that the teacher unions were not exaggerating when they said that the NCER members were 'Nakasone people' (interview with Kawai Naoki, May 16, 1991).

It would be wrong to expect so many people to be able to discuss a subject like education without disagreement. As Schoppa describes it, there were internal conflicts in NCER particularly between the First and the Third Subcommittees and this probably was the reason for a number of vague formulations in the reports — they were compromises (Schoppa, 1991, 242). It then follows that when terms like 'NCER recommended' are henceforth used they concern these compromises, the contents of the NCER reports. The reports represent what NCER could agree on, so no total consensus in NCER is assumed. Rather, such inclusive terms are used in order to describe what is said in the reports, the official NCER statements.

As NCER was placed directly under the Prime Minister, the education reform issue was emphasised as a particular concern of the Prime Minister and further, the Prime Minister had considerable influence on the direction the reports took. Not only were the NCER members mostly people with whom Nakasone had worked before, he was also to provide NCER with its tasks and references. In his address to the chairman of NCER, Okamoto Michio, on September 5, 1984, he first reiterated the calls for 'basic strategies for reform', and then added, in the section called 'Reason for the Reference', that 'a variety of problems' had arisen due to changes in the social environment and great quantitative expansion in education. He stated that the reforms should be 'in accordance with the spirit of the provisions of the Fundamental Law of Education' (*Kihon Kyooiku Hoo no seishin ni nottori*) (Rinkyooshin, 1988, 322).

Nakasone as the provider of tasks and guidelines, and as the person who was to receive the end result, was immensely influential. His goal of reform, liberalisation, furthering economic growth and the wish that Japan should take responsibility in the world community, made a strong imprint on the work of NCER. To take an example, the issue of internationalisation under the headline of which NCER strongly recommended that Japan should place itself as a responsible member of the international community while maintaining its unique Japaneseness was a direct reference to statements made by Nakasone.

The legal foundation for NCER is found in the Law for the Establishment of a National Council on Educational Reform (*Rinji Kyooiku Shingikai Setchi Hoo*). Here the council's affiliation with the Prime Minister's office was firmly established and the purpose was stated as that of 'designing necessary reforms with regard to governmental policies and measures'. The council also was to examine contemporary educational policies and express its opinion to the Prime Minister, and in return the Prime Minister should 'pay due regard to the reports submitted by the council'. The Prime Minister also had to report directly to the Diet when he received deliberations from the NCER.

Concerning the members of NCER, the law stipulated that there should not be more than twenty-five members, consisting of 'citizens whose character and views are exemplary' (*Jinkaku shikken tomo ni sugureta mono no uchi ...*), who would be appointed by the Prime Minister on the advice of the Minister of Education. The two Houses in the Diet were to give their consent to the appointed members. Unfit members could be removed, and no member was to reveal confidential matters even after retirement. The members were to serve on a part-time basis.

Specialist members (see Appendix 3 for a list) were to study 'certain specialised matters' and were also recommended by the Minister of Education and appointed by the Prime Minister (Rinkyooshin, 1988, 357-59).

In all, the NCER issued four reports between 1984 and until its end of term in 1987, and those reports have served as the starting point for further work on educational reform. The deliberative council to follow NCER, the 14th CCE (*Dai Juuyon Ki Chuuoo Kyooiku Shingikai*), explicitly took its key issues from the NCER reports. The NCER reports are central to understanding the direction of Japanese educational reform at present because they are the foundation on which the present 14th CCE and the Ministry of Education work.

The NCER, as mentioned above, started its work at a time of high public concern about violence and misbehaviour in the schools. This meant that a large majority of the public was convinced that some change was needed. The ground was cleared for reform. Despite this broad support, NCER ended up producing reports containing only vague recommendations. For instance, NCER considered Nakasone's suggestion that the national university entrance examination be abolished, but in the end it merely suggested that the old examination be replaced by a new one. NCER also failed to agree on a shift of the starting date for the school year from April to September — a shift that would make it considerably easier for international exchange of education and research to take place (Schoppa, 1991, 5). So, despite the fact that NCER was bred in Nakasone's hothouse, realism or maybe timidity towards public reaction, or perhaps even internal disagreement, prevented it from endorsing truly radical reforms.

Taking a closer look at the actual NCER proposals, we find that the central issues of the NCER reports are declared in the Fourth and Final Report (1987) in chapter two 'Basic Direction for Educational Reform' as:

1) The principle of putting emphasis on individuality

2) Transition to a life-long learning system

3) Coping with changes:

   (a) Contribution to the international community,
   (b) Coping with an information-oriented society.[4]

   (Rinkyooshin, 1988, 265)

---

4. 1) Kosei juushi no gensoku.
   2) Shoogai gakushuu taikei e no ikoo.
   3) Henka e no taioo.
      (1) Kokusai shakai e no kooken.
      (2) Joohoo shakai e no taioo.

The five ground rules LDP started out with had become four, and the difficult subject of liberalisation incorporated into point one and two in particular, along with the issue of diversification. Business requests as well as Nakasone's ideas on an internationalised and responsible Japan as a forerunner in technological development were amply represented.

3.1.1 Conclusions

The NCER was conceived in a climate of apprehension for the national economy's future and an increased aplomb on the part of the conservatives which made them more confident in their demands for a 'clearance of the post-war political accounts'.

The four main issues of the NCER reports were all based on what should be cleared up and what was deemed necessary for the future. Individuality was supposed to link up with creativity and work against the rigid standardisation which had hitherto characterised Japanese education. With new and more diverse manpower needs, education had to produce more diverse talent. The individuality concerned here was more in the genre of diversification of the choices offered in education than a characteristic of persons. This is no surprise when one refers to the initial conservative ground rules where diversity was one of them, side by side with respect for the individual.

Life-long learning, which incorporated diversity as well as liberalisation, had two objectives. One was further manpower development, re-training and up-to-date training. The other was that of activating people in old age and leisure time. Increased learning, especially about the information media, was considered indispensable in the future. This linked with the adaptation to the information society expected to materialise in the next few years, a concept mainly concentrating on the computerisation of society.

Finally there was the issue of internationalisation. With its emphasis on a 'good Japanese' it looked more like nationalist propaganda for traditional values than internationalisation. The NCER did not make any policy plans except pointing out that a Japan isolated from the rest of the world would face economic disaster. Nakasone's aim of making Japan take responsibility was central in NCER's deliberations but the lack of concrete proposals turned it into just another round of verbal support for Nakasone's policy. This makes the NCER enterprise stand out as a conservative attempt to regain the lost central control over education as well as making such changes in the educational system as are necessary for Japan to survive as an economic superpower. The background is political as well as economical but *not* pedagogical.

The very modern rhetoric — words such as individuality, internationality, information society — employed by these conservatives served a multiple of purposes. One obviously was to indicate that reforms of the areas criticised by the opposition were indeed being contemplated. Another probably was to demonstrate how eminently suitable this conservative policy was for future requirements. For this, traditional conservative rhetoric would have seemed archaic, and in all probability explains the rhetorical differences between the five ground rules initially set by the LDP and the four major matters treated by the NCER. But one must not be fooled by the modern terms. They cover, as I will show one by one in the sections dealing with the four main issues, the traditional hallmarks of conservative Japanese politics — central control, commercial liberalism and traditional values.

3.2 Teachers' Organisations — History and Position

3.2.1 Teacher organisation in Japan

Today the picture of Japanese teacher unions is quite polarised. The Japan Teachers' Union (*Nihon Kyooshokuin Kumiai, Nikkyooso*, hereafter JTU), which used to be the largest teacher union by far, split in two in November 1989 when the factions supporting the Japan Socialist Party (JSP) on the one side, and the Japan Communist Party (JCP) on the other, could no longer agree on a modus vivendi, resulting in the communist faction leaving. This has meant a significantly weakened JTU, and a new actor on the arena — the All-Japan Teachers' Union Council (*Zen Nippon Kyooshokuin Kumiai Kyoogikai* shortened as *Zenkyoo*, hereafter ATU), which is where those who left JTU went. The result has been confusion at the lower levels of the unions. New groups emerged such as 'I'm 89', a group which was formed at local level to express teachers' dissatisfaction with both communist and socialist control (*Japan Times*, 1990, 21).

Though the physical split was new, the existence of conflicting opinions was not. From the early postwar period two groups in JTU, supporting socialists or communists respectively, had been in rivalry over issues like formal affiliation to political parties, strike action, and whether a teacher should be defined as a 'labourer' or a 'professional' (Oota, 1989, 256-57).

Efforts to unionise the teaching force before the Second World War had been sporadic and isolated and never successful in attracting the majority of teachers. There were plenty of reasons for this. Donald Thurston in his book *Teachers and Politics in Japan*, which is an extensive study of the subject of teacher unionisation, explains it in the following terms:

The natural inclination of Japan's modernising elite ..., was not to encourage the development of independent employees' organisations ... emphasis on harmony, coupled with the need for national unity in order to build as rapidly as possible a strong and wealthy Japan, tended to inhibit the growth of labour unions.

Also, the 1889 Meiji Constitution in its article 29 stipulated that Japanese subjects were permitted to associate only 'within the limits of the law', which made suppression of undesired organisations very easy. Groups deemed 'public peace problems' by the government could be disbanded. Further, there were no laws guaranteeing the basic rights of unions in pre-war Japan (Thurston, 1973, 24). Legal limitations on union activity were contained in the following laws and ordinances:

> 1881 'Instructions for Elementary School Teachers'
> 1887 'Peace Preservation Regulations'
> 1894 'Order Restricting the Liberty of Speech'
> 1901 'Peace Preservation Police Law'
> 1925 'Peace Preservation Law'
> (Thurston, 1973, 22)

Union activity was treated as a potential threat to public peace and order. These provisions rendered teachers politically impotent and it can hardly come as a surprise that under these circumstances unions did not do very well.

Further, as education was regulated by Imperial Ordinances, not by parliamentary law, it was normal for teachers to regard the Ministry of Education's educational policies as 'right' or 'correct' and in any case 'absolute, impartial and non-political' (Thurston, 1973, 25). In this light even the idea of making education an issue that could be questioned, would be unthinkable. To join groups like, for instance, unions opposing the Ministry of Education and the system created by the Ordinances, even more so.

The decade after the First World War was comparatively liberal and many unions were created in this period and continued to operate until the mid-1930s. The Western democracies had won the war and in Japan there was a demand for parliamentarism and democracy. The emergence of bolshevism in Russia stimulated socialist and labour movements in Japan as well.

In 1925 the Universal Manhood Suffrage Act was passed, reflecting the dawning concern about the people's involvement in government.[5] But it would be wrong to think that the ruling elite was ever seriously challenged by the liberal mood of those years. In 1925, a little earlier than the Suffrage Act, the Peace Preservation Law had been passed, prohibiting the formation of groups advocating a change in the Japanese national polity (*kokutai*), or the abolition of private property. In 1928 the terms were made even more harsh for use against the Japanese Communist Party (JCP). The Suffrage Act and the

---

5. The electorate by the act grew from three million to over twelve million. (Reischauer & Craig, 1989, 240)

Peace Preservation Law indicated both a willingness to accept a certain political potential in every man, as well as a desire to limit the range of political alternatives to which the public would be exposed (Reischauer & Craig, 1989, 240).

In 1930, after several battles with the government over salary decreases, all union activity was suppressed by invocation of the 1925 Peace Preservation Law. Union members were arrested, fired, suspended or reprimanded. After this, independent unions were illegal (Thurston, 1973, 35-37).

The pre-World War II teacher movement was part of the liberal or reformist movement and as such had been reluctant to profess socialist sympathies, but by 1931 it had come to correlate with the socialist movement openly, apparently provoked by the pressure the government was exerting on labour unions.

3.2.2 Postwar teacher unionisation

With the Allied Occupation, left-wing parties and unions once again became legal. JSP and JCP struggled for influence in the House of Representatives, and while the latter was numerically the weakest its influence on the emerging labour-unions was stronger. Desperate living conditions after the war fuelled the growth of labour organisation and within two years from the end of the war, the unions felt strong enough to announce a general strike in February 1947. But the strike never came to fruition. General MacArthur as the leader of the Allied Occupation outlawed the general strike and the use of 'so deadly a social weapon in the present impoverished and emaciated condition of Japan' by issuing a 'Statement Calling Off General Strike' on January 31. 1947 (Thurston, 1973, 40-44, 67).

Teacher unionisation had started as early as December 1945 when one 'left-wing socialist' union — the All-Japan Teachers' Union (*Zen Nihon Kyooin Kumiai, Zenkyoo*) — and one 'right-wing socialist' union — the Japan Educators' Union (*Nihon Kyooikusha Kumiai, Nikkyoo*) — were founded (Thurston, 1973, 52). In 1947 they amalgamated into JTU, but the left/right dichotomy remained and in the end lead to the split of the JTU in 1989.

The organisation of JTU was — and still is — complementary to the way their 'counterparts', the school boards, were organised. Thus there was a local level of the union, a prefectural level and a national level. They negotiated with local school boards and prefectural school boards and there was considerable overlapping at local and prefectural level, but none whatsoever at national level. Initially, when JTU had the right to bargain collectively, there was contact between the top levels too, that is between JTU and the Ministry of Education, but this right was denied the teachers by the Occupation Authorities in 1947-48.

The Local Public Service Law (LPSL) of 1950 outlawed collective bargaining and strikes for all public employees and it replaced the Trade Union Law for the public employees. The LPSL classified JTU as a 'personnel organisation' (*shokuin dantai*), not a union, and in this way the Trade Union Law with its guarantees of rights to strike and bargain collectively had no bearing on teachers or any other publicly employed personnel. The LPSL gave local employees the right to organise and they were also allowed to federate up to prefectural level and 'negotiate' with the prefectural board of education. Federations above this level had no legal right to negotiate and JTU thus had no right to negotiate with the Ministry of Education.

The result of a negotiation — significantly, the word was not 'bargain collectively' — was a 'written agreement' which was by no means the same as a 'collective agreement'. It was far less binding as the legal foundation merely stated that it was to be 'carried out with sincerity'. Otherwise, its legal status was unclear (Thurston, 1973, 180-82).

Of course JTU fought — and still fights — to regain the right to bargain collectively and to strike, but in this matter it faces opposition from the public as well as the government. As Thurston puts it:

Without question, there is a general consensus among the Japanese public that teachers ought not to participate in such activities, that such behaviour has an unfavourable influence on children, and that in some way striking is not consistent with the image children should have of their teachers. (Thurston, 1973, 182)

This makes the right to strike a question of morality and not a question of whether or not the children are victimised in a strike situation. This problem is also known from other professions whose strikes affect parts of the public, such as firemen, police, doctors and nurses. When the question has become moral, it also becomes infinitely more difficult to handle, because it then concerns deep rooted beliefs of right and wrong, and in recent years the incidents of illegal strikes by teachers in Japan have declined dramatically, on the one hand because they have public opinion against them, and on the other hand because the Ministry of Education never hesitated to punish those who took part in illegal strikes. Punishment measures have been wage decreases, arrests, interrogations, suspension, warnings and dismissals. By 1970, 250,000 teachers or about half of the JTU membership had suffered different kinds of punishment and more than half of those had had financial losses (Thurston, 1973, 184). This made the JTU change its action policy, and though it is still demanding the right to strike, it has given up the illegal strikes as a pressure device.

The demand for the right to bargain collectively does not meet with popular antagonism as does the question of strikes, but it is resisted by the Ministry of Education. As a more realistic course of action JTU initially demanded 'central negotiations' along the lines of the local negotiations, but the Ministry has refused to grant this, arguing that JTU does not organise all teachers and that it would therefore be unfair just to negotiate with JTU (Thurston, 1973, 188). Obviously, the same could be said of the negotiations at local level, but it would seem that the interest at this level was in peaceful coexistence with the union rather than the Ministry's conflict approach.

With respect to its lack of means for influencing government decisions, JTU is a typical 'opposition interest group'. JTU is excluded from bureaucratic advisory councils, greatly limited in their official and unofficial contacts with government policy makers and isolated in general by an official attitude which places them outside the circle of power. Further, the groups have been locked in this position virtually since the formation of the LDP in 1955 (Schoppa, 1991, 149).

3.2.3 Major union issues

The estimated membership of JTU in 1947 was an impressive 98% of all elementary school teachers. Unionisation was stimulated by grievances against the government's unlimited authority over teachers in particular. Main causes for the new union included issues such as:

a) substantial salary increases;
b) abolition of government interference in the rights of teachers to:
    — partake in labour and political activities
    — join independent organisations
    — bargain collectively
    — strike
c) a new educational system;
d) issues raised before the war, such as democratisation of education, equality of opportunity, independent education and abolishment of standardisation.
    (Thurston, 1973, 33, 44-5)

The issue of democratisation of education focused on the conflict between education for the good of the state and education for the good of the individual. This is a problem which is continually on the agenda in the Japanese educational debate, particularly in connection with central control and centrally issued guidelines for education. At the heart of the debate is the question: with whom lies the authority over education? Professor Horio of Tokyo University is not in doubt. He argues:

The right to learn and know is the most basic human right without which democracy becomes meaningless. To know is to govern. Thinking activity is what characterises Homo Sapiens. It then follows that people have a right to education. As the people are the master of the government — this is stipulated in the Constitution — they are also the master of education — the people have educational authority. (Horio, 1991, 3-4, 7)

Presumably, the consequence of this view would be to give decisive power to local, elected school boards and reduce the power of the Ministry of Education to providing educational facilities. Though this view is rarely, if ever, challenged openly, circumspect invalidations of it have been numerous. Acknowledging that authority lies with the people, the government through the democratically elected parliament sees itself as the lawful representative of the people, and as such it administers the people's authority over education. The government's interests and by extension, the Ministry of Education's, are assumed to equal the people's interest.[6]

Equal opportunity and free education until university level was another major issue. The principle of equal opportunity is of course not objected to by anyone, on the contrary, it is held up as a successful characteristic of Japanese education. The disagreement rather lies in the *nature* of equal opportunity. For instance, does stratification of clever and not so clever students constitute an example of inequality because students are divided and hence do not receive the same teaching, or is it on the contrary equality because both groups are taught according to their abilities?

Equality of opportunities, which means that everyone in principle can choose between the same options, should not be mixed up with equality of results, which would mean educating all people to the exact same level of knowledge. Bringing everyone up to the same level is not what one is concerned with here. Neither are culturally based inequalities the target. Here it is clearly a question of material equality, as demonstrated by the proposed solution, which is education at public expense up to university level. On this issue teacher attitudes have changed over the years. Acknowledging that equality of opportunities and facilities exists — in principle at least — in Japan, the teachers point out that people should be helped in such a way that everyone can actually take advantage of those opportunities. The attitude today in the teacher organisations is focused more on equality of results.

---

6. It would be folly of course, to assume that institutions consisting of several individuals have total internal — or even external — agreement on all issues. Thus when the 'interests' of such large institutions are mentioned, what is referred to is the policy statements and reports issued by the institution, which are taken to represent a compromise of whatever diverse opinions there may or may not have been. Though the institutions are referred to as one, this is not to be intrepeted as meaning that there is no internal diversity, it is just a convenient means of reference.

Today elementary and middle school is free in Japan. To obtain free education up to university level, organisations like ATU have proposed that compulsory education be prolonged to twelve years, that is, to include high school, and thereby make payment a public matter. In practice high school is already virtually compulsory, since 95.8% of a relevant cohort attend high school and it has been over 90% since 1975 (Shimizu, 1996, 9). The effect of prolonged compulsory education would then presumably be that fewer students were withheld for economic reasons from applying to high school, but the question is how many this in fact would really be with the attendance rate already so high.

Other sources of inequality such as gender, family background or geographical background are not taken into consideration by this measure. The hierarchy between universities has already seeped down to the high school level and even if high school is made compulsory, there are bound to be some schools which are more prestigious than the rest, unless radical changes in admission procedures are made as well. The cause of the hierarchy lies with the universities and the employers' recruitment procedures. As long as there is a hierarchy among institutions of education and firms, people — especially those with financial means — will find ways of gaining advantages, for example by buying extra tutoring and the like.

Perhaps the 5% (or less) that do not attend high school do so for economic reasons, but apart from this small segment of the cohort, it seems economy is not what is hindering total equality of opportunity. The other sources to inequality — social status, geography, gender — however, are not easily dealt with. A change here has cultural implications, it would mean breaches with tradition and are matters which can only be changed slowly. Those sources of inequality are rarely made an issue — the gender problems, for instance, have only recently become accepted issues (James & Benjamin, 1988, 49).

The call for the abolition of bureaucratic control over educators was prompted by the fact that the Ministry of Education had strengthened its grip on educators rather than loosening it by issuing legally binding guidelines for the curriculum and by issuing directives for textbook authorization.

Lastly, there was a demand for the abolition of standardisation. Efforts are still being made to create a more flexible system, though the Ministry of Education seems unwilling to entirely give up the idea of uniformity and standardisation. It is claimed that without uniformity and standardisation, it is difficult to ensure equal opportunities. An additional reason, though not openly stated, could be that a standardised system is very easy to control and push in the desired direction.

Instead of standardisation the teachers called for freedom in the system and freedom for teachers to select textbooks. The definition of freedom seems to create disagreement, with predominantly teachers and academics advocating total non-intervention on the part of the government and the educational bureaucracy, while the Ministry of Education is more inclined towards the 'freedom and responsibility' approach, whereby, for example, teachers can 'freely' choose from a list of approved textbooks.

Postwar teacher unions seem to have toned down the issue of salaries, while the issue of central control over teachers and their political activities is still debated heatedly. There can be said to have been four great struggles in the postwar years. They are 1) The struggle for regaining the right to strike and bargain collectively; 2) The struggle to make school boards elective again and the question of textbook authorization procedures; 3) The struggle against the status of the curriculum guidelines as binding rather than suggestions; 4) The struggle against the efficiency rating system for teachers.

As mentioned above, the right to bargain collectively as well as the right to strike were denied the teacher unions in 1947. Both the JTU and the Ministry of Education had been extremely unwilling to cooperate and agreement in the collective bargaining was reached only with great difficulty. Neither side had any experience with building a constructive relationship, and tradition ran counter to accepting free unions as necessary as well as against using collective bargaining as a means of settling any conflict in the public sector. Further problems may be rooted in the tradition of paternalism as Thurston suggests. This tradition assumes no contradiction in interests between employer and employee whereas in collective bargaining conflict of interest is the rule rather than the exception (Thurston, 1973, 69-70).

The struggle to regain the right to strike and bargain collectively became one of JTU's main issues. JTU also engaged in other political issues such as opposition to the security treaty with the United States, opposition to military activities in Japan, opposition to treaties with South Korea etc. JTU in these matters enjoyed much popular sympathy, but only as long as tactics were non-violent and did not disrupt education in the schools. Some of the rank and file teachers opposed the engagement in matters remote from their daily lives, just like the more radical teachers wanted greater vigour in opposition to, for example, the Vietnam War (Thurston, 1973, 73). Those are clear examples of JTU's policy of engaging in issues other than the immediately school related ones, issues that will influence people's way of, and view of, life in a political way.

In 1970 JTU ideology took a new turn. There had been a successful wage struggle where JTU ended up defining teachers as 'professionals' rather than 'labourers', and demanding compensations as such. This greatly perturbed the 'left-wing' of the union, since this redefinition would most certainly weaken solidarity with the working class. In 1971 it even came to physical attacks on the JTU headquarters by members of the left-wing faction (Thurston, 1973, 75). Clearly the union had internal conflicts of ideological nature. The definition of the term 'teacher' is still one of the crucial points of argument between today's JTU and ATU, the former calling them 'professionals' and the latter insisting on the term 'labourer'.

The major struggles where the JTU tried to exert power in the first 25 years of its existence were in administration of education. JTU strongly opposed that the government made school boards appointive. The background for this decision was complex, but an incident which certainly influenced the decision to make school boards appointive was the so-called 'Yamaguchi Diary' case which occurred in 1953.

It was revealed that JTU through branch affiliates compiled and published quasi-textbooks for class room use in the form of workbooks and supplementary materials. Of course, they were not authorised by the Ministry of Education and they contained very provocative passages on the relationship between socialism and capitalism. This material was widely used in the schools of Yamaguchi Prefecture. It chastised capitalism for exploitation of workers and farmers, and exalted Russia as a fine example of a socialist country. The Yamaguchi Teachers' Union was by no means the only union to issue such material.

The reaction of the Ministry of Education to this was to publish three reports entitled *The Deplorable Textbooks* (*Ureubeki Kyookashoo*) which marked the beginning of an increasingly rigid system for textbook authorization. Further, the Ministry of Education was not comfortable with JTU publishing textbooks as well as partaking in the selection of textbooks through the school boards. It was felt that the JTU could gain a monopoly if this practice was allowed to spread (Duke, 1978, 257-58).

The problem for the Ministry of Education was that in 1952 a third of the elected school board members were union-dominated teachers. Of course, JTU felt that teachers were in fact the ones best qualified to take care of the school board functions. Though the boards were conservatively controlled, the JTU was able to exert considerable pressure with its share of the membership. But despite JTU opposition the school boards were made appointive in 1956 and teachers were reduced to eleven percent of the school board membership. The conservatives had gained full control of the boards.

Another field of conflict between the Ministry of Education and the JTU was — and is — textbook authorization. In 1956 the government tried to pass a Textbook Control Bill. It was pressured, however, by the JTU, JSP and intellectual members of other unions to withdraw the Bill. The Ministry instead used directives to narrow down the limits of 'suitability' of textbooks for use in the schools, and the authority to choose textbooks was moved from teachers to the prefectural boards of education (Thurston, 1973, 75-6; Duke, 1978, 259).

The third great struggle of the JTU in its first 25 years has been against the curriculum guidelines (*Gakushuu Shidoo Yooryoo*), which have been issued regularly by the Ministry of Education since 1958. JTU maintains that changes in the curriculum should come from the teachers, but as it is itself shut out from influence in the Ministry, in order to influence decisions, the tactics have been those of non-compliance at school level. Particularly moral education has been regarded with discontent and uneasiness (see also 4.1).

The fourth great struggle to be mentioned here is that of the efficiency rating system of teachers which was presented by the Ministry in 1957 (see 2.1.3). JTU interpreted the system as being designed to control teachers and weed out those considered politically undesirable. By means of non-cooperation the system was in the end rendered largely ineffective (Thurston, 1973, 77-78; Horio, 1988, 215).

From the beginning, the ideology of JTU was predominantly Marxist. However, much of the support JTU gained was not based on this ideology but on the general wish to prevent government control of education. For this reason, JTU had a high degree of support from non-Marxist members as well. The Marxist view dominated the Code of Ethics for Teachers which was drafted in 1952. The drafting committee included Marxists as well as progressive liberals, but the result was much coloured by the Marxist view that history is class struggle. JTU explicitly stated its policy as one of fighting 'to the finish to eliminate reactionary forces that would spark a war' with special address to the attempts by the government to revise the Peace Constitution and the conservative pressure for rearmament (Thurston, 1973, 83-7).

Though an amended version of the Code of Ethics for Teachers with softened Marxist terminology was presented in 1961, the Code still was the embodiment of the aim of fighting reactionary forces. The main slogan — which is still in use today both in the JTU as well as in the ATU — is 'never again send children off to the battlefield' (*Kodomo o futatabi senjo ni okuru na*). The slogan is printed on JTU's envelopes right under their address. It is argued that if teachers refuse to train children in patriotism or any military-like discipline, and furthermore oppose conscription, the sending of troops overseas, and rearmament for any purpose other than that of defence, this will in time influence the views of large segments of the population and in the end make aggressive actions impossible. The Code articulated the antipathy of many teachers to the pre-war authoritarian educational system, and it claimed the right to fight for the livelihood of the teachers.

During the sixties there were slight but significant changes in the interpretation of the union's ideology and the Code of Ethics. The class aspect was played down and the earlier classification of teachers as 'labourers' was modified and the 'wage earner' nuance of the word was emphasised instead. Teachers were wage earners and professionals, and as such they should have the right to decide on educational policies — they were after all the professionals (Thurston, 1973, 88-91).

In the labour movement as a whole there were changes under way. In 1970, JTU still adhered to the ideology based on class consciousness and it was fighting against a general tendency in the unions for moving to the right and for 'private' unions to become stronger. Also there were internal conflicts in JTU such as a danger of a split by radicals in Kyushu. This is why JTU, even if it softened its terminology, could not under any circumstances accept cooperation between labour and capital. It maintained its position as an anti-status quo interest group within the mainstream of the left-wing of Japanese politics (Thurston, 1973, 92-3). In this way it managed for a time to keep the radicals within the union.

In the beginning of the seventies the following objectives characterised JTU policy and they are still representative of teacher union policies. 1) Education is to be for the people and by the people, that is, it is to be democratic; 2) Moral education should not be re-introduced into the curriculum; 3) The creation of a democratic peace loving country; 4) Avoiding ministerial control with teacher training; 5) Fighting against administrative centralisation; 6) Wage struggle.

The first objective was of an ideological nature with its concern for education for and by the people and was not new on the agenda. While the government had slowly started reclaiming various central powers over education as explained above, it had not succeeded in modifying the *laws* which laid the foundation for 'democratic' education: the Constitution and the Fundamental Law of Education. With these two documents in hand, the JTU (and later also the ATU) attempted to prevent centralisation of power in the educational administration. The extent to which the unions valued the two documents was clearly demonstrated in the answer given by ATU representative, Kawai Naokito, to my question in 1991 about what 'ideal' education would be like: '... it is important to realise the ideas in the Constitution and the Fundamental Law of Education. It wouldn't be ideal but very close to ideal anyhow' (interview with Kawai Naoki, May 16, 1991).

The system of education as it was in the 1970s when these objectives were first formulated, was seen by the teacher organisations as non-democratic and beneficial only to the ruling class. The government had, in union eyes, disfigured a fundamentally democratic system of education. To create real democratic education, JTU maintained in its 1970 manifest, that this state of affairs had to be overturned, and a new political situation with the people in control of education had to be established — a higher standard of democracy approaching a general consensus. JTU proclaimed that education and politics could not be separated and that there was no such thing as 'politically neutral' education. JTU claimed that 'Political neutrality' was just an excuse for fostering partisan views of the LDP. On the other hand, JTU's affiliation with JSP was not viewed as partisan because JSP's educational policy was thoroughly dictated by the JTU. For instance, in the sixties and the beginning of the seventies, JTU held about two-thirds of the JSP seats (which amounted to one-third of the total) in the standing Education Committees in the two Houses of the Japanese parliament (Thurston, 1973, 94-95, 249; Schoppa, 1991, 151).

Article 10 of the Fundamental Law of Education (*Kyooiku Kihon Hoo*) constitutes the basis for much JTU argumentation on the subject of 'improper control' (*futoo na shihai*), which is what JTU claims is a result of the LDP partisan views gaining influence on education. The article says:

Education shall not be subject to improper control, but shall be carried out with direct responsibility to the whole people. School administration is required, on the basis of this realisation, to be conducted in a way so as to provide the various necessary conditions and facilities for fulfilling the aim of education. (Roppoo, 1991, 28)

In 1971 a primary JTU concern was the attempts by the Ministry of Education to reinterpret this Article 10. The Ministry's interpretation, as explained earlier, was that the government, as the elected representative of the people, was responsible for, and rightfully held authority over, education. JTU on the other hand, insisted that the provision against improper control was intended to prevent government excesses in the area of education. JTU also fiercely attacked the suggestions in the NCER reports of reinterpretation of Article 10 in particular (Schoppa, 1991, 151).

Based on Article 10, JTU also maintained that a school administration 'that concerns itself with the content of education constitutes improper control'. On this background it fought against the appointive school boards, the rating system for teachers and principals, and the nationwide achievement tests. (Thurston, 1973, 96-97) The term 'improper control' for JTU covered all conceivable manifestations of central influence on educational content and method as well as attempts to control the practitioners.

The second objective of JTU's 1970s policies was a combination of ideological and practical struggle. It concerned moral education. Moral education had been abolished by the Allied Occupation Authorities, but there was a widespread feeling in the conservative group, that moral education was a necessary component of education.

From 1953 onwards, it was the Ministry of Education's policy to reform the social studies curriculum and strengthen moral education in its place. In 1958 moral education was reintroduced in the curricula of elementary and middle school (Nakano, 1989b, 43). In the curriculum guidelines special moral education classes are set up, a regulated curriculum is in use, and NCER has proposed the use of government-prepared 'special materials' for moral education courses.

The JTU was not in principle opposed to instilling in students a certain sense of morality, but the way the government was realising moral education was in JTU eyes reminiscent of pre-war practices. In a response to the second NCER report it said:

There is a danger that [the policies recommended by the NCER] neglect the scientific consciousness of education, that they would wrap-up the whole school system in moral education, and that they could lead to a re-establishment of the pre-war system under which a moral code was enforced through militarism, the Imperial Constitution and the Imperial Rescript on Education. (Schoppa, 1991, 152)

ATU, in a pamphlet issued in 1990 in response to the new curriculum guidelines which were inspired and legitimised by NCER recommendations, stated that:

We all want our children to mature with a sense of public morals and respect for human rights. We are not saying that moral education is not important but we find it problematic to make its aim in elementary school that of 'respecting and revering beautiful and noble things beyond the explanatory power of humans'. (Zenkyoo, 1990, 19)

ATU was referring to a passage in the NCER reports. It is easy to see in the call for respect for superhuman things the shadow of the pre-war and wartime emperor worship as evidently ATU did.

The third ideology related objective on the 1970's JTU agenda was the creation of a democratic, peace loving country, a term also found in the Constitution. Adhering to Marxist tradition it was the opinion that democratic education was impossible with capitalists in power and further, that a democratic country was ipso facto a force for peace.[7] JTU was anti-American but it warmly supported the postwar reforms instigated in effect by the USA, as the overwhelming majority of the personnel in the Allied Occupation Authorities were Americans. The reason for the antipathy probably was the

---

7. It would seem that this preoccupation with securing peace was dominant among the more radical members of the JTU. When I interviewed the JTU and the ATU (which is where many of the radical members went after the split) none of my questions were about peace, and it was never mentioned during the JTU interview, but it came up several times during the ATU interview and received extensive covering. Now, this may be a coincidence, but in view of the character of the above 'vital measures' for securing peace and the anti-American flavour of them, it is not unreasonable to think that it was the more radical members that were most interested in the peace issue.

'reverse course' in 1949 when union rights were suddenly diminished as well as Marxist dislike of what was considered *the* capitalist country.

JTU was also fighting against every attempt by the Ministry to increase control over teacher training. Efforts by the Ministry to increase course requirements for university training programmes as well as government-run teacher training colleges, and training of veteran teachers, were met with strong opposition by the JTU. It was feared that teachers would be turned into government tools and that the usual broad range of graduates who became teachers would be narrowed. Grading teachers according to their level of training — the top grade would be graduate teacher training — and other such administrative means of control were opposed by the JTU because it was feared that such measures would enable the government to force teachers to quit the union and ingratiate themselves with administrators to secure their jobs and chances of promotion and further training (Schoppa, 1991, 152).

An objective related to this was the struggle against increased admini- strative centralisation. The government has already succeeded in introducing centralising policies such as a national curriculum and the school board reform. Recent JTU efforts have concentrated on the opposition to the strengthening of ministerial textbook authorization (Schoppa, 1991, 153). Because these control measures are passed administratively and not via the Diet, strengthened control has been possible despite opposition in the Diet itself.

A more practically oriented objective was the wage struggle. A general salary increase since the war indicates a certain JTU success in this area — at least the members are convinced of this, and thus have an economic reason for supporting the JTU, even if they do not agree entirely with the union policy. This is clearly illustrated by a survey made by Donald Thurston in 1965. He found that 97% of the teachers in the survey thought that the union was necessary for the protection of their livelihood, but at the same time the survey showed strong disapproval of JTU's emphasis on political matters. The average teacher felt the JTU did not in fact consider *his* opinion (Thurston, 1973, 102, 163).

The highly political nature of JTU's activities was not necessarily caused by the opinions of rank-and-file members. From the time of Thurston's survey the discrepancy between the political outlook of the union leaders and the rank-and-file members has been mirrored in declining membership. Whereas official statistics recorded the membership of JTU as 86.3% in 1958, it has been around 50% or slightly less for the last decade[8] (Schoppa, 1991, 284).

8. Note: Figures used in the official survey may not give the whole picture, as persons not allowed to be union members, e.g. principals, are included in the total (from which the percentage is calculated), but overall decline in membership is a reliable finding.

It is noteworthy that all the foregoing aims and objectives are based on opposition to change, preservation of the Fundamental Law of Education and the Constitution. Accordingly, the JTU has quite often been criticised for going against reforms because it was opposed to the government, not because it was opposed to the contents of the reforms. The government wants to increase teacher training requirements, moral education and centralisation. It turns out that the *reformers* are the *conservatives*, while the ones who want to *preserve* and stick to the values listed by the Occupation reforms, the Constitution and the Fundamental Law of Education, are from what is generally considered the *progressive camp*. In this case conservatism does not necessarily relate to preservation of the existing, but the reforms are conservative in the sense that their ideals are those known from liberal, conservative political ideology, in short, emphasis on liberalisation, the free market forces and individual responsibility.

The JTU was not without programmes for positive action in education policy. It proposed the 'substantialisation' (*juujitsuka*) of what was already there in the Constitution and the Fundamental Law of Education. Specifically, it proposed that teacher training be left to teachers, that the curriculum guidelines were limited to function as guidelines, that school boards become elective again and that textbook regulation be limited to an absolute minimum. These proposals have not changed much since the middle of the seventies, and given the out-of-power position of the JTU, they did not have much prospect of being implemented. Their effect was mainly to illuminate the points on which the JTU opposed government policy on education. It was perhaps only natural that the JTU, limited to a role of opposition as it was, could only react by defending the status quo (Schoppa, 1991, 153).

3.2.4 The split of JTU

In November 1989 the internal conflicts in JTU had come to a point of no return. There were several issues of conflict, but a very serious disagreement arose from the question of whether to associate with the central labour organisation *Rengoo* (*Zen Nippon Minkan Roodookumiai Rengookai*). Up till then JTU had been associated with the central organisation *Soohyoo*, and it had been quite influential there, but with the aggravated internal strife between left and right factions, JTU lost influence in *Soohyoo*. Also *Soohyoo* was weakened by a loss of membership caused by the privatisation of the national railways, and by the declining influence of the Japan Socialist Party (JSP) with which it was associated. All central organisations in Japan were losing ground and influence at the time, and in order to gain strength a number of them decided to unite. This meant that *Soohyoo*, which had up till then been rather radical in its action policies, had to find a balance with the more moderate organisations (that is, those who did not use measures like strikes) such as *Doomei*, organising labourers, and *Chuuritsurooren*, organising people in private enterprises.

Rengoo, the new central organisation, was decided upon on November 20, 1987, and the final fusion with *Soohyoo* took place in 1989. In *Rengoo* the privately employed were the majority and this influenced the action policies in such a manner that they became considerably more moderate and 'establishment friendly' than had been the case of *Soohyoo*'s action policies (Pohl, 1988, 60-61).

The leftist faction of JTU found this very disturbing. In a speech at the founding meeting of this union, Mikami Mitsuru, chairman-to-be of the new teachers' union, criticised *Rengoo* harshly. He quoted a *Rengoo* publication for stating that any association with the JCP would mean 'loss of rights and freedom' and pointed out that the reason for protesting against this was not that the leftist faction of JTU wanted to support JCP in particular, but that it strongly disagreed with the way communism and 'the reds' were used to frighten people. The anti-communism of *Rengoo* was bound to influence JTU, he said, and added the question: 'How can we postulate to represent truth and justice if we accept a thing like anti-communism?' (Mikami, 1990, 48).

Mikami argued that it was folly on the part of JTU to surrender to *Rengoo* in order to avoid being popularly associated with JCP and the subsequent risk of being deserted by the members. His point was that while *Rengoo* was undoubtedly not interested in communism, it was also highly questionable whether it was at all interested in the kind of education teachers should be interested in. There had been no assurances whatsoever that *Rengoo* would be the slightest bit interested in education or that it valued educational freedom. The association with *Rengoo* could not be for educational reasons. He did acknowledge, though, that a larger organisation was in some cases stronger, but at the same time he warned against the fallacy of thinking that 'big is better' or that a large organisation such as *Rengoo* could be changed from within (Mikami, 1990, 47).

The unification of the central organisations into *Rengoo* triggered the split of JTU. The JSP and JCP factions had been there throughout JTU's history but, up until 1989, in a precarious coexistence. This ended with the formation of *Rengoo*. The left-wing of JTU feared that in a huge organisation like *Rengoo* they would have difficulties being heard, educational matters would be difficult to champion and further, they feared that reformist and even anti-communist policies would be forced upon them. The reason for the split of the JTU was political.

The purpose of the new teachers' union named *Zen Nippon Kyooshokuin Kumiai Keimeikai* (in short *Zenkyoo* and hereafter ATU) was to 'continue the original JTU line', as it was put. To be on the children's side, to fight against central control of education, to protect educational freedom. Freedom, peace and democracy were the key words, and results were to be reached by uniting efforts with parents and local Parent-Teacher Associations (PTA). In effect ATU was not a new creation, but a continuation of *true* teacher union activity, Mikami maintained. No opinion would be excluded and in this they were not like *Rengoo*, which excluded communism. It would only be a matter of time, Mikami warned, before JTU would have to succumb to the *Rengoo* policies of not associating with communists and not using strikes or other drastic action measures in labour struggles. Further, Mikami predicted that *Rengoo's* attitude would eventually exclude cooperation between the two teacher organisations (JTU and ATU) as ATU would probably, in *Rengoo* eyes, be 'infected' with communism (Mikami, 1990, 49-51).

A further complication arising from the affiliation with *Rengoo* was the question of the attitude towards NCER's reports and proposals. *Rengoo* wanted to support the reports as they were. Mikami argued that the purpose of NCER was, in unison with business and large-scale industry, to establish a manpower policy for the manner in which children should be 'formed' (*hito tsukuri*) or brought up. To achieve this, new curriculum guidelines were issued. However, as Mikami saw it, these guidelines in fact fostered discrimination by separating and streaming children at an early stage into 'students' or 'workers'. He stated that NCER would make *tools* out of the children as it did not consider their souls (Mikami, 1990, 16-17).

The act of supporting NCER's reports placed *Rengoo* in the government friendly camp as far as the left-wing of JTU was concerned. Further, *Rengoo's* refusal to employ drastic means of protest was interpreted by the left-wing as an attempt to please the government and big business. The consequence was that the left-wing could not possibly accept an association with this central organisation.

When Rengoo's views on education became known, the left-wing of JTU considered them plainly conservative, a sharer of the NCER's view of children. In Mikami's opinion this NCER view of children should be of deep concern and this he demonstrated with a quotation from the book 'Introduction to Future Learning' (*Mirai Gakunyuumon*) written in 1967 by the NCER member-to-be Kooyama Kenichi[9] in which it was said that:

What population researchers point out with apprehension, is that the growth in birth rates is particularly high among people with a low IQ. Birth rates among people with high IQ's are much lower, and there is a danger that the quality of mankind will deteriorate as a result. In the long run this degeneration of mankind

9. Kooyama Kenichi was a professor at the Gakushuuin University; a former advisor to Prime Minister Oohira and he became one of Nakasone's chief 'brains'.

by bad genes is a serious problem that cannot be ignored. (Kooyama quoted in Mikami, 1990, 18)

Before this quotation, Kooyama had stated that in our 'industrial civilisation people with an IQ below 110 are not useful'. Kooyama evidently was proposing that the well-educated should have more children. His openly discriminatory remarks stopping short of suggesting genetic hygiene, brings back to many Europeans unpleasant memories of Nazi ideology. Such remarks would be highly unsuitable or even unthinkable and, at the very least, unwise in Europe.

But in Asia, Kooyama was not the only one to voice such ideas. In Singapore, for example, part of dealing with the population problem was discouraging the 'irresponsible, the social delinquents' from producing children until they were persuaded to use their limited resources on 'one or two children giving them maximum chances of climbing up the educational ladder', as it was put by Prime Minister Lee Kuan Yew in 1969 (Salaff, 1985, 167).

An interesting aspect of this discussion is the question of how the Japanese can earnestly say such things — Kooyama was by no means the only one to express such opinions — which are definitely not considered comme il faut in most democratic countries. Former Prime Minister Nakasone's famous remark about the lowering effect ethnic groups had on average American IQ is another example of — in the eyes of most of the Western world — an outrageous comment, but apparently Nakasone did not have the slightest compunction about making it. It is possible that the reason why a Japanese can say such discriminatory things is because he feels he is just stating an obvious fact. Like low-income strata will affect average national income, so low IQ's will affect the average national IQ. Assuming that low IQs are associated with race is, however, a blatant display of racial intolerance or perhaps plain ignorance.

Examples of Japanese intolerance of other races are legendary, and in addition there is apparently an intolerance (particularly among the politically conservative) towards the weak. This may be due to their liberalist 'everyone-for-himself ideology' and to the fact that the political tradition in Japan — as well as in the Western countries — has been that the left made the poor, the weak and the workers their concern, while the right concerned itself with industry and private enterprise. At any rate, consideration of the weak has become a hallmark of the left-wing in Japan just as it often characterises left-wing political rhetoric in other parts of the world. In this respect Mikami is a typical left-wing representative, and with regard to Kooyama's IQ theory, he referred to Kooyama's suggested solution to the perceived problem:

Only people with superior genes (*sugureta idenshi*) should be allowed to have more than three children and they should be subsidised in various ways, and all others should confine themselves to less than two children. A policy like this could be imagined. (Kooyama quoted in Mikami, 1990, 18)

Such a policy may have been imaginable to Kooyama, but certainly not to Mikami who called the plan 'unthinkable' (*tondemonai puran*). The Kooyama views were represented in NCER as Kooyama himself was a member, and Mikami saw elements of Kooyama's views in the official view of children held by NCER. This view was described by Mikami in the following terms:

They see children as rockets born with a certain amount of fuel. When this is used up they cannot possibly advance further. This is at the heart of NCER thinking. (Mikami, 1990, 19)

Mikami explained that if this is the basis of the reform proposals, the task of teachers becomes the determining — preferably as fast as possible — of how much fuel is on the rockets, and teaching accordingly. He condemned the new curriculum guidelines as selection devices aimed at sorting out 'workers' by compressing the curriculum to a ridiculously difficult degree. The curriculum changes consisted of additions such as the teaching of millilitre in the 2nd grade of elementary school (whereas before it was in the 6th grade) and the introduction of 19 more Chinese characters during the first two years of schooling. The addition of more Chinese characters, it was feared, would make pupils worse at spelling, since the only way to get time for the new characters was by speeding up the learning of hiragana and katagana[10] (Mikami, 1990, 19-26; Interview with Kawai Naoki, May 16, 1991).

This was one of the reasons why the ATU could not tolerate the Rengoo recommendation of the NCER reports. Other issues of conflict based on the NCER reports were the 'creation of a better Japanese' (*yoki nihonjin o tsukuru*)[11] and particularly the method by which this was to be done. Again *Rengoo* was involved because its Vice-President Kanasugi was also a member of NCER and had argued for the creation of a better Japanese by stating that 'if you are not able to explain about Japanese things like the Meiji Restoration and

10. *Hiragana* and *katagana* are syllabic writing systems. They can be used for writing any word, but the *hiragana* system is usually used for writing particles and endings, while *katagana* is used for foreign names and loan words.
11. The expression stems from the following passage in the introduction to the first NCER report: 'Understanding that to be a good world citizen (*kokusaijin*) one must be *a good Japanese*, we find it necessary to establish education which teaches love of country, deep understanding of the uniqueness of Japanese culture, as well as deepening the understanding of foreign cultures and traditions' (Rinkyooshin, 1988, 15-16).

Admiral Toogoo[12] you will not be valued as an international being by other countries'. He stated that it was crucial for an internationally minded Japanese to have knowledge of the following four subjects: Admiral Toogoo, the Meiji Restoration, Kabuki and Zen. As this was said by an official from *Rengoo*, Mikami took it to represent Rengoo's official views. To Mikami, the core of the problem here was the way these four things were explained to children. The story of Toogoo Heihachiroo was the example he used.

Formerly Toogoo was not part of the curriculum, but a lot of people seemed to think that as an important historical person he should be known. However, Mikami found the way the Toogoo story should be taught, according to the guideline recommendations, to be highly questionable. The story of an aggressive war waged by Japan which made people in a third country (China) suffer, was told as an example of how Japan gained international esteem and was related to the children in such a way as to make it extremely exciting. The atrocities were omitted, and Mikami felt it was not right but rather frightening, that children in this way were seduced to enjoy a tale of war. In general, Mikami criticised the recommended treatment of the wars in which Japan was involved. They were always portrayed as having been necessary for the protection and security of Japan, and the positive outcomes were always emphasised. The Pacific War was a case in point.

Mikami summarised the guidelines on this issue: The Second World War was Asia's fight against imperialism. The Japanese may have been cruel, the Nanking Massacre may have taken place, but look at the many sovereign countries that came into existence after the war! (Mikami, 1990, 40-44).

The idea of Japan as Asia's liberator can and will certainly be contested by many, but this was not Mikami's main concern. He was more concerned about the way war was turned into an adventure, the way it became a fairy tale of 'how the ancestors suffered for our sake'. It gave children a dangerous idea of what war was, because it left out the true suffering, the injustice and the cruelties, instead glorifying it as actions of heros (Mikami, 1990, 42).

The preceding makes it clear that certain groups within JTU, notably what was known as the 'left-wing', could not live with an affiliation with the central organisation *Rengoo*, which was ready to condemn communism and support NCER and what the left-wing saw as nationalistic influences on education. It came as the last straw in a series of internal disagreements plaguing JTU and the result was the establishment of an alternative to JTU, which had as its expressed goal to become a truly *national* teacher organisation with rights, as such, in relation to the Ministry of Education.

---

12. Toogoo Heihachiroo is one of the heroes of militarism. He is famed for his surprising victory over the Russian navy in the straits of Tsushima during the Russo-Japanese war of 1904-5.

3.2.5 Conclusions

In view of the history of teacher organisations in Japan it is no wonder that they have had so little influence on the policy making of the Ministry of Education. Their influence was cut short by the restrictions on public servants' means of action as well as the re-definition of teacher organisations as 'personnel organisations' rather than 'unions'. This re-definition meant that no trade union law applied to teachers, or other public employees for that matter.

Thus, effectively put out of circuit as a union, stripped of any right to negotiate on a national level, the only road of action left to the teachers has been at school level. Numerous tactics of non-compliance with new directives, and interpretations slightly different from that of the Ministry of Education have been devised, and strikes have been used as weapons. The strikes, however, were given up in the seventies as the personal costs became unreasonably high for the teachers.

The teacher organisations, of which JTU is still by far the largest, suffered losses of influence not only due to external pressure (from the Ministry of Education), but also due to fractionalising internally. The fundamental disagreement was over whether to engage in party politics, and in that case, whether to affiliate with the Socialists or the Communists. The final split was brought about by disputes over the affiliation with the central organisation *Rengoo*, which for many in JTU was too interfering and too establishment-friendly, or even reactionary, to be trusted. The split in 1989 only served to reinforce a long standing argument of the Ministry of Education against negotiating with JTU — it would be unjust to negotiate with just one organisation as they did not organise all teachers. The result of the split has been an amputated JTU and a more radical ATU with a strong ideological basis.

However oppressed teacher organisations may have been since the war — and of course they were even more so before the war — they have not been entirely without influence, albeit influence of an unofficial nature. By using different tactics the teachers have been able to render government directives ineffective.

In connection with reforms, the problem of teacher influence arises as the teachers demanded influence in the *making* of the reform proposals, instead of being content with trying to alter the ready made policies seeping down from the government. Though public hearings were held concerning the NCER reports and teachers were invited to these, the hearings did not seem to have had significant effect on the contents of the reports. Objections were listened to but not dealt with. The hearings did not provoke alterations. Still the hearings have been used by the Ministry and NCER to legitimate their actions, as a proof that the teachers were in fact heard — and they were — but apparently to no effect.

As for the implementation of the reforms proposed by NCER, the attitude of the teacher organisations will greatly influence in practice the shape of the reforms. As the ones to translate the reforms into actual teaching, the teachers are the first to detect problems, and in most cases the first to react. They have a unique chance of interpreting what is dictated in the course of their teaching practices, and no doubt this will often be done. Therefore it is interesting to analyze the position of the teachers in relation to the NCER reforms, as their reaction will have influence on the implementation of reforms and on their success.

The two organisations discussed here, JTU and ATU, agree by and large about the NCER reports, but JTU's reactions are tempered by the desire to be a mainstream organisation and the desire to be on good terms with the Ministry of Education in order to play a more important part at the policy making stage. The JTU rhetoric is less dramatic and not so studded with ideological terms as that of ATU. While JTU tries to transmit its criticism of the NCER reports in terms of the children's interests, the ATU, while doing the same, is also more openly political.

The reactions of the teacher organisations to the NCER reforms are by and large political. The whole issue of education in Japan is a highly politicised area and even in the discourse of the teacher organisations, pedagogical concerns are given little space. Pedagogy and discussions of it, are largely matters for individual teachers. It is a quite natural reaction to the NCER reports in which the pedagogical element is virtually non-existent. NCER made no attempt to propose methods, analyze existing methods or define the needs of a child.

The politically determined reaction to these educational reforms by the pedagogues was caused partly by the highly political content of the reports, partly by the history of educational discourse in Japan where it has always been a highly politicised issue in which government control and government aims have set the agenda, not pedagogical concerns or discussions of the nature of education. Educational debate has moved within the realm of politics and neither the split of the teacher organisation nor the NCER reports have changed that.

3.3 Other Opposition Groups

Besides the teacher unions there were several other groups protesting against the reforms proposed by NCER. Among these were researcher groups, citizens' groups, independent parents' and teachers' groups.

In the following, two groups who opposed the full implementation of the NCER reforms have been chosen as examples. The groups are the Women's

Democratic Council on Educational Reform (*Josei ni Yoru Minkan Kyooiku Shingikai*), and the Academic Society for Research on the Educational System, under the organisation Study Group on Japanese Education (*Nihon Kyooiku Gakkai no Kyooiku Seido Kenkyuu Iinkai*). The first group has been chosen because — as a group of women — it stood in sharp contrast to the male dominated NCER, and because it did its best to represent views close to the grass roots level. It very consciously tried to deal with the problems drawn to its attention by the public as well as those placed on the agenda by its own members. It was, as such, an interesting example of the 'grassroots' level movement for educational reform and can show us the extent of the differences between the official agenda for educational reform and the grass roots level agenda.[13]

The second group derived — and still does — its importance from the many renowned scholars participating. It was called upon from time to time by the NCER to give specialist opinions on various matters, but despite the chance to get heard this group had little or no influence on NCER's agenda-setting and its deliberations. It represented a section of the reform movement dominated by academics who were critical of the government, often from a left-wing viewpoint.

3.3.1 Women's Democratic Council on Educational Reform

The Women's Democratic Council on Educational Reform (hereafter WDCER) was established in April 1985 as a reaction to NCER, which was perceived not to be representative of the views of women and particularly not of those held by mothers and female teachers. Indeed, of the 25 members of NCER only three were women, one of whom was also the only regular school teacher to be member of NCER.

WDCER was a voluntary group and it consisted of teachers from universities, schools and kindergartens, journalists, housewives, authors, and a paediatrician. Stating that their aim of reform was fundamentally different from that of NCER, the WDCER in 1987 issued a publication containing over a hundred different reform proposals. It was issued in June 1987, just before the last report from NCER (August, 1987), so as to enable NCER to 'consider the proposals of WDCER in its last report' (*Asahi*, 1987, 3). It is doubtful, however, whether they were really in time with their report to be included in NCER deliberations. The idea of giving NCER a chance to consider the proposals before issuing their own final report is more likely to be wishful thinking on the part of WDCER and a good story for the press.

---

13. By 'grassroots' I mean groups created by users, people directly involved, on their own initiative and with no control relations to any public administration.

In the opening of its publication on reform, WDCER emphasised that the changes they were envisaging were not for the sake of the nation or the economy, but for the sake of the suffering children. The children were seen as pressured and maimed by the current educational system, and WDCER felt that in order to ensure that in the future there would be kind, healthy (*kenkoo*) and brave (*takumashii*) citizens with a democratic outlook, the adults (parents) had to provide the required conditions. The most urgent problems as seen by the WDCER were: the excessively bureaucratic anti-human system of education, bullying, truancy — which was seen as a desperate cry for help — and at the root of it all, the entrance examinations (WDCER, 1987, 90-91).

The words *kenkoo* and *takumashii* are extremely value-loaded and deserve special attention since they were both used repeatedly by the different parties of the debate. *Kenkoo* (health/healthy) means that you are strong in body, not sickly or frail, and the strength of the body is associated with strength of spirit or mind. The Ministry of Education in its White Paper from 1992 says:

Sport is a fundamental thing in human culture because it not only answers the body's basic need of movement, but it also provides a completeness of mind, it helps improve the health (*kenkoo*) and bodily strength and thus works for both mind and body. (Monbushoo, 1992, 6)

In this way *kenkoo* and mind is directly connected. A person who is *kenkoo* is usually also expected to be *takumashii*. WDCER also associated the two above. *Takumashii* signifies the ideal of an unafraid, active, strong person, and no Japanese would dream of rejecting the desirability of either of these two attributes. The protagonist of a folk-tale often possesses these character traits, for example *Momotaroo* is a *kenkoo* and *takumashii* character. By using such words, the groups try to assure positive reception by their readers.

WDCER took great pride in its openness and in the process of identifying the problems to be dealt with, displayed a very open and public procedure. Before going to work in the council, telephone lines were established for parents, teachers, students or anyone who wished, to air complaints or put forth reform proposals concerning the educational system. This took place in March 1985, and based on 273 calls from all parts of the country, the WDCER identified the problems that should be dealt with first of all. Although 273 calls are not many with a population of more than 120 million, it did at least constitute a more popular basis for deliberations than was the case in most other groups dealing with educational reform notably, of course, the NCER. The low number of calls could also support the assumption that the NCER reform deliberations were not answering a popular demand for educational reform. As mentioned earlier an official survey in 1985 found 42% of the surveyed ignorant of the publication of NCER's first report (*Mainichi*, 1985b, 3).

The theme occurring most often in the calls to WDCER's lines was complaints about the school itself. This concerned the bureaucracy in the schools and the stiffness that inevitably seeped into teaching as a result of this, the dress codes, the rituals concerning the Japanese flag (*Hinomaru*), and so on.

The second most occurring theme was about bullying (*ijime*). Many children called to relate their experiences with this and parents called to get advice on how to react to the fact that their child was being bullied. It turned out that a lot of the callers felt that the teachers did not in any way try to support the victims of bullying, rather the victim was reproached by the teacher and told that it was his own fault (*omae ga warui*). The number of calls for the five most mentioned themes was as follows:

1) Complaints about school	95
2) Bullying	54
3) Reform proposals	35
4) Family problems (manners)	16
5) Truancy	15

(*Mainichi*, 1985, 13)

The callers were mostly mothers, but 15 children under 18 years of age also called and a number of fathers and teachers.

Among the more concrete complaints in the category of 'Complaints about school' were grievances over corporal punishment exercised by teachers, and in particular the use of *naishinshoo* as a weapon against the pupils. The *naishinshoo*, the internal report card, evaluates not only academic performance, but also the personality of the student. The student has no right to see it much less to correct or criticise it. The *naishinshoo*, as described earlier, is primarily used in the admission procedures for high school, and it can carry decisive weight as to whether a person is admitted or not (see Section 2.2.3).

The WDCER demonstrated its members' awareness as women, complaining that the educational system and all government councils were, and had always been, male dominated. To correct this, WDCER would present the female point of view. But the female aspect was not the only one. Also they saw themselves as representatives of the parent group, as representatives of the guardians of the direct users of the system, and as such they displayed much concern for the happiness and the future of the children. The tone of the language in their proposals was refreshing because it did not hide the heartfelt emotions involved, compared to the rather theoretical tone of the NCER reports, but the contents of the WDCER report were in no way 'soft' or dreamy. The proposals were concrete and deliberate.

WDCER in the first chapter outlined the areas in need of immediate reform. Apparently, great care had been taken to propose *actually feasible* reforms, as opposed to elaborating on dreams and ideals which were not readily realisable, and therefore more vulnerable to charges that they were unrealistic.

Areas urgently in need of reforms were:

1) Abolition of the relative evaluation report card (*Sootai Hyooka Tsuushin Hyoo*).
2) Better conditions for the children. To make children understand their lessons better and to increase their confidence and joy of learning, direct experience should be emphasised.
3) Teachers. The administration should ease the administrative burden on the teachers to release more time for the teachers to be with the children.
4) A local body to settle conflicts.
5) Working parents should have better opportunities for receiving education.
6) Mobility between high schools should be facilitated.
   (WDCER, 1987, 97-101)

WDCER dealt with reform issues which corresponded nicely with the problem areas identified by the telephone session which had initiated the council's work. Great pains were taken to accommodate the popular demands thus voiced, emphasising the WDCER claim that they were on the people's side in the issue of educational reform, rather than the NCER and official side. The pressure on children to compete and be the best was sought alleviated through the abolishment of some of the evaluation devices and the high school entrance examination. Also this measure was supposed to be remedial in the fight against bullying and the violence that sometimes accompanied bullying.[14]

The relative evaluation report card came in as a Number 1 concern for WDCER. It was seen — along with other evaluation devices — as being

---

14. It is worth noting that the incidents of violence in Japanese schools have indeed become more numerous, but still the problem is small compared to the situation in many West-European countries and in the United States in particular. Thomas P. Rohlen quotes the following Japanese and American figures. In 1976 the arrest rate per 1000 young persons in the United States was 79, whereas in Japan it was 4. Young persons constituted about 24% of the total population in both counties. Juvenile arrests for violent crimes in the United States was 6 per 1000, whereas in Japan it was 0.5 per 1000 (Rohlen, 1983, 296). Police reports on violence in Japanese middle schools in 1994 was 0.4 incidents per 1000 schools and 3.8 incidents per 1000 high schools. (Calculated on the basis of Shimizu, 1996 & Soomuchoo, 1996).

responsible for many of the problems which plagued the educational system. This report card listed the members of a class in the order corresponding to their relative standing in the class, and was issued three times a year. The procedure of relative evaluation meant that some children would never experience the feeling of 'having done well' as a good mark may convey.[15] Instead they may find themselves always placed behind a few or several friends in the class. It puts great pressure on the children to advance, or at any rate not to slide down the ranks.

WDCER pointed out that this method created a lot of losers, and that it was not pedagogical. It caused jealousy, anger and pressure, and provided causes for bullying, it was said. The WDCER pointed out that this last problem was due to the fact that the teacher by the sheer act of ranking — and always ranking the weakest pupil lowest — signalled in a sense that picking on the weak was all right. Hence, the recommended remedy was to abolish the relative evaluation report and instead devise another way of evaluating, which would make a child happy about his/her own *progress* instead of being disappointed that it was not enough for a top-rank in the class (WDCER, 1987, 97).

Along with a reform of the report card a reform of the *naishinshoo* was suggested. The *naishinshoo* and the report card were seen by WDCER as sources of competition and stress in the schools. Hence WDCER recommended not only the abolition of the relative evaluation report, but also the abolition of the entrance examination for high school. This last reform would render the *naishinshoo* superfluous as its prime reason for existence is the use made of it as a report card between middle school and high school.[16]

Realising that the call for abolition of the entrance examinations for high school may not be quite realistic for yet some time, the WDCER proposed the following remedial measures in the meantime: a) the *naishinshoo*'s name

---

15. This experience is possible with the provision that marking is not conducted according to guidelines prescribing certain percentages of every mark in each class, because with this method only a fixed number of a certain grade would be available. This means giving 10% A's, for instance, and no more, instead of giving the number of A's warranted by performance, regardless of whether this means that 20% or more students in a class receive A's.

16. An example of how the *naishinshoo* is used is quoted in Horio 1988, 281-82. A student was denied admission to one public and three private high schools despite the fact that he had met the required academic standards. He was denied admission because of an unfavourable *naishinshoo* report, and he was even barred from participating in the graduation ceremonies of his middle school because of the *naishinshoo*. The unfavourable report concerned his 'behaviour' ranking, which was consistently the lowest or next lowest rankings possible. The teacher's 'special comment' explained that the background for the negative evaluation was the student's political activities in a student organisation.

should be changed to 'Report Card' (*Seiseki Shoomeishoo*); b) the new Report Card should not be directed by the curriculum guidelines, but by the guidelines issued by the WDCER; c) only academic performances were to be evaluated. The highly biased evaluations in the *naishinshoo* robbed parents of their trust in teachers; d) The Report Card had to be open for comment by pupils and their guardians, and amendments resulting from such comments may be made.

Further, WDCER proposed to prohibit that the school disclosed details of the pupils' or their home's private affairs to any investigative body, and all reports from school concerning individuals — be it to the police, the school board or others — should be presented to the pupil and the guardians for approval or denouncement.

The responsibilities of teachers, parents and pupils were to be made clear in a new School Charter (*Gakkoo Kenshoo*) which established how information was to be distributed and what the responsibilities of the different groups were. Also, a body should be established at every school to review the many rules and regulations. The profuseness of rules caused violence, bullying and truancy because the rules provided ample opportunity to point fingers at those who did not conform, WDCER stated. The new body should investigate which rules were indispensable and which were redundant or unnecessary. The members should be pupils, teachers and local representatives (WDCER, 1987, 99-100).

With regard to the second issue on the list, that of bettering children's conditions for learning and developing, WDCER had the following remarks: The task of learning was so concentrated upon memorising huge amounts of facts that the joy of learning by doing was in practice not experienced by the children. In order to introduce more direct experience the curriculum should be eased. Also the school should accept 'second attempts'. The current tendency that once you fall behind you will never catch up again had to be reversed, or the label of *ochikobore* (slow student) would stick to a person for the rest of his life and direct him to a life on the fringes of society, WDCER warned. The remedies for this were:

a) to offer sabbatical years from school and accept returning drop-outs;
b) make it possible for students to work during enrolment in school, so that a student who tires of studying may work for a while and then return to studies later[17] (WDCER, 1987, 97).

17. It is interesting that this is counted among changes to be desired. In Denmark for instance, the present policy is wary of such initiatives because working usually involves increased consuming and an increased need for money, which makes it difficult to return to school later.

Children should be provided with more diverse choices. They should not be confined to books if they do not have the urge, but instead be allowed to go out and get other experiences by working. This option was of course also available at the time, but a return to studies as WDCER was envisaging, was virtually impossible in the contemporary school structure. Returning to school should, WDCER requested, be an actual option for youngsters.

Also, children should to a greater extent learn by direct experience. Subscribing to the theory that 'learning by doing' not only would give more joy of learning but also would provide the children with a better understanding of what they learn, the WDCER recommended easing the curriculum and allowing more time for seeking direct experiences during lessons.

In this discussion of in-and-out-of-school, WDCER seemed to overlook the effect of popular opinion. Would someone who left school to work for a while and then return to school later, not suffer a loss of prestige? And would this stigma be significantly different from that attached to being an *ochikobore*? — Even if the individual was successful in learning better after gaining work experience, the social aspect would still be likely to influence his life. It is unlikely that a person who has left school for a while is ever going to accumulate the same degree of social prestige as someone who has stayed on the fixed path of the educational system. To avoid this, a change in the background for social evaluation would be necessary. The NCER often mentioned the necessity of such a change in connection with life-long learning and the evaluation of learning acquired late in life, but the WDCER did not deal explicitly with this problem. Perhaps the WDCER took it for granted that the problem would disappear by itself once new procedures were introduced and accepted?

To combat bullying, WDCER proposed that children should experience more autonomy and know that they also have human rights like everyone else. WDCER felt that bullying could not be remedied solely by counselling and supervision by adults. Also, children should be given responsibility, good surroundings free of adult supervision, and the feeling that they had some power to decide themselves. To achieve this end, pupils' committee activities at school needed to be appreciated by everyone, there would have to be local support for children's group activities, and finally, children's playgrounds should not be artificial environments but resemble nature as closely as possible (WDCER, 1987, 97).

The WDCER pointed out problems in club activities. Under the heading of corporal punishment;[18] which was denounced as most improper, the

18. Corporal punishment is not deemed legal in Japanese schools, but incidents of it are not uncommon, as the ATU representative regretfully pointed out. (Interview with Kawai Naoki, May 16, 1991)

volunteer after-school-hours club activities were mentioned. Apparently, some of these were quite rigid and military-like in structure and corporal punishment of members had been known to take place. As this was an obvious extension of bullying, WDCER naturally proposed to prohibit such procedures in clubs and also wanted to relax the structure and nature of club activities. And further, club activities should not be compulsive in middle and high school, and they should never take place on Sundays. This day, in WDCER's opinion, was to be spent with the family (WDCER, 1987, 100).

Finally, WDCER proposed that in the case of both parents working, there should be better facilities for taking care of children after school . At the time there were only child-care facilities up to the third grade, but WDCER felt that was insufficient, and should be extended to the end of middle school (WDCER, 1987, 101).

With regard to the teachers mentioned under item No. 3, WDCER suggested that they should not separate themselves from the children during breaks or leisure time but should be with them under informal circumstances as much as possible. This should be supported locally by the provision of a house for the use of teachers, where they could stay overnight with groups of students for leisure and learning activities. Such activities should be voluntary (WDCER, 1987, 98-99).

Through more direct contact, WDCER expected teachers to understand the individual needs of the children better, to get to know their charges better, and thus become better teachers. Also, the presence of a teacher and the involvement of a teacher in the daily activities of the children might put the teacher in a better situation to deal with bullying and those who bully, rather than blaming the victim.

WDCER regretted the antagonism between different teachers unions and between the unions and the Ministry of Education. This should be settled so as to make school a nicer place to be and work. WDCER, as a representative of parents, did not welcome the fractionalising of teachers due either to adherence to different organisations or non-organisation. They feared that it would make team-work impossible and in the end affect the teaching and the children. The proposed solutions were the following: a) If possible, all teachers should belong to only one organisation; b) The Ministry of Education or the administration was not to put any kind of pressure on union members because of their union affiliation; c) the Ministry of Education should not be involved with current political power holders. The Minister of Education should be appointed from among people with occupational experience with education, not from among politicians; d) the teacher unions should not associate themselves with political parties (WDCER, 1987, 98-9).

This could seem quite reactionary but it did not place the WDCER on the side of the Ministry of Education in this matter. It is clear that WDCER realised the importance of the independent organisation of teachers, while at the same time wishing it not to be a conflict area with regard to the Ministry of Education or to be the cause of internal conflicts of which the children would be the victims. It was apparently an attempt to move the focus of the debate towards addressing pedagogical issues rather than politics.

Of the areas urgently in need of reform, items 4, 5 and 6 concerned more detailed and concrete problems than the previous points. The fourth point on the list concerned the way conflicts were dealt with. WDCER aimed at creating more democratic structures in the following manner: To settle conflicts WDCER wished every school to have a special body for this purpose. The members may be those partaking in the body evaluating school regulations. Anyone should be allowed to air complaints to this body, and if a problem proved too difficult to solve for the school by itself, the school board may be called upon for help. The most significant characteristic of this body was that it should have pupil representation. Pupils were not usually involved in such things, just as they were cut off from any influence or even knowledge of the evaluation of themselves.

WDCER took up the question of adult education and was very realistic about the time factor involved in this. It proposed that adult education could take place in night schools or, in cooperation with the workplace — during working hours.

In order to remedy a situation where families could be separated due to a family member changing his/her place of work, WDCER called for more flexible high school structures in order to promote mobility between them. At the time, if a member of a family — usually the father — was forced to move for occupational reasons, it was difficult for the family to move also if a child was enrolled in high school. This meant that families had to live apart. If a move became necessary under the current circumstances the child would be set back in learning because he/she would usually have to start high school all over again, primarily because of the entrance examination, and the ensuing differences between schools. NCER did not consider this problem and WDCER attacked it for this. The concern for the life of the family was a trademark of the WDCER.

WDCER argued that a change in procedures would definitely be possible, especially if the entrance examination for high school was abolished. Also WDCER proposed a credit system in high school so that the students may choose subjects according to interest and abilities. In this way the credits could just be moved along with the student and a lot of the curriculum problems avoided. As a result of this change, texts and lessons would become less standardised (WDCER, 1987, 100-1).

The measures for flexibility proposed by the WDCER were not those most readily realisable as they involved the abolition of the high school entrance examination and the creation of a credit system in high school. There is no doubt, however, that facilitating moves between individual high schools involved reforms like these. Or at least a more accommodating attitude towards the problem on the part of the administration of education.

It seems unrealistic, though, to think that the high school entrance examination would ever be abolished. Whereas differentiation of individual high schools was certainly on the agenda of the Ministry of Education, entrance examination reforms were a tricky area. The Ministry had for years proclaimed that entrance examinations were in need of drastic reform, though not being specific as to what the character of the reforms should be. The need for reform as seen by the Ministry, concerned university entrance examinations in particular, for, as WDCER rightly pointed out, the NCER (and the Ministry of Education too) did not concern itself with the high school entrance examination. WDCER agreed, however, on the importance of reforming university entrance examinations, because they feared if this was not done, the harmful effects — excessive competition — would still seep downwards in the educational system even with an abolition of the high school entrance examination (WDCER, 1987, 139).

The only result of years of discussion about university entrance examinations, crowned by NCER deliberations, had been the proposal of a new common test to replace the old one(s). Can this be considered progress? Judging from WDCER's opinions about entrance examinations at a lower level, and the effects that the university entrance exams are accused of having on the educational system as a whole, the WDCER would hardly think so.

With its list of areas in need of urgent reform, WDCER made clear its alternative approach compared to the NCER and it claimed that the most fundamental difference between them and NCER was that whereas NCER contemplated reform for the good of the country, WDCER put the individual at the centre of its deliberations. WDCER thus placed itself within the context of a conflict dating far back in Japanese education, namely the conflict over whether education is a *duty* the people have towards the state, or whether education is an *undisputable right* the people have, and over which they should have *authoritative power*. With the stand WDCER took, it firmly placed itself in opposition to the Ministry of Education, viewing it as a massive bureaucracy whose main interest was to control education for the good of the state.

While it is clear that the WDCER has been quite conscious of the danger that their proposals might be turned down as unrealistic, and thus apparently has tried to propose intermediary remedies until proper reforms could be worked out, it is still unclear what they thought their chances were of getting the attention of the NCER. They did have some attention in the press and in academic circles as well, but there was no tradition for taking much heed of opposition interest groups. Hence the most probable road to influence would be through the socialist bloc in the Diet, but it is doubtful whether that would be possible with the very explicit demands of WDCER that teachers' unions should not get involved with political parties. Certainly, the goodwill WDCER could otherwise have had in the socialist bloc and the teacher organisations must have suffered because of this. It may also be that WDCER did not wish to associate itself directly with any political group. At any rate, its attack on the very politicised teacher organisations and their relations to political parties served to diminish any possibility of political influence through the Diet.

Summarising WDCER opinions Higuchi Keiko, a WDCER member, writer, critic and professor of *Tokyo Kasei Daigaku*, stated that the biggest problem of Japanese education today was that the school simply was too strong an influence on children's lives. Its interests directed their activities and set standards for their behaviour to an extent where it was almost ridiculous. She quoted a recent example of a girl who sued her high school. She had been expelled because she'd had her hair permanently waved, which was prohibited by school regulations. Though she had only a few months left of her schooling, she lost the case and could not graduate. In Professor Higuchi's eyes, this was a clear indication that school matters more than individuals. She did not want schools to have no regulations but she criticised the way the rights and needs of the school seemed to have gained precedence over the rights of parents and students.

Though WDCER was in opposition to the Ministry of Education, this clearly did not mean that it allied itself with the unions. As was evident from WDCER's worries concerning teacher unionisation, there was a somewhat ambiguous feeling about unions.

Professor Higuchi (interviewed on June 27, 1991) clearly defined her point of departure as that of a *parent*, not to be confused with the unions *or* the Ministry's point of view: 'I speak from the point of view of a parent, and from this viewpoint, the JTU, the Ministry of Education, principals and school boards amount to much the same.'

This has been a line up of the most important reform areas proposed by WDCER. The more detailed reaction to NCER reports will be discussed in Chapter 4.

3.3.2 The Study Group on Japanese Education

The Study Group on Japanese Education — *Nihon Kyooiku Gakkai* — (NKG hereafter) is a group of Japanese academics conducting research in the field of education. At their 42nd annual conference held at Hoosei University in Tokyo in 1983, they decided to initiate preparations for an educational-system research council (*Kyooiku Seido Kenkyuu Iinkai*) within the organisation, in order to be able to deal more actively with the anticipated government moves towards reform of education. This research council started its deliberations in 1984, shortly before the NCER, and in the following years closely followed the proceedings of the NCER. NKG issued a number of reports on various topics in the NCER reform proposals, and was in general highly critical of the proposals and of the intentions of the government (Oota, 1988b, 1).

The NKG was not a group striving to express one united opinion on everything, rather it was a discussion forum trying to relate and react on an informed basis to the work done by NCER. It represented the different views of the participating scholars rather than a unified ideology, the common denominator being criticism of the government and its educational policy. This is clear in many places in the writings of NKG, which are mainly essays contributed by the participating scholars and summaries of discussions. An example of the pervading critical attitude is a remark by Professor Hirabara of Kobe University:

It is hard not to deem [the NCER proposals] inadequate in all aspects. Though there is a great variety of opinions, even within NCER, reforms are hurried on as if there was a consensus, and further, the debate is totally estranged from the schools and the people, so it can properly be termed a 'battle in thin air'. When the heart is not in the work, ensuing reforms are bound to be hasty, so in effect, the provision that the Prime Minister must 'duly respect the reports of the NCER' has become a liability. (Hirabara, 1985, 33)

She further argued, by extensively quoting a survey on educational reform aspirations in the population which was conducted by the Yomiuri Shimbun, and which clearly proved her point, that the topics most emphasised by NCER were in fact not in accord with the wishes of the people. Speaking at a very early stage of the NCER deliberations, Hirabara based her analysis on the Second Summary of NCER activities, which was issued in April 1985. The Yomiuri survey was published in February 1985 and asked people which areas they felt were most in need of reform. The answers converged around concerns about violence and misbehaviour in the schools as follows:

School violence and misdemeanour	47.6%
Teacher quality	39.7%
Cramming in education	37.3%
Moral education	30.5%
Streaming	29.8%
(Hirabara, 1985, 34)	

Asked which of the areas emphasised by the NCER deliberations were of most concern the answers showed the same areas of prime concern, namely

teacher quality, streaming and moral education, but as NCER did not deal
with violence in school, the top priority for the common man was of course
absent from this next list:

Teacher quality	49.3%
Streaming and ability-oriented education	49.2%
Strengthened educational role of the home	40.8%
De-emphasis of school certificates	35.5%
Entrance examinations	24.9%

(Hirabara, 1985, 34)

Especially the complete lack of concern for violence and bullying (*koonai
booryoku, ijime*) in the NCER summary, prompted the above remark from
Hirabara about the inadequateness of the NCER work. The effect of NCER's
agenda-setting is clear here. The topic that seemed to worry the population
most at the time was simply not on the agenda at this stage.

More generally, NKG was critical of government attempts to revise or
reinterpret the Fundamental Law of Education (FLE). They shared this fear
with the teacher organisations. NKG's reasoning was that because NCER in
the second summary called the FLE 'a breach with tradition' there was reason
to fear for its fate, particularly if the initial NCER statement that the FLE was
created in a united effort by the Japanese and the Americans was to be substituted
with the quite popular conservative attitude that the FLE — like the
Constitution — was actually *forced* on the Japanese.

NKG called for a realisation of the 'spirit of FLE' — the very same
wording as employed by ATU. They argued that because this spirit had not
yet been invoked, Japanese education floated around without a well-defined
goal, with no common ideology for teachers to base their efforts on. This, in
NKG's opinion, was one of the main causes of the much discussed
'devastation of education' (*kyooiku no koohai*), (Hirabara, 1985, 37-8).

A year later, in a comment to the second NCER report, an NKG member
pointed out that NCER was dealing only with fragments of the FLE, in fact
only with the first paragraph, concentrated as it was on developing the
individual and creating a peace-loving, cultured nation and society. The rest
of the FLE which was about democracy in education, was conveniently
ignored by NCER.

So, whilst that part which NCER did deal with was indeed within the
scope of the FLE spirit — as was stipulated in NCER's references — the
NCER apparently chose to ignore a substantial part of this basic law (Ootsuki,
1986, 80).

NKG agreed with the NCER that post-war Japanese educational ideology had been in confusion but whereas NCER blamed it on the 'breach of tradition' that the FLE constituted, NKG felt it was caused by the non-implementation of the FLE spirit.

On receipt of the second NCER report NKG member Ootsuki, a professor at Waseda University, further elaborated on NCER's reaction to the so-called 'devastation of education'. He summarised NCER's countermove to this devastation as founded on the assumption that economic affluence had weakened traditional values and morals and that the solution would be to revitalise the 'centripetal forces' of society (Ootsuki, 1986, 79). NCER was ascribed an altogether very emotional approach to the problem, a traditionalistic approach which sought to solve problems by reverting to former practices.

NKG also attacked the nationalistic mood of the reports referring to such expressions as the 'awareness of oneself as a Japanese' as well as the call for strengthened moral education and the moral and emotional interpretation of issues in the FLE. All these things combined equalled the contents and aims of the Imperial Rescript on Education, it was claimed (Ootsuki, 1986, 80).

The recurrent references to the 'end of the catch-up phase' in the NCER reports signalled change, but NKG feared that the nature of this change would turn out to be nationalist and militarist, just like the slogan of 'freeing education' in 1927 had paved the way for nationalism and militarism in education. In more specific terms the NKG line went against streaming in middle school, against the calls for heightened 'awareness as a Japanese' and 'respect for things beyond our comprehension', both of which were seen as an attempt to foster nationalism, against extended cooperation with private educational enterprises and finally, NKG criticised the almost mantra-like invocation of 'sports' in NCER's reports and summaries. It was included repeatedly but its role was never clarified (Kawai, 1986, 81-82).

As a scholarly group NKG did not have a specific programme for reform like WDCER but concentrated on discussing and analyzing the reports and summaries NCER issued. The members had different ideas concerning education when it came down to details, but overall agreed that the NCER was undemocratic, seeking centralism and nationalistic reforms, and that it was aiming at a revision of the FLE to use it as a substitute for the Imperial Rescript, thereby installing an official state ideology in education.

In 1987, six weeks before the third NCER report was due, NKG Chairman Oota Takashi, sent an address to the NCER chairman Okamoto Michio. NKG had had contacts with NCER, its members had been called upon to give lectures on reform issues to NCER, and Oota had made two previous addresses as NKG chairman. NKG was thus by no means ignored by the NCER, nor was its opinions unknown to NCER. In this respect the status of

NKG was very different from that of WDCER which did not have official contacts with NCER.

The access to the NCER forum, however, did not help NKG much in the struggle for getting influence on the reform discussions. The address sent by Oota in 1987 recapitulated NKG's ideas in a list of issues. It recommended the clearance of the legal status of the curriculum guidelines, preferably making it explicit that they were to be seen only as *recommendations*. It called for *approval* of text books rather than authorization and for the abolition of the practice of censoring drafts of textbooks. Approval should be made by an independent scholarly organ and new text books should concentrate on making children think rather than cramming facts, Oota and NKG recommended.

Additionally, a thorough revision of the entrance examination system would be necessary to remove the impetus for cramming and teachers should be trained to match children and teaching material optimally. Oota, on behalf of the NKG, condemned the 'new teacher' envisaged by NCER in its third report as only being able to 'kill individuality in education'. No matter how good the text books, Oota continued, all effort at individualisation and democratisation of education by teachers whose training was based on the NCER model would be to no avail (Oota, 1987, 35-36).

When the third report came it was clear that these recommendations had made no difference. NCER did not deal with the problem of the entrance examinations in other ways than by proposing a new common test and there were no ideas for reform of the basic philosophy of the educational system or any thoughts about the nature of education. To NKG this was unsatisfactory and demonstrated that NCER was not ready to deal with the problems which NKG and that segment of the population which was articulate about these matters considered most pressing. The official agenda of educational reform had been set and fixed long before NCER ever started its deliberations.

Another area in which NKG became deeply involved was secondary education. As partakers of the activities of a Ministry-sponsored research group on secondary education, NKG in 1988 produced a summary of the work done by the NKG members of this group. NKG described the importance of adolescence as lying in the fact that it was the time when a person was to become independent and choose his occupation. The schools, in NKG's opinion, did not teach the children how to make such choices, nor were they able to support children who tried to make choices on their own.

For secondary education in particular, NKG listed the following four points of special concern:

1) Entrance examinations. They owe their existence to the importance allotted 'manpower needs' in the Japanese educational system. Rather than diversifying the curriculum because of manpower considerations one should diversify it, keeping in mind the opportunity for children to be able to make their own choice. If children were allowed individual choices and in addition were allowed to change their minds, as NKG wanted, it naturally followed that the entrance examinations in their present form would be obsolete.

2) In principle NKG supported the idea of a unified six-year secondary school. This idea was also aired by the WDCER. But NKG had some reservations. Secondary school should be flexible to the extent that one could attend for the time needed for acquiring the required amount of credits, regardless of whether that be four or eight years.

3) As it would be difficult for one single school to satisfy to all the individual wishes of the students, NKG proposed that all the schools within a particular area cooperated on providing as many different choices as possible, allowing the students on a flexible basis to choose any subject from any school.

4) Finally, to assist the students in their choices of subjects and guide their choice of further education, an elaborate guidance system supported by the educational administration would be necessary. (Oota, 1988a, 155-56)

These four points of particular concern as listed by Oota were not among the items high on NCER's priority list. Entrance examinations were difficult to deal with. It was anticipated that students and parents engaged in the examination competition would object to the prospect of being the last to have to deal with the examination hell and with the added pressure of having no insurance that this would not deteriorate their chances of landing the desired job, it could create an uproar. The topic was politically unattractive.

The six-year secondary school was a detail for NCER but certainly not one without appeal. It seems clear though, that the flexible structure and the emphasis placed by NKG on the free choice of the individual was not the major aim of such a structure for NCER. Rather, it would for NCER mean earlier selection and streaming. The main problem with this six-year structure for the education administration, however, was probably the cost of prolonging compulsory education with three years, which would be the natural consequence of such a change.

The NKG disregarded the limitations of the official agenda and primarily treated problems that had been listed by the public in major surveys. In this respect they were similar to WDCER. But it is also significant that despite explicit public concern, the NKG did not take the problems of violence and bullying up as separate issues the way WDCER did. The idea was that with more flexible schools occupied with assisting children in building character and adapting education to their individual needs, rather than trying to fit them into a particular mould, children would generally experience greater satisfaction and have less reason to resort to violence.

NKG's critical attitude towards government policy placed it in the opposition camp but, due to its membership perhaps, it was not a grass-roots organisation like WDCER, a fact made further clear by the lack of direct dealings with bullying, violence in schools and the preservation of the family. NKG took up most of the popularly experienced problems, but it was more involved with ideology and politics than WDCER, hence the very different manner of dealing with the problems. WDCER can be seen as representatives of the popular level of opposition and NKG as the supplier of the ideological background for the opposition demands and proposals.

3.4 Industry

Over the years, various business groupings have commented on the educational system. In light of the often voiced accusations against NCER, and the Nakasone cabinet, of being concerned first and foremost with the needs of industry and the national economy, it is all the more interesting to see what the business world had to say about education around the time of the establishment of NCER. The fact that the following two groups issued reports just before the NCER started its work has greatly influenced the nature of the task given to NCER. Also, influential businessmen were members of the NCER and thus in a position to have business priorities written into the NCER reports.

That groups other than those directly concerned with education were interested in educational reform had been evident for long. An omen of things to come was a report issued by an Industrial Structure Council under the Ministry of International Trade and Industry in 1980. This report charged that the established uniform and exam-oriented educational system had failed to produce the *creative, diversely talented* and *internationalist* workers required to meet the nation's economic needs. It argued for greater flexibility and speci-fically for the abolition of high school entrance examinations and for the creation of a six-year unified secondary school. Those ideas were echoed in reports produced by business groups later in the 1980's. (Schoppa, 1991, 214)

Clearly, already in 1980 some of the later NCER key phrases were used by a group with industrial interests at its base, namely internationalisation and diversity. The Kyoto Group for Study of Global Issues (*Sekai o Kangaeru Kyoto Zakai*), headed by industrialist Matsushita Koonosuke, and the Education Council under the Japan Committee for Economic Development (*Keizai Dooyuukai*) both publicised their views on educational reform in 1984. The Government sponsored Foreign Press Centre collected excerpts from these as well as other material on education and the need for educational reform, in a booklet entitled 'Discussions on Educational Reform in Japan' in 1985.

The Kyoto Group as well as the Education Committee both offered reform proposals which called for more diversity, less public involvement and the application of free market forces to education.

3.4.1 The Kyoto Group

The Kyoto Group, as mentioned above, was headed by the successful industrialist Matsushita Koonosuke, and among its members were such well-known names as Kumon Shumpei, a leading force behind Nakasone's *Rinchoo* ideology who was known for having the opinion that a wealthy Japan did not need any longer to depend on public education, but should allow the expansion of private education, even at compulsory level (Schoppa, 1991, 68-9). Other members included businessmen like Ushio Jiroo (vice-chairman of Japan Committee for Economic Development, *Keizai Dooyuukai*) as well as leading academic and government figures who later served as members of NCER: Amaya Naohiro (chairman of the first NCER subcommittee), Ishii Takemochi (chairman of the second NCER subcommittee) and two specialist members (Schoppa, 1991, 132-33).

In practice the Kyoto Group was set up and managed by the Matsushita controlled publishing house, Peace, Harmony and Prosperity Research Centre (*PHP Kenkyuujo*), which was responsible for the publication of the journal 'Voice' and numerous books presenting the views of the reform-oriented wing of the business community calling for deregulation, privatisation and reduced government spending (Schoppa, 1991, 282).

The Kyoto Group issued its 'Seven Recommendations to Revitalize School Education' in March 1984. It concerned itself with elementary and secondary education only. The recommendations were clearly made from a business standpoint, as was evident from the opening section on the principle of fair competition. This was applied to education as a means of motivating students to learn, to compete with each other and to encourage teachers to compete among themselves to become better educators. As in liberalist business philosophy fair competition was seen as the prerequisite of progress, and in connection with education fair competition meant that education ideally 'should be free and independent of constraints and interference from public authorities as much as possible' (Kyoto Group, 1985, 31). In other words a fiercely liberalistic version of education, and if this had succeeded it would probably have become even more liberal and free of central influence than Japanese industry and business itself!

The key element in securing fair competition was 'decontrol'. Through decontrol the evils caused by standardisation would be remedied. Among the evils engendered by the standardised school system and the standardised teaching materials were, in the group's view, a 'monolithic value system' and the creation of an 'environment in which children's aspirations and motivations were easily stymied'. The group felt that there was a risk that children would become disillusioned with school and perhaps drop out if a new flexible and free system was not created, and this was not necessarily to be along the lines of a 6-3-3 system.

To the Kyoto Group a more flexible system was one that provided the children with more freedom to choose what they wanted to study once having mastered the basics of learning. They ought to be able to 'seek new areas where they will be more comfortable', the group requested, while also suggesting that there should be made provisions for the child to choose either further study or job experiences before a return to schooling. The institutions of education on their side were requested to practise greater flexibility in their selection of students, thus avoiding a standardised section of students at a given institution. Students should be valued for their distinct personalities, it was emphasised, for only such people could 'truly adjust to the anticipated social changes of the next century' (Kyoto Group, 1985, 32). These proposals were remarkably like those aired by the WDCER especially and by the NKG to some extent.

But the agreement lasted only as long as the issue lay in the category of *aims*. When it came to *means* disagreement was prevalent. In order to make school more flexible and diverse on an overall scale, the Kyoto Group proposed a gradual shift from the present reliance on public schools to private schools. Free competition should be encouraged to enhance the quality of education. The group envisaged private schools established on the basis of philosophies and ideas held by individuals. A comparison was made between the Meiji Restoration when a lot of new private schools were created to 'generate a new wave of education', and the contemporary situation when the creation of private schools on elementary as well as secondary level should be welcomed as providing a wider range of choices for the children (Kyoto Group, 1985, 32). Such ideas of privatisation of the compulsory school system were not acceptable to any of the opposition groups.

Emphasis on moral education was another key issue for the Kyoto Group. This was moral education in the sense of teaching social norms, the 'certain rules vital to society's sound functioning and progress'. In this connection the educational role of the home was highlighted and it was made clear that instruction in morals was not really the responsibility of the school, but in essence the responsibility of the home.

The group proceeded with listing their seven recommendations which were as follows:

1) *Diversification of school education through the relaxation of rules on the establishment of new schools*
   The group was of the persuasion that anyone who was truly interested in education should be permitted to open a school, thus creating a variety of schools with distinctive characteristics run by dedicated educators.

2) *Relaxation of the school zone system*
   Children should be able to attend the school of their choice, not necessarily the one in their zone. The group recognised the effect school zones had had as a means of creating equal educational opportunities, but stated that 'now that equal educational opportunities exist virtually for all, we think it is high time that a new system which gives students greater freedom of choice be considered'.

3) *Employment of dedicated teachers*
   This entailed a revision of the current licensing system which would allow unlicensed people to teach, provided they had the ability, the aptitude and the interest. Also, there should be a system of limited periods of service and reappointment of teachers according to circumstances.

4) *Greater flexibility in the years, content and methods of education*
   The core of this suggestion was to make it possible to jump classes, repeat classes, or attend advanced classes in particular subjects. School operators should be able to freely decide upon contents and methods of education, provided they lived up to a national minimum standard in the basics.

5) *Review of the present school system*
   The decision whether to adhere to the 6-3-3 system or to employ another system should be left to the individual schools and further, any person who lived up to the national minimum standard in the basics of education should have the freedom not to attend school.

6) *Abolition of the 'deviation value' (hensachi)[19] system*
    Students should no longer be instructed to choose schools based on
    their examination marks, and school guidance should be based on
    what is suitable for the student. Also, each school should have its
    own entrance examination system.

7) *Enforcement of moral education*
    The group listed the social norms to which all human beings were
    expected to conform as:

    a) Taking responsibility for one's words and actions,
    b) kindness and consideration for others,
    c) respect for law, social rules and justice.

The group felt that home and society carried principal responsibility for
helping children to understand those norms through real-life experiences.
(Kyoto Group, 1985, 33-4)

The group's influence was not so much in the impact of this report, but rather
in the fact that it managed to establish itself as an actor and participant in the
actual formulation of reform policies through supplying members for the
NCER. Thus the issues discussed in the Kyoto Group were bound to be dealt
with in the NCER.

The Kyoto Group was apparently fiercely liberalistic wishing the schools
to be governed individually and for everyone with an interest in education
to be allowed to participate as educators.

The report, however, presupposed a lot of things lying at the basis of this
liberal educational system. It was, rather than a new liberalistic system, a
liberalisation of the old one. The Kyoto Group stated that 'equal educational
opportunities exist virtually for all', an equality — if it was truly there —
established by the old centralistic system. Further, the Kyoto Group recommended that school guidance 'should be based on what is *suitable* for the
child' (*kodomo no tekisei o kangaeta shinro shidoo*). This is a very vague formulation. Who is to decide and how?

As mentioned, the significance of this group lies not so much in its

19. The *hensachi* system is based on students' grades. According to examination marks,
    students are ranked in a hierarchy which, in principle, is national. If a student wants
    to apply to a certain high school his marks will be compared to those of the other
    applicants and he will be ranked accordingly. Thus, from previous experience,
    everybody knows that certain marks are necessary for getting into a certain high
    school and thus the *hensachi* value determines how high a student's aspirations will
    be.

concrete ideas but in the influence it had at government level. It had direct relations to the government and even managed to be represented in the NCER. What the Kyoto Group contributed to NCER was the liberalistic view of education, consideration for manpower needs and high priority of moral values supporting the status quo.

3.4.2 The Education Council

The Education Council was a body under the Japan Committee for Economic Development (*Keizai Dooyuukai*) which issued its report on educational reform in July 1984. From the viewpoint that 'acquisition and fostering of human resources' was of prime importance if one was to entertain any hope of expanding corporate activities, this council listed the qualifications to be expected of young people in the future as *creativity*, *diversity* and *internationalisation*. The same themes that the Kyoto Group emphasised.

Of these, *creativity* was in the Education Council's opinion the most desirable and it was linked closely with diversity, which was defined as the antonym of uniformity. The two features combined would be a source of strength for an enterprise dealing with an uncertain future.

Internationalisation was called for because the council felt that other than exporting Japanese products, Japan had failed to open itself up to the world and play its part in the international community. Education was seen as a particularly closed area in this respect (Education Council, 1985, 35).

Higher education and its content was the immediate target, and realising that the institutions of higher education were tied hand and foot by the recruitment procedures, the Education Council initially proposed a revision of evaluation standards in business enterprises and government agencies, in effect a change in recruitment procedures. It stated that enterprises should realise 'that their philosophy and methods in employee relations policy (especially in recruiting) have great impact on the educational field', and that qualifying examinations (for government employees, diplomats etc.) had to be reviewed in the same light.

The subsequent ten point list of areas in need of changes is summarised here: individuality in employees should be valued and specialists respected and utilised. Also, female employees should be encouraged more and overseas activities should under no circumstances be a liability. As for recruitment, conscious efforts to recruit from as many different schools as possible should be made, and personal traits and life style should also be considered during the recruitment procedures (Education Council, 1985, 36). A list of proposals with which few people would disagree.

As for higher education the Education Council continued in the same line and stated that higher education in general and the universities in particular, should concentrate on reforms to alleviate the effect of the 'national character of the Japanese, who tended to lean towards uniformity'. This has led to a uniform evaluation of the universities and hence the well-established hierarchy among them. In order to meet the future needs of the 'Japanese people' the council recommended that among other things each university should develop its own characteristics with unique curriculums, new teaching methods and individualised screening methods for admission (Education Council, 1985, 37).

The Joint First Stage Achievement Test came under heavy fire as having been instrumental in the excessive standardisation the educational system had witnessed. While wishing to maintain Japanese language and mathematics as subjects to be tested, the council otherwise suggested that the universities should devise their own unique testing methods for the remainder of the subjects of the Joint First Stage Achievement Test, in view of the undesirable effects the university entrance examination was having on the rest of the educational system.

Concretely the proposal operated with a first stage test in only Japanese language and mathematics, which should be carried out 3 to 4 times per year, and this system should also be employed by the private universities. As for other testing, for which each university should create its own methods, foreign languages, in the Council's opinion, should be tested in such a way as to consider auditory comprehension and speaking, as well as reading and writing. The ordinary test only concerned itself with the two latter and thus had a bad effect on English education in middle and high school. As social science had the tendency of becoming a mere memorisation of facts it was to be eliminated from the test along with natural sciences, instead using report cards from earlier schooling and special tests to assess the efforts a student had put into these subjects.

To diversify the system of education further, a relaxation of the 6-3-3 system was proposed. The idea was for schools to be free to use other demarkation systems than 6-3-3, and the council wanted to establish it as a rule that 20% of the schools should shift to a 6-6 year system (a unified secondary school). Also, general qualifying examinations should be abolished and the acceptance or refusal of entry into schools of higher education should be left to the schools' own discretion. This was expected to vitalise the system and increase social mobility (Education Council, 1985, 38-39).

With regard to internationalisation the council took the stand that tolerance towards other people should be fostered by education, but that education also had to teach affection and mastery of the students' own culture in order to establish true understanding of other cultures.

The mastery of spoken foreign language naturally took high priority and also changing the beginning of the academic year from April to September was recommended as a means to facilitate exchange of teachers and students with foreign countries, thereby promoting internationalisation. Lastly, the council recommended that it should be made easier to employ foreign teachers in schools and companies and that more foreign students be accepted in schools and that added curricula in English should be offered to them (Education Council, 1985, 40).

Advancing to a more general level the lack of basic research in Japan was lamented and the need for creativity in this field was emphasised. Increased budget, and company involvement in basic research and cooperation between universities and industry, were among the suggested remedies.

Another area where Japan was seen as lagging behind, was in the utilisation of computers in education. As one anticipated a growing need for manpower in software as well as in hardware this was problematic. To prevent regression in the mastery of the basics, the area was to be studied closely and all involved parties should be sought out for advice. The United States was mentioned as an example of how attractive computer educational programmes could be developed (Education Council, 1985, 41-42).

The echoes of the earlier Ministry of International Trade and Industry (MITI) report are clear. Creativity, diversity and internationalisation were concepts used in the MITI report as well. This is probably not so much a sign that business was being lead on by the MITI but rather the reverse, that the MITI was actually voicing the wishes of the business world quite well in its criticism of education.

The Education Council was not as loudly liberalistic as the Kyoto Group. It concentrated on higher education and was of the opinion that the key to reform of the educational system lay in reformed recruitment procedures. In this Education Council report we also find the idea that one can only be a good internationalist if one's international orientation is based on a firm Japanese identity, a concept which was elaborated by the NCER.

3.5 Conclusions

These early business reports on education were in content similar to what LDP was discussing at the time. The Nishioka-memo of 1983 was the basis for Nakasone's campaign for educational reform and his 'seven issues of educational reform' were a popularised edition of this memo. Nakasone's seven issues were:

1) Revision of the 6-3-3-4 system.
2) Revision of the entrance examination for high school and career guidance based on streaming.

3) Revision of higher education and a common first test in the university entrance examination.
4) Training at school in service and group life.
5) Moral education and rectification of sentiments.
6) Internationalisation.
7) Improvement of teacher quality.
   (Mikami, 1984, 17)

The only apparent conflict with the business groups was over the question of entrance examinations. The Kyoto Group wanted no common tests, while the Education Council wanted only a very limited number of subjects to be tested in this way. But all in all the agreement in the conservative camp — the LDP, the government, NCER and the business world — on what is important in educational reform, was admirable.

In the progressive camp things were more polarised. While all the agents described here agreed on rejecting NCER's proposals — or most of the proposals — their internal relationships were of a nature to prohibit them from forming a united front against official reform efforts. The two teachers' organisations had ideological grievances against each other, the WDCER suspected the official side as well as the teacher organisations of being equally obsessed with politics at the expense of the individual's interests, and the NKG as a scholarly discussion forum did not have the texture to enable it to play the role of an activist, though perhaps this group alone could have commanded the respect of all the others and united their efforts. The result was a polarised and weak opposition trying to stand up to a comparatively unified conservative group. The best hopes left for the opposition for influencing the reforms were left-wing opposition to legal measures in the Diet and non-implementation tactics at local level.

The educational debate at this level, that is the official-organisational level, tended to (and still does) concentrate on political issues rather than pedagogical issues.

CHAPTER 4

ATTITUDES TO NCER'S PROPOSALS

NCER's proposals clustered around four main issues which will be discussed in detail in this chapter. The four issues were individuality (*kosei*), life-long learning (*shoogaigakushuu*), internationalisation (*kokusaika*) and the adaptation to the information society (*joohooka*). These were the issues NCER considered central in the reform efforts, which were, as we recall, intended to prepare Japan and its people for the challenges of the 21st century.

But before discussing the four issues and what they mean, it is important to take a closer look at the new curriculum guidelines issued by the Ministry of Education in 1989. They were the first major tangible changes the Ministry carried out after the NCER reports had been issued and as such make a powerful policy statement.

4.1 The New Curriculum Guidelines

In March 1989 the Ministry of Education issued revised curriculum guidelines. The old guidelines were from 1977, and it was felt that in order to adapt the educational system to the information society and to internationalisation it was necessary to revise the curriculum. Ostensibly the revisions were based on a report from the 'Council on Course of Study' (*Kyooiku Katei Shingikai*) issued in December 1987, but the concerns listed as reasons for the revisions were similar to those raised in the NCER reports. New curriculum guidelines had not been an explicit concern of the NCER but for their proposals to have any effect and for the proposals to materialise at all, a new revised curriculum was definitely necessary.

The revisions fitted the recommendations made by NCER very well and the guidelines were, as usual, made by the Ministry of Education singlehandedly. There was, and is, no precedent for inviting, for example, teachers to participate in the formulation process.

In Government White Papers on education from 1989 and 1990, the purposes of the new curriculum guidelines were stated as follows:

Therefore [in order to adapt to changes in society] we must make plans for educating people who can live vigorously and with rich hearts and who have the strength to learn by themselves. Also, we must emphasise basics and foster individuality in our education while respecting culture and tradition. (Monbushoo, 1990, 295)

The new guidelines were to be enforced on a gradual scale, starting with kindergarten in 1990, elementary school in 1992, middle school in 1993 and high school in 1994.

The basic policy behind the revisions was explained in terms of the need for life-long learning, and the need to foster a person who was able to adjust harmoniously to the changes bound to come with the 21st century. Creativity, desire to learn, individuality, a rich heart (*yutaka na kokoro*) and the ability to live vigorously and powerfully (*takumashiku ikiru ningen*) were key words in the efforts to revise the curriculum. Also, an important consideration was that education should respect Japan's culture and traditions, while also deepening the knowledge of other cultures and traditions in the world, and in this way foster a Japanese individual who is able to live in the international world (Monbushoo, 1989d, 68-70; Monbushoo, 1990, 295).

Again we see the plus-word *takumashii* in use, as well as the equally positively loaded *yutaka* (rich, abundant), a word often used to describe not only the desirable state of a country or society, but also a desirable state of mind. As is the case with *takumashii*, there is guaranteed positive reactions to stating that *yutaka na kokoro* is the aim of reform.

Despite the humane touch in the wording, the 'heart' and 'human beings', the net result of the curriculum revisions as they have been implemented so far, has been that the workload has increased in the younger classes and elective subjects have increased at middle school level.

Mark Lincicome's comment on the way the text of 'General Policy for the Organisation of the Curriculum' opened, analysed the seeming conflict between words and actions in the following manner:

The opening section of this text (...) is a model of ideological compromise that reads as though it were deliberately crafted to silence the charges of conservatism and nationalism that critics (...) had levelled against the NCER's proposals for reform. (Lincicome, 1993, 146)

Indeed, both during and after NCER's deliberations the use of certain terms which were used in popular discussions and in criticisms of Japan were employed as a rhetorical means of refuting criticism.

4.1.1 The new kindergarten curriculum

Continuity in guidance and curriculum was a main concern for the Ministry of Education and the subjects in the kindergarten curriculum were divided into five categories: health (*kenkoo*), human relationship (*ningen kankei*), environment (*kankyoo*), language (*kotoba*) and expression (*hyoogen*). As described earlier in the section on pre-school, the minimum number of school weeks was set at 39 with 4 classroom hours per day. In the earlier curriculum the required time in kindergarten was set in terms of days (220 days), but this division would be troublesome if the five-day week was later to be introduced so it was given up (Monbushoo, 1989a, 59).

In the kindergarten curriculum continuity to elementary school curriculum was emphasised strongly.

4.1.2 The new elementary school curriculum

In elementary school the emphasis of the activities was directed towards learning, particularly towards learning the Japanese language. The new curriculum allocated 34 more school hours to the subject in first grade, and 35 more in second grade. Also, the two first grades were to have the subject 'Life Environment Studies' (*Seikatsuka*) in place of Science and Social Studies (Monbushoo, 1989a, 61).

The contents of the new subject of Life Environment Studies were not necessarily the combined contents of the old subjects. ATU quoted from the new guidelines for Life Environment Studies for the first grade:

By letting the children raise animals and cultivate plants, they are to understand that animals and plants have life (*seimei*) just like they themselves, and thus they will learn to feel close to all things living and treasure life. (Zenkyoo, 1990, 11)

In the old guidelines for Science in the first grade, the subject of plants was treated as follows:

By letting the children sow seeds and regulate the conditions for the plants, as the plants grow, they will learn that water is necessary and they will learn about the remarkable changes plants undergo as they grow. (Zenkyoo, 1990, 11)

There are other examples of a similar tendency to play down the scientific approach to nature in Life Environment Studies, and critics such as ATU fear that the introduction of this new subject with its emotional approach will, as a consequence, damage the budding scientific consciousness of children.

Even though it is a more emotional approach, ATU's rock hard opposition is perhaps a little too automatised here, making it look like opposition just for the sake of opposition. This approach of teaching young children that plants and animals are living things rather than just teaching about scientific facts, could also be interpreted as an ecological approach, and ATU has in plenty of other places made its concern with ecology quite clear. As the 'emotional' or 'ecological' approach does not necessarily rule out the later introduction of a more scientific approach, ATU's harsh denouncement leaves them open to attacks for being automatically in opposition. However, the opposition here is probably guided by the 'to-know-is-to-govern' idea, meaning that it is dangerous for a democracy if knowledge is kept from the general public and it is instead fed with emotionally based conceptions. Such a situation would lead to a more susceptible population and this is most probably why ATU is so critical.

Apart from this perhaps slightly overdone opposition, to ATU the most significant change in the elementary school curriculum has been the move of items of learning, particularly in mathematics, to lower grades, and the step-up in the pace of learning Chinese characters — in short, the increase in workload.

4.1.3 The new middle school curriculum

The most significant change here is the breach with the long established principle of non-stratification. Hitherto, middle school has been exactly the same for everyone, but with the new curriculum the Ministry has wished to offer instruction in accordance with individual character and ability from this level on, and therefore different levels were introduced in the new middle school curriculum. In the first and second middle school grades one can now choose between different levels of Foreign Language, Music, Art, Home Making, Health and Physical and Industrial Arts. In third grade streaming was also introduced in Japanese Language, Social Sciences, Mathematics and Natural Sciences (Monbushoo, 1989a, 61).

Supposedly, different levels would be better at accommodating individual abilities, but it was criticised by ATU, among others, for only benefitting the bright students and neglecting the not-so-bright ones. It was attacked as gross stratification, as un-egalitarian and as only fit to make children feel like failures at an early stage (Zenkyoo, 1990, 14).

The number of elective subjects was increased and in all, the changes actually made possible the emergence of both an elite course and an ordinary course, in so far as weak students might feel encouraged to select lower level courses and leisure oriented electives.

4.1.4 The new high school curriculum

In the new high school curriculum the overall tendency was to increase the number of required lessons, only Foreign Language decreased, but here more conversation practice was introduced. Particularly in Mathematics, Social Sciences, Japanese, and Natural Sciences the number of required lessons was raised and streaming was introduced in those subjects. The total number of credits required for graduation was raised from 32 credits in seven subjects to 38 in 11 to 12 subjects (Monbushoo, 1989a, 63).

New subjects were Modern (Japanese) Language, Reading and Reciting Classical Japanese, Oral Communication, Reading, Writing (the preceding three all in English), German, French and 'Life Techniques' (*seikatsu gijutsu*) (Monbushoo, 1989d, 75-6).[1]

This increase in demand for high school graduation of course makes it all the more necessary that those not fit for high school realise this before entering, that is, upon graduation from middle school. Some kind of sorting mechanism would be necessary, in this case an entrance examination. This is the selection process that ATU was so worried about when it talked about inequality at middle school level. It is debatable, however, how much effect middle school streaming is going to have on the proportion of students advancing to high school. One should not forget that the Ministry of Education is actually proud of the high proportion of the age-cohorts entering high school (over 95%) and it seems unreasonable to believe that the Ministry would deliberately want to lower this rate.

What stratification in both middle school and high school will probably do is to ensure 'suitable' education for each individual, not over-educating anyone not fit for it, and securing optimal conditions for the brightest. This will not necessarily mean that fewer students receive higher secondary education, but it will mean that more students will be directed — more or less willingly — to the vocational courses in higher secondary education rather than the academic courses. What ATU evidently fears, is that if a student is labelled 'not so fit' both the student and the teachers will cease to make an effort, and the student's abilities will not be developed in full. In other words, ATU fears a return to elitist education, in which slow learners are lost because the system provides no real second chances.

4.1.5 Teacher reactions to the new curriculum guidelines

The new curriculum guidelines have been the topic of much debate in the teacher organisations. ATU in 1990 issued a small publication on the issue, which was entitled 'A Child's Smiling Face is My Smiling Face' (*Kodomo no Egao wa Watashi no Egao*). In it the new curriculum guidelines were described and criticised subject by subject.

1. One may ask why English, German and French are the preferred foreign languages. These are the classic European choices. But with a location in Asia, Chinese or Korean would seem a more natural choice for the Japanese. Apparently, the focus here is more on tradition than on logic. See also the section on 'Internationalisation' wherein it is noted that NCER does emphasise Asia and Asian languages more.

The main point of criticism was that the curriculum since the end of the war had become increasingly demanding and that items of learning progressively had been moved from elder classes to younger. An example was in mathematics where first graders according to the new curriculum would learn three digit numbers whereas they only learnt two digit numbers in the former curriculum. Also millenary units would be introduced in second grade according to the new curriculum. Earlier this was taught in the sixth grade (Zenkyoo, 1990, 8).

The subject of Japanese, which is, as ATU rightly points out, basic to most other learning, also has become much more intensive in the years which have passed since the war. The amount of Chinese characters to be learnt in first grade, as stipulated by the new curriculum guidelines grew by four, which may seem quite insignificant but, in ATU's opinion, considering complaints that it was not possible for every child to learn all the *then* prescribed 76 Chinese characters, an increase in this number was going to make matters even worse. The following chart shows how the number of signs to be learnt in first grade has grown since 1971:

Chart 11: Number of signs to be learnt in first grade of elementary school

CHARACTERS	Before 1971	1977	From 1992
Hiragana	71	71	71
Katagana	Only reading	71	71
Numbers (0-9)	10	10	10
Kanji[2]	46	76	80
TOTAL	127	228	232
Weeks/school yr.	34	34	34
Characters/week	3. 7	6. 7	6. 8

(Zenkyoo, 1990, 6)

The most significant changes were introduced by the new curriculum guidelines in 1977. The total number of signs grew from 127 to 228 — a number which grew to 232 with the new guidelines. This meant teaching 6.7 signs per week, or 6.8 with the new guidelines, in practice more than one sign per day, even if the six-day school week is maintained.[3]

2. *Hiragana* and *Katagana* are the syllabic alphabets and *Kanji* are Chinese characters.

ATU members teaching in elementary school complain that they have to pace the children too hard. When they have barely learnt how to use the *kana* (syllabic alphabet, 71 signs) they have to hurry on with the Chinese characters, and since it is generally impossible for the children to learn 76 Chinese characters during school hours, they have to be tutored during breaks and to do characters for homework. In this way, the love of learning that most first graders initially feel is replaced by loss of self-confidence and complexes. This, ATU members predicted, was bound to have an effect on other subjects as well.

Incidentally, ATU warned today's adults against using examples of their childhood workloads and their childhood school successes to inspire their children, because the workload children face today is double that of their parents, and hence any comparison would be highly unjust, particularly as this is often used as a device to daunt a complaining child (Zenkyoo, 1990, 6).

The 1977 curriculum guidelines were accused of causing dislike of school (*gakkoo kirai*), and the increased numbers of children who could not keep up with the rest of the class (*ochikobore*). A new, and even if only slightly more compressed, curriculum would aggravate the situation. The numbers of children who did not understand what was going on in class was already considerable, judging by ATU's figures. Chart twelve shows the self evaluation made in February 1989 by 531 elementary school pupils in a school in Tokyo:

Chart 12: Self-evaluation, elementary school

	Understand well	Under-stand	Average	Not much	Not at all
Grade 1	29%	22%	37%	8%	4%
Grade 2	9%	23%	49%	13%	6%
Grade 3	4%	21%	52%	21%	2%
Grade 4	16%	33%	33%	13%	5%
Grade 5	14%	23%	46%	16%	5%
Grade 6	0%	14%	54%	21%	11%

(Zenkyoo, 1990, 2)

The reason for the small size of the group 'understand well' may of course be modesty, but if so, one would expect the next group 'understand' to be large, but it is not. The largest is, perhaps not surprisingly, the 'average' group. Not surprisingly, because there is a distinct dislike among children in general, and Japanese children in particular, of standing out, being 'weird'. Therefore 'average' or 'normal' is a popular choice. The proportion of pupils feeling at ease with their school work apparently declines as they advance in school. Or, if we are to be a little critical of the survey, it may also be that the pupils become more self conscious as they get older and the desire to belong to the 'normal' group rather than the more 'bright' group increases in relation to this. For whatever reason, the 'understands well' group is absent from sixth grade answers, whereas the average group is by far the largest.

It is difficult to assess with any certainty whether or not the children have been guided by modesty in the manner of evaluating themselves. On the other hand it is rare to willingly admit not understanding at all. So, the figures for those who do not feel that they understand what is going on in school ought to be fairly reliable. In this context those who do not feel at ease with their school work are those who answered 'do not understand much' and 'do not understand at all'. Those two groups progressively grow over the six years in elementary school. In first grade they constitute 12% of the total, in second grade 21%, in third grade 23%, in fourth grade it drops to 18%, in fifth grade it is 21% and finally in sixth grade 32% say that they do not feel they understand much, if anything at all.

Though the figures are not as baffling as those often cited in the anecdotes told by the teacher organisations — that is, that the rate of children not understanding grows proportionately with the years they spend in school, making the rate ten percent in the first grade, twenty in the second, thirty in the third and so on — they are certainly worrying. Doubtlessly, they are tendentious as they were collected by an organisation in serious opposition to the Ministry of Education who of course have responsibility for the curriculum guidelines, but this is not a good reason for total dismissal. The extent of the problem may be exaggerated, but even the ATU is not able to create a problem which is not there. If figures like those were utterly nonsensical, the Ministry of Education should have no difficulty disproving them, but I have not been able to find official surveys on this question.

Why does the Ministry want to make the curriculum even more difficult if students are already having problems with keeping up? The ATU's explanation is the need for earlier selection and stratification for the benefit of industry. An

3. Proposals are being made regularly to introduce the five-day school week in Japanese schools, and as more and more employers convert to five-day work weeks, the schools are bound to follow suit sooner or later.

earlier selection would identify those destined for a life as a common worker to avoid their 'wasting time' on academic tracks at high school or the like.

From the viewpoint of the Ministry, one of the reasons for tightening the curriculum is the obvious low standard of many children in, for example, Chinese characters, and a concern that the Japanese performance standard in mathematics, on a worldwide scale, will drop. Teachers say that declines in performance are brought about by the workload — but it would seem the Ministry is of the opinion that this is simply a question of 'learning more', demanding more, and that children are in fact showing signs of not having a suitably demanding curriculum.

An important issue in the new guidelines, which has been discussed widely and which has created much discomfort even outside Japan, has been the introduction of the national flag (*Hinomaru*) and the Emperor song (*Kimigayo*)[4] in the schools. This was to happen, according to the new curriculum guidelines, all over Japan in the Spring of 1990 at the graduation and entrance ceremonies, but not all schools complied with the guidelines. The following figures were collected by the Ministry of Education:

Chart 13: Schools using flag and Emperor song at ceremonies, 1990

	Elementary school	Middle school	High school
Using flag	95.7% (89.9)*	95.5% (90.2)	90.1% (81.3)
Using song	75.1% (46.4)	76.8% (62.3)	64.8% (49.0)

*The figures in brackets are from the admission ceremonies in 1985. (Monbushoo, 1990, 299)

The figures for schools which flew the flag are hardly worrying, but the figures for schools which sang the Emperor song are probably of more concern to the Ministry. Clearly, many schools distinguish sharply between the flag, which is in reality used as a symbol of Japan internationally, and the song, which in its wording is unquestionably worship of the Emperor. On the other hand, the figures in brackets indicate that the stipulation in the curriculum guidelines has in fact made a difference, increasing the number of schools using the national symbols from the year 1985 to 1990.

The Ministry views the flag and the Emperor song as essential parts of training to become a good citizen and a good worker, and urges the full implementation of the curriculum directives (Monbushoo, 1990, 299). This new

4. *Kimigayo* is termed 'Emperor song' here because of its content and because it does not have legal status as the national anthem of Japan (Mogi, 1989, 6).

feature of the curriculum is not seen as questionable in any way by the Ministry. The argument is that any country has its own flag and song — why shouldn't Japan? In ATU's eyes, as well as in the eyes of many other critics, this is just another attempt by the government to glorify militarism and war in the minds of children, a sign of the basically nationalist orientation of the ruling party (Zenkyoo, 1990, 1; Horio, 1988, 149).

ATU criticised the fact that the flag and the Emperor song were introduced in the new curriculum guidelines despite the lack of legal foundation for such a move, and further criticised the government in this matter for displaying complete disregard for children's right to freedom of thought and religion. ATU made this one of the cornerstones of its opposition to the new guidelines and expressly vowed to fight against their implementation (Zenkyoo, 1990b, 19).

4.1.6 Conclusions

The new curriculum guidelines explicitly stated that one must 'develop the attitude of respecting the culture and tradition of Japan', which was a new thing compared to the old curriculum, and the overall mood of the guidelines was one of strengthening subjects which related to the creation of a good Japanese, but also to the creation of a good Japanese with communicative skills in foreign languages.

There was also an explicit attempt to direct more students away from elite academic tracks by means of earlier selection. 'Ability oriented education' was the means by which this was to be done but the expression is problematic. While on the one hand it can mean adapting the teaching to the student's individual abilities, in order to help him or her reach a common level, it can also, on the other hand, mean streaming students and dividing them so that teaching can be differentiated and students can thereby reach different levels. The latter interpretation tends to focus on the bright students but neglects the weak. The introduction of streaming into middle school, and the nature of the new curriculum guidelines, would suggest that the Ministry of Education was working by the latter interpretation.

There are many references to national identity. The introduction of *Hinomaru* and *Kimigayo* being the most explicit manifestations of the national orientation, but also, for example, the intensifying of *Japanese* as a subject of study demonstrates the preoccupation on the part of the reformers with the goal of strengthening the national identity.

4.2 Individuality

The concept of individuality and its meaning in a Japanese context is a subject which has received a huge amount of attention. In this respect NCER was no exception when it chose the term as one of its key phrases. As a concept originating in the Western philosophical and scientific tradition it has been taken up by the Japanese and fitted into their internal cultural debate, but it has not altogether remained the same as in the Western philosophical tradition.

When interpreting other cultures it has been common to emphasise the differences in order to prove a point. Thus, when Europeans or Americans have described Japan, the 'everything-is-opposite' model has been very popular. This typically included statements saying that the Japanese were group oriented rather than individualists or that they were emotional rather than rational, in short, the opposite of our *ideal* selves. Individualism has been a cherished concept in Western culture and hence it has often been claimed by Westerners that non-Westerners — such as the Japanese — could not possibly possess this character trait, merely because they were 'opposite' (Rosenberger, 1992, 2).

The Japanese for their part have also used this approach to affirm Japanese identity by using a systematic taxonomy of the 'Other' (China/the West). As a consequence, what is attributed to Japan must be denied the 'Other' and vice versa (Dale, 1990, 39).

Edwin O. Reischauer, who has produced a lot of books on the Japanese and their history, describes in one of his later works this apparent 'oppositeness' as being a difference of *myths*. Americans and Europeans, he says, were likely to see themselves as independent individuals and as more free than facts actually proved. The Japanese on the contrary are 'much more likely to operate in groups — or see themselves as operating this way' (Reischauer, 1990, 128).

In the same work, he also touches upon the idea of the emotional Japanese versus the rational Westerner:

The Japanese have always seemed to lean more towards intuition rather than towards reason, to subtlety and sensitivity in expression rather than to clarity of analysis, to pragmatism rather than to theory, and to organisational skills rather than to great intellectual concepts. (Reischauer, 1990, 200)

Though very cautious about emphasising that exceptions can always be found and that we are dealing with conceptions — not necessarily facts — his work otherwise reflects the traditional binary way of describing a foreign culture, exoticising it by emphasising differences rather than similarities. In the earlier part of his career he was much more black-and-white in his analysis of East versus West, but an apparent awareness of the budding criticism of this mode of interpretation inspired him to be more relativist in wording though not necessarily in content (Minear, 1980, 511-12).

The approach of seeing Japan as opposite an undefined 'West' — which is by the way usually the United States — is characterised by Peter Dale as being in danger of *exoticising prejudice* instead of creating an objective picture because of its denial of homologies between otherwise similar situations. Additionally, the focus on differences and the refusal by the Japanese to acknowledge the value of Western theories carries with it the danger of making the culture unable to understand its own human predicament, deprived as it is of using analogies and foreign experiences, he warns (Dale, 1990, 7, 40).

This approach is used in the literary genre called *nihonjinron* ('Theories of Japaneseness' which attempts to identify the uniqueness of being Japanese) which, among other things, deals with the concept of individuality in a Japanese context. This genre has been criticised particularly strongly by Peter Dale (1990) and Mouer & Sugimoto (1986) for failing to take into account regional and class variations, the difference between voluntary and coerced behaviour and the role of conflict in its attempt to present Japan as a harmonious, homogeneous society.

Peter Dale in a particularly acrimonious attack calls *nihonjinron* 'an expression of an intense tradition of intellectual nationalism' which emerged around 1909-11 as a reaction to the crisis faced by the late Meiji leadership, and which is all the more menacing because it fervently denies having anything to do with ideology or politics. *Nihonjinron* describes a Japan, seen through the eyes of conscious nationalists, which is out of touch with both reality and the principles of logic and method, he states (Dale, 1990, 9, 38).

Despite the apparent unreasonableness and tendentiousness of the genre it is necessary to take it into account when dealing with things like self and individual in Japan because *nihonjinron* is quite influential. Often the authors of such works are acknowledged scholars respected for their intellectual credentials and acting as spokesmen for the 'inarticulate soul of the national essence', though the inspiration for writing such works may often just have been the allure of money. *Nihonjinron* material is immensely popular in Japan and widely read so its doctrines are well known to most Japanese and thus constitute common knowledge on the nature of the 'Japanese' as opposed to the rest of the world.

A Nomura Survey of publications on the theme of Japanese identity showed that from 1946 to 1978 approximately 700 titles were published on this subject, 25% of which were issued in the peak year period 1976 to 1978 (Dale, 1990, 14-15, 17). For this reason, it becomes important to deal with the ideas expressed in *nihonjinron* in the attempt to analyse the nature of Japanese 'individuality'.

Well-known examples of the *nihonjinron* tradition are Nakane Chie, 1970, *Japanese Society*; Doi Takeo, 1973, *The Anatomy of Dependence* and Tsunoda Tadanobu, 1978 *The Japanese Brain*. Nakane Chie became the most famous, though by no means the only, advocate of the theories on the group orientation of the Japanese. These theories became so popular that her work was published by the Japanese Ministry of Foreign Affairs in an abbreviated form and distributed through Japanese embassies and government agencies.[5] Clearly it was seen as an ideal picture of the Japanese culture, a picture to be presented to the world's public. Statements such as the above by Reischauer have been supported by this supposedly 'native' and in effect semi-official way of interpreting Japanese society, but Reischauer's background for his statement on the group-oriented Japanese more probably stems from the binary model in which Western individualism is seen as opposed to Eastern groupism.

As for the Japanese version of individualism, it has usually been characterised in terms of group orientation, as seeking identity through relationships with other people, and the perceived egotistic character of Western individualism has been distinguished from the relational individuality of the Japanese (Rosenberger, 1992, 12-13).[6]

The theory of group orientation has also been applied to schooling. Roger Goodman quotes an example from a school he visited. This school based itself on group action and claimed that 'success is not an individual success but that of the group' (Goodman, 1990, 121).

The difference between Western and Japanese ideas of individualism is also revealed in the terminology applied by the Japanese. Japanese type individualism is termed *kosei* whereas Western individualism is termed *kojin shugi*, which signals selfishness and immaturity (Hendry, 1992, 56).

As Brian Moeran points out in his book *Language and Popular Culture in Japan*, the term *kosei* only seems to consist of the 'good' side of individualism, that is, individualism devoid of such aspects as selfishness and irresponsibility. The West is left with the entirely negatively evaluated term 'individualism' (*kojin shugi*) (Moeran, 1989, 70). This is a telling example of the way the binary model works. *Kosei* is attributed to the Japanese and hence the same characteristic is necessarily denied the 'Other', here the West. To make this distinction clear, the terms are translated into 'individuality' for *kosei* and 'individualism' for *kojin shugi* respectively.

Takie Sugiyama Lebra in the article *Self in Japanese Culture* deals with two types of 'self', two types of actors — whether capable of individual action or not is secondary to this distinction. One is the socially regulated self, which is more universal and cross-culturally accessible than the other, the inner self, which is a meaning-loaded self based on local culture and history (Lebra, 1992). The term

5. Nakane Chie, 1972. *Human Relations in Japan*, Ministry of Foreign Affairs, Tokyo. Nakane's field of research is social anthropology and her work has mainly been on India, China and Tibet. She calls the group theory a by-product of her studies in India. (Hendry, 1989, 645)

6. F.L.K. Hsu in his article 'The Self in Cross-Cultural Perspective' in *Culture and Self* edited by Marsella, DeVos and Hsu (1985), described the Chinese and Japanese conception of man as based on the 'individual's transactions with his fellow human beings', thus also supporting the relational type of individual in Japan.

kosei clearly belongs to the inner self-sphere, as it is connected with local definitions and interpretations, but the problem is that because it is translated into 'individuality' it would seem at first glance to belong to the socially regulated and universally understandable self-sphere, which this special Japanese definition of individuality clearly does not, at least not in the Japanese interpretation. Joy Hendry in an article on individualism and individuality emphasises:

... it is important to make a clear distinction between individualism, with its connotations of self-assertion and individual rights, and individuality, or the opportunity for an individual to develop his or her own particular talents or character. (Hendry, 1992, 56)

Hendry sees *individualism* as a strategy for survival in response to the increasing complexity of society, and *individuality* as existing in any society recognising individual differences and qualities. The latter would not necessarily presuppose the former. It follows then, that it is perfectly thinkable that a Japanese could possess individuality without being an individualist.

The emphasis on group life, for which Hendry traces the foundations back to early childhood, is thus not an obstacle to individuality in Japan. On the contrary, offering individual skills for the benefit of the group becomes an important part of group activities. Every group member can thus take advantage of the individual characteristics and abilities of the other members of the group (Hendry, 1992, 60-61).

A further characteristic facilitating this acceptance of a common goal, is that group tasks often rotate among the members. Everyone has to take turns acting out particular roles and thus will know and understand the tasks when they are performed by others. An example is the village or neighbourhood, where houses take turns to collect the community funds. This ensures that most people not only pay but also thank the collectors for their trouble. In hierarchical relations this aspect of role may also be strong inasmuch as the individual knows that he or she may someday be called upon to act in the role of the superior (Hendry, 1992, 62). The role structure is supported by the traditional *soto-uchi* (outside-inside) distinction of public face and private self. Though the public face may be a rigidly defined role which has not been chosen by the individual, the fact that this distinction exists makes it possible for the individual to have a completely different identity in the *uchi*/inside sphere, to be considerably more 'individual' than would be possible if the culture did not allow for this distinction (Hendry, 1992, 63). Hence it would be wrong to say that the Japanese are incapable of being individualistic because of their rigid social customs. On the contrary, Hendry makes a case for saying that it is indeed *because* of the rigid social customs that a Japanese can sometimes be individualistic.

Brian Moeran explains the role of *kosei*-individuality in the traditional system of Japanese values by linking it to *kokoro* — 'heart' or 'mind'. *Kokoro* is one of the most popularly used words in advertising, in the press and when explaining the Japanese mind. It covers a wide range of aspects having to do with feelings, sensibilities, intimacy and spontaneous feeling (*ninjoo*, another traditional factor in the group model) and is an ingredient in what Harumi Befu has termed the 'social exchange model', a model based on the assumption that individual resources are exchanged for resources that he or she does not possess. The individual will maximise his opportunities by strategically allocating his resources. The social exchange model was created as an alternative to Nakane's group model, because the latter failed to account for behaviour going against group norms (Befu, 1980, 179-80 in Moeran, 1989, 65).

Thus a concept seemingly alien to Japanese social structure such as individualism, is transformed into individuality (*kosei*) and manifested as individual freedom of action within the bounds of the group, as described by Hendry and others, or as individual actions in a social exchange model, as described by Befu and Moeran.

An important characteristic of this particular brand of Japanese individuality is that it is not a threat to the established system, because it is firmly placed within the traditional social hierarchy. Though the concept of collective or interpersonal identity has often been criticised by Western-trained scholars, they usually agree that Japanese conceptions of self are still embedded in interpersonal relationships (in the group model or the social exchange model). They also agree that growth towards individuality consists of aesthetic polishing towards a final unity of non-self, rather than individualism in a sense of essentialism and consistent identity (Rosenberger, 1992, 13).

The interpretation by Western scholars ranges from relativist theories at one extreme, insisting on the uniqueness and the difference between cultures which would render any comparison useless, to a universalistic approach at the other extreme which tends to think that all things are really the same, that they are just different manifestations of the same basic human phenomena. The *nihonjinron* and much of the officially sponsored rhetoric on individuality is of the relativist persuasion, while the Japanese progressive camp's interpretation of individuality tends more towards the universalistic approach concentrating on paroles such as peace on earth and human rights for children.

Reflecting these two completely different foundations the two main parties in the debate on individuality in Japanese education have argued heatedly against each other. Many problems arose from the choice of words signalling things which were never the intention. Though the government persistently used the Japanese term *kosei*, there was apparently no consensus as to what this term actually covered. The definitions made by people such as Joy Hendry and Brian Moeran apparently were not commonly accepted. Though both sides acknowledged that individuality had nothing to do with egotistic intentions, it was clear that for the opposition *kosei* entailed individual choice of goals and freedom to act to a much greater extent than it did for the government.

4.2.1 Individuality as defined by the NCER

Initially there was much discussion in NCER itself about how to express the idea of individuality properly in Japanese. It has consistently been translated into the English 'individuality', but in Japanese it was important to avoid expressions that would indicate any kind of egotism, since this was very often associated with expressions denoting some kind of individuality or individual activities. In the beginning, NCER used the expression *kosei shugi* ('individualism'), but this was criticised at ensuing public hearings for smacking too much of ideology, probably because of the word *shugi*, which means something like '-ism' — indicating an inflexible approach to things — and it was further criticised for being too difficult to understand (interview with Minakami Tadashi, May 31, 1991).

So NCER changed this key expression to *kosei no sonchoo* ('respect for individuality') or *kosei juushi* ('attach importance to individuality'). The discussion on the respect for the individual was based on a broad idea of freedom or liberalisation (*jiyuuka*) in the educational system, which meant that the definition of individuality was actually much more broadly defined in Japanese usage than the English expression implied. NCER in an explanatory paragraph in its first report defined individuality as linked to the perception that 'each individual is a distinctive independent human being' and went on to say:

Individuality means not only the individuality of each person but also the individuality of each family, each school, each local community, each industrial firm, each nation, each culture etc. These individualities do not stand isolated from one another. Only those who really know their own individuality, develop it and fulfil their own responsibilities, can fully respect and help develop the individuality of other people. (Rinkyooshin, 1988, 12)

Minakami Tadashi, a former NCER member, further elaborated on the relational character of this particular brand of Japanese individuality:

I believe the goal is the development of the individual's personality, not as an isolated individual but as an individual in a group. Man is a social being. If the personality is well developed it will benefit society, the country, the world.

The individual was firmly defined as existing within a group, within society, in the world. The main concern was clearly not with the individual as such but with its *relations* to other units of social organisation. Minakami further recollected that:

We [the NCER] did not think of the individual in particular. It was part of it, but we also emphasised that the families, the schools, the Japanese culture, society and the country had to have their own peculiar characteristics. A very broad definition. (interview with Minakami Tadashi, May 31, 1991)

Individuality was closely linked with freedom or liberalisation of education (*jiyuuka*), as was evident from the NCER report as well as from a remark made by Minakami that:

freedom to make choices in education must be increased for the students, and this also goes for individuality. The schools have to change, to create a more varied curriculum, — this is also what *kosei juushi* is about.

During their discussions NCER, according to Minakami, identified several different 'freedoms'. For instance, was there to be freedom of method, freedom to choose whatever textbook one found to be best, freedom not to go to school at all? In the end NCER decided that doing away with standardisation and protecting the individual was to be considered real freedom. Teachers were to choose and be responsible while staying inside the framework set up by the school boards. It was felt that expressions of personal ideologies could only be tolerated at university level. Liberalisation and freedom apparently did not go well with basic education in NCER's view (interview with Minakami Tadashi, May 31, 1991).

The tendency to concentrate the efforts around liberalising schools and structures rather than working on the way people judge and treat each other was evident. The emphasis was on institutional individuality from which individual individuality was expected to follow. Professor Saitoo Taijun from the University of the Air, and a former Ministry of Education employee, saw NCER's attempts at individuality as aiming at less control, and at deregulation, which would in the end lead to more emphasis being placed on the individual (interview with Saitoo Taijun, May 17, 1991).

Freedom of choice and individuality was seen as possible by NCER only if schools were more differentiated in their offers. In a manner of speaking, students should, rather than choosing between different flavours of ice cream, be given the choice between ice cream and fruit. If schools became distinctly different, students would have a better base for choosing and for securing the perfect surroundings for the development of their individuality (interview with Minakami Tadashi, May 31, 1991).

In this way a close connection between conditions in education and society and the development of personality was established and this was part of the reasoning behind emphasising institutional individuality over individual individuality.

While analyzing the policies carried out under the headline 'respect for the individual' as well as the criticism of it, one should at all times keep the NCER definition of individuality in mind. A lot of problems arose from the fact that the interpretation of the word — whether it be 'individuality' or *kosei juushi* — differed considerably in NCER and the groups in opposition to it. If the opposition expected *kosei juushi* to be primarily concerned with the individual, it was only to be expected that the measures taken by the government in this area would disappoint them.

The essence of the NCER individuality was institutional individuality and this was qualified later by a general director of the Ministry of Education, Satoo Jiroo, who, perhaps influenced by new reports issued by the NCER's follower 'Central Council on Education' stated that:

The task of Japanese education is to preserve quantity while enhancing quality — to adapt education to the different talents and needs of the individual. (Interview with Satoo Jiroo, June 6, 1991)

This added a twist to institutional individuality — the institutions were to individualise their programmes for the benefit of the individual, but it was still the educational institutions which were the point of departure. In the call for adaptation to different talents we recognise the concept of diversification which has been on the agenda of the conservative government since the 1960s. Such ideas may well, as has been claimed by JTU now as then, be a result of the desire to create elite education.

4.2.2 Why more individuality?

NCER's reason for emphasising individuality and putting it at the top of the priority list was its expected effect on a problem NCER had considered very seriously, namely the uniformity, rigidity and closedness of Japanese education, which were said to be 'deep-rooted defects' of the system causing problems with educating and providing future manpower with suitable qualifications and in the immediate present, problems with bullying and violence. Instead, values like the 'dignity of individuals, respect for personality, freedom and self-discipline, and individual responsibility' were to be established.

To achieve this, it was said that areas like 'content and methods of teaching, educational structures and government policies in education, should be reviewed drastically' (Rinkyooshin, 1988, 278).

Minakami Tadashi, former NCER member, felt there were two central problems in current Japanese education: Lack of respect for children's personalities and lack of adjustment to society's evolution. He saw these two factors as causing most of the problems in education (interview with Minakami Tadashi, May 31, 1991). The problems mainly lay in lack of creativity and the so-called 'devastation' (*koohai*) of education, the rising rates of truancy, violence and drop-outs. The conservative call for diversification originating in the 1960s had the same root: anticipation that the standardised educational system could not produce people who could be part of future development.

The proposed measure against the uniformity problem was the establishment in the educational system of such principles as dignity of the individual, respect for personality, freedom and self-discipline, and individual responsibility. Individualised educational institutions were also expected to be able to divert more students away from the traditionally much coveted universities:

Certain Japanese universities — such as the universities of Tokyo and Kyoto and Waseda for example — have too many applicants. They have long traditions and highly qualified teachers and students, which makes everyone crowd around these few universities and this makes the competition for entrance hard. But we have 500 universities. If every institution had distinctive characteristics I think this situation could get better. (Interview with Satoo Jiroo, June 6, 1991)

Reflecting on the history of Japanese education NCER pointed out that efficiency, continuity and stability had been emphasised in the educational system at the expense of respect for the individual and the fostering of free spirits. It went on to elaborate on the need to be able to cope 'flexibly with the social changes expected in the rest of this century and in the next', and emphasised that this necessitated the fostering of 'creativity (*soozooryoku*), thinking ability and power of expression'. The purpose of it all was to produce 'more human resources with distinctive personality and creativity' (Rinkyooshin, 1988, 278). Clearly, one was worried whether Japan would be able to turn out enough creative talent, whether Japan would be able to secure a vanguard position in global research and trade.

Soozoosei or *soozooryoku*, perhaps more accurately translated into 'power of imagination' than to 'creativity', is positively loaded and is what both foreign as well as domestic sources have accused Japanese education of lacking. Creativity was seen as closely linked to individuality, and further along to manpower needs (human resources) in industry and research, thus reflecting the strong influence of the business world on NCER. The business world's requests for educational reform ran along those lines of argument with statements like:

Creativity should be ranked as the most desirable qualification ... The development of diversity, the antonym of uniformity, is hoped for in many areas in society. A combination of human resources each having a variety of unique characteristics is the source of strength for an enterprise, assuring flexibility in dealing with an uncertain future. (Keizai Dooyuukai, 1984, 35)

The invocation of a term like *soozooryoku* thus was a reaction to criticisms of excessive uniformity and also at the same time elicited support for proposals claiming to work for increased *soozooryoku*.

The notion of individuality as something for the benefit of the individual, and individual development, was not absent from NCER's discourse, but it was not considered to be the core of the issue. Rather it seemed that NCER felt there was actually plenty of 'individual individuality', presumably in the sense of relational individuality *kosei*, as was clear from the following lines: '... people's mental attitudes have been individualised and diversified, and their demand for freedom of choice has been increasing.' NCER wanted to support this development as a measure against standardisation in education (Rinkyooshin, 1988, 279). It would seem then, that NCER would have us believe that it was reacting on the impulse of popular demand, not on the impulse of worries over manpower supplies. NCER proposed a review of contents and methods of teaching, educational structures and government policies in education and based on this, one can only assume that the lamented lack of creativity and power of expression was judged to be *caused* by the educational system, since NCER apparently saw no innate lack of individuality (*kosei*) in the people.

The same belief in the beneficial effect deregulation and liberalisation in itself would have on education was aired by the business world and to some extent by Professor Saitoo from the University of the Air. Business groups such as the Kyoto Group emphasised free competition among students as well as teachers as the ideal of an education 'free and independent from public authorities as much as possible' (Kyoto Group, 1984, 31).

The bottom line of it all, for NCER, apparently was that individuality was primarily a characteristic to be desired for developing society and industry and for staying among the economic superpowers. In the process the individual would of course be developed too, but it was not directly emphasised, and was never intended to be so, as Minakami pointed out. This influenced the measures taken in policy-making on the issue of individuality where the emphasis was on creating institutions of education with different characteristics.

4.2.3 Views on individuality

In opposition to the idea of individualisation of institutions was the notion that individuality was primarily a question of free choice for the individual, less central control of the curriculum and the freedom to have and maintain different traits of character, as it was expressed by the teacher organisation ATU (interview with Kawai Naoki, May 16, 1991).

The ATU and Professor Horio as part of the NKG, when dealing with individuality, emphasised people's right to be different, to be given the chance of exploiting their particular strong points. Realising that at the bottom of the controversy with NCER were different interpretations of the expression 'individuality' (*kosei*), ATU explained that individuality in NCER terms was all about streaming and separation, in other words, that NCER was mainly concerned with providing elite and ordinary education, giving the not-so-clever pupils no more than an elementary education. This claim they based on the NCER proposition of streaming in middle school and emphasis on vocational secondary education, which in effect, they foresaw, would mean that less students would get academic high school education (interview with Kawai Naoki, May 16, 1991; Horio, 1988b, 6). Their claim was further supported by the likeness of the concept of 'individuality' to that concept of 'diversification', which had been on the conservative agenda since the 1960s. Another NKG member pointed out that liberalisation and individuality were in many cases confused by the NCER and as a result what could be expected from NCER in terms of individuality was: 1) more flexible rules for school establishment; 2) more flexible school districts; 3) flexibility in teacher qualification demands; 4) public exposure of the educational philosophy and methods of each school (Hirabara, 1985, 36).

This constituted the basic framework necessary for giving private educational enterprises a role in the public educational system. Further, NKG equalled NCER's individuality to standardisation based on the following example:

Amaya of NCER claimed that our national flag *Hinomaru* was an expression of the individuality of the Japanese, but if it is flown indiscriminately from every school it is really just a sign of standardisation. This kind of individuality connects to the notion of 'a group-oriented Japanese' and NCER's individuality is exactly the opposite of true individuality. (Horio, 1988b, 7)

NKG's representative went on further to state that the Japanese administration was seeking 'optimal result — minimal individuality' and had got people involved in the common goal of securing Japan's future to an extent which made people find individual expressions difficult (Horio, 1988b, 3).

The perception of individuality and what it was supposed to mean, for the teacher organisations clearly implied if not total abandonment of group activities, then at least a shift in emphasis away from it. JTU asserted that individuality certainly was part of the Japanese character, 'we just do not try to develop it in our education' (interview with Sakai Tomiko, May 7, 1991). Further, the state of affairs in education was described by JTU as being characterised by too much irrelevant knowledge which had to be taught, by contempt for manual work and by a too rigid scale for evaluating people.

ATU, the more radical of the two teacher organisations, lived up to this label and went somewhat further away from the traditional emphasis on the group in its characteristic of individuality, claiming that 'every child has good and bad character traits and education must help them modify the bad traits. ' Children should learn that people are not all alike — and indeed should not be — and that Man is not perfect but can be taught to emphasise his positive sides. How, ATU asked, can children possibly be expected to understand the diversity of Man if they themselves are treated alike? (interview with Kawai Naoki, May 16, 1991).

Both organisations agreed on the difficulties of treating a class of 40 to 45 students as individuals and on the danger of losing a substantial proportion of the class in the race for keeping up with the curriculum standards. In this connection ATU was particularly incensed by the efforts at streaming in middle school.

In order to create real individuality, ATU asked for such measures as reducing class size to 20 pupils (it has only recently been reduced to 40) in order to make the individual more visible to the teacher in the class. If the teacher was unable to teach every child individually it would be impossible to instill in the children a sense of the value of each individual regardless of ability, ATU maintained. They saw it as the task of the adults, teachers and parents, to be good examples for the children, while the task of the government was that of ensuring that the necessary facilities were available (interview with Kawai Naoki, May 16, 1991).

In the guise of taking care of individual needs, ATU argued, the Ministry of Education just tried to separate the clever from the not-so-clever, and ensure that the latter would get only compulsory education and choose vocational careers at an earlier stage. Industrial needs as summed up by the ATU were as follows: 5% academics, 10% with intermediate education and the rest for peaceful obedient workers. Based on a 1963 survey of future manpower needs, NKG stated that the government foresaw a need for 3-5% highly talented manpower and that the government on this basis was attempting to create an elite which could preserve Japan's advantages in the world economy (Horio, 1988b, 5).

Though recognising that this aim of early separation and the creation of an elite was not actually spelled out in the NCER reports, ATU and NKG, based on the actual policies carried out after the NCER reports had been accepted as indicators of the course of the government's future educational policies, analysed this to be one of the covert aims. A further argument for this was found in the business paroles for educational reform, paroles such as 'free and fair competition in education' of the Kyoto Group, and further, the Kyoto Group's professed ideal of 'giving ample leeway to those who are eager to study' by, for instance, encouraging attendance at private academies before university entrance (Kyoto Group, 1984, 32).

ATU felt that, ideally, education should cater for the individual character traits of the child, not just be a means for separation and selection, and children should be taught to genuinely value the differences involved in individuality, not just see them as a means of selection. While for ATU teaching according to ability would be a means of helping all students reach the same level, and NKG said that it meant teaching 'appropriate to the level of development', the NCER's version of teaching according to ability was criticised for being solely a means of selection and separation.

The business groups attacked the inflexible evaluation standards and the relative standing evaluation system (*hensachi*) in the name of free competition. Choice of school should be left to the student, although with the due amount of guidance from school authorities, and each school should have its own entrance examination system (Kyoto Group, 1984, 34). The Education Council also elaborated on the desirability of individualised admission screening methods for universities (Keizai Dooyuukai, 1984, 37).

The Women's Democratic Council on Educational Reform (WDCER) and NKG linked individuality to the question of human rights. Education in school should be conducted in such a way as to respect the human rights of every single child. This would include the child's right to be an individual with its own powers to grow and learn. As WDCER stated:

All children are individuals who cannot be compared with each other by one single standard. Education should be a common public enterprise, free of competition and bureaucracy, with children at the centre. It is wrong to think of education as something given by the state. (WDCER, 1987, 93) (See also section 4. 2.5 on children's human rights)

In this respect teaming up with the business groups, WDCER's first and most urgent reform proposal was the abolition of the relative-standing evaluation system. Further proposals from WDCER were all very concrete in their content centring on securing the right to make choices, to complain and to change schools. Like ATU, WDCER also wanted class size to be reduced to 20-30 pupils to make more individualised and democratic teaching methods possible. As they said: 'With classes of 40 pupils it can only be done the hard way' (interview with Higuchi Keiko, June 27, 1991).

WDCER clearly saw individuality as something closely related to the individual and not as a general feature applicable to institutions as well as persons, which was the way NCER had primarily defined it. As mentioned earlier ATU was also inclined to interpret individuality more in terms of individual rights than as a general characteristic of persons and institutions. ATU chairman Mikami said on the subject:

We all have individuality (*kosei*), but not the kind of individuality that NCER deals with, which separates people into those who can and those who cannot. Our kind of individuality is the uniqueness of each and every human being. (...) Individuality is when you are loved by many people, not the way NCER has it. (Mikami, 1990, 34)

He further elaborated on this remark by pointing out that special traits of personality were often treated by the educational system as flaws to be corrected, rather than advantages inseparable from the personality. In Mikami's opinion the idea that there is one special foolproof recipe for getting particularly desirable results from children, the search for which he saw as lying behind many of the official reform attempts, was fallacious. Methods should be adapted to the needs of the individual child, he felt (Mikami, 1990, 37).

More concretely ATU criticised the way they felt individuality was being hampered by the curriculum guidelines urging the teachers to introduce national(ist) symbols such as the Japanese flag and the Emperor song as well as teaching pre-schoolers to have a 'respectful heart'. This, in ATU's opinion disregarded all concerns for the pupils' individual tastes and opinions as well as those of the teachers and the parents (Zenkyoo, 1990, 17).

JTU, the other large teacher organisation, took the same side as ATU in this respect. The schools, in their opinion, were to be places where children could work according to their different interests, and schools were to provide a creative atmosphere where individuality (*kosei*) could prosper. (Nikkyooso, 1991, 9). They pointed out the apparent commercial liberalism attached to NCER's use of the word freedom in education (*jiyuuka*), and the economic and materialistic connotations of this, and they doubted whether a liberalised educational system would be able to secure social equality and equality of opportunities, because equality could not be expected to be profitable and hence it would not be interesting for private enterprisers.

The liberalisation theme was treated at length by NKG, who interpreted it as plain privatisation of education. In view of the business groups' calls for liberalisation and their earlier quoted remarks on the subject, it is indeed hard not to interpret liberalisation as privatisation, especially since NCER was obviously much inspired by the business groups.

The official attempts at lowering public spending on education and the willingness to let private enterprises participate in the educational system had made education look like a marketable good. Parents would do anything to secure optimal conditions for their children and in the process of commercialisation of education, true learning would disappear and people would start to exploit education for their own purposes and feel that it was something which could be owned, NKG warned (Horio, 1988b, 6).

Individuality, in the opposition's view, was a thing which concerned the individual as such, just like ATU defined it, and while JTU definitely thought that individuality did exist innately in the Japanese, they accused such educational practises as rote-learning and standing/walking in rows, of making it bothersome for children to think for themselves, thereby precluding manifestations of individuality. A recurrent theme for both of the teacher organisations was the standardising effect Japanese education was seen to have on children. As the JTU representative put it, children were 'taught how to memorise, not how to think' (interview with Sakai Tomiko, May 7, 1991).

The effect streaming might have if it was effectuated in middle school, as proposed by the Ministry of Education and NCER, was of grave concern to JTU. Separating pupils according to ability would only aggravate the pressure of competition, they feared. In additon, the Ministry of Education introduced an even more compressed curriculum in 1989, while at the same time entertaining ideas of a five-day school week.

JTU was not opposed to the idea of a five-day school week, but they maintained that without curriculum reductions it would have ominous consequences for the pupils, who would have even less time to learn the increasingly compressed curriculum. Instead JTU wanted educational reforms to emphasise areas which could bring back elbowroom (*yutori*) in children's lives and be of use to them in the 21st century. These were things like peace, human rights, environment, development, training in the use and processing of information, in short what was needed to become a world citizen and a people capable of ruling themselves. They therefore saw Saturday as a day to be used for activities which would enhance children's independence and autonomy. This meant that JTU discouraged school-club activities and cram school lessons on Saturdays and Sundays (Nikkyooso, 1991, 3-4, 18). With this last proposal they were in accord with WDCER.

So, while both the opposition and NCER were concerned with educating for the future, the central figure for the opposition was the individual, whereas for NCER it seems to have been the national economy.

A common theme for most of the opposition was the fear that the liberalisation component of individuality would mean privatisation of education. As previously quoted, NKG saw the mix-up of liberalisation and individuality as a mix-up which equalled liberalisation or privatisation of education and individualisation of education. The government made it no secret that more private initiative, especially in elementary education, was desirable for budgetary reasons as well as for diversification in the offers of education.

This was a stand strongly supported by the various business groups. One of the major reasons for the worries of the opposition was that values such as equality of opportunity would be infinitely more difficult to uphold if part of the education was taken care of in private institutions where perhaps ulterior motives, like money, may matter more than in a publicly run system.

With the discourse on individuality taking such different starting points as it evidently did in the government and the opposition, it was of course difficult to reach any form of consensus. Fortunately for the government there was no reason for them to actually take into consideration the views of the teacher organisations, much less the other organisations taking part in the debate. The exclusion of teacher organisations in the policy formation stage may seem strange or even impossible, as it would be in Denmark, but it must be remembered that there were, and are, no formalised ties or procedures for national negotiations between the Ministry of Education, the state and the teacher organisations (see also 3.2.3).

4.2.4 Why the term 'individuality'?

It would appear that at the root of at least many of the problems was the expression the NCER had chosen. Though it had been discussed extensively within the NCER itself, the term *kosei* and especially the English translation 'individuality' led many to the conclusion that this was about the 'uniqueness of every human being', as ATU chairman Mikami termed it. But as NCER had already explained, this was not all there was to it. If, for instance, the NCER had chosen instead 'differentiation' (*tayooka*), a lot of the problems may have been avoided. Judging from the concrete reform proposals presented under the heading of 'individuality', the term 'differentiation' would have been more precise for NCER's aims. *Tayooka* was indeed initially used along with *koseika* by the CCE in 1971, but was given up as a key-phrase though not as a concept. NKG analysed the official individuality ideas as a mix-up not only of the two concepts 'individuality' and 'liberalisation' but of diversification as well, and made clear that since *tayooka* did not mean *individualise* but *standardise*, this mixture was undesirable (Mikami, 1984, 23; Horio, 1988b, 3). The mixture of the three phrases does suggest an explanation of the curious flavour of standardisation and privatisation pervading the attempts of the NCER and Ministry of Education at individualising.

To adjust the system to the new demands, NCER deemed it necessary to make the structure of both schools and educational administration more flexible and decentralised. With regard to individuality, it was said that: 'there must be relevant deregulation in the field of education' (... *kanren suru shokisei no kanwa ga hitsuyoo de aru*). However, the sheer vagueness of the phrase and the use of the word 'relevant' (*kanren suru*), seems to offer some leeway for any interpretation the users of the report may find useful, and may as a consequence render the whole argument for deregulation powerless (Rinkyooshin, 1988, 279). The option of non-implementation was certainly visible in this section. The reason for including such a vague statement at all probably was that business groups had made deregulation of education a central theme in their deliberations and NCER in this way acknowledged its familiarity with this proposal. However, NCER seemed to prefer terms like 'making flexible' (*juunanka*) or 'decentralisation' (*bunkenka*), perhaps in order not to sound as if condemning the educational administration as overly regulatory (Rinkyooshin, 1988, 279).

If decentralisation meant a wider range of choice for the individual and opportunities of realising individual ideas, decentralisation could of course work to promote individuality. However, judged in the context that the decentralisation, or decontrol and free competition referred to concentrated on *institutions* and *institutional status* as publicly or privately financed, this is certainly not an obvious promotion of the individuality of the individual. It leads to the assumption that the individuality talked about here is not the property of an individual, but something that should characterise and distinguish the institutions in the educational system.

On how to emphasise individuality more in practice, NCER talked about the 'diversification and reform of institutions of higher education' and 'enrichment and reform of elementary and secondary education'. The overwhelming emphasis was on individualising and diversifying the institutions of education, and those of higher education especially, expanding cooperation among them, evaluating universities and making those evaluations available to the public; reforming the procedures for selecting university entrants and so on. There was no reference to *persons*, it was the *institutions* which were to have individual characteristics, such as producing a wider range of choices, making the credit system and the academic years and terms more flexible.

In the end such changes may all add up to more individuality for the individual but judging from the way the issue was treated by NCER it was seen more like a device to secure the diversely talented manpower needed. For instance, there was no proposal for such things as supporting the individuality of those not feeling at home in the current educational system, no added emphasis on humanistic subjects for character development, no suggestions relating to pedagogy.

But why choose officially to limit the discussions to a problematic expression like 'individuality/*kosei*'? There was nothing in the foundation on which NCER was created to necessitate this. The various reform requests from the business world and internal LDP memos such as that produced by the LDP member Nishioka, *all* concerned such subjects as the standardisation of Japanese education and the harmful effects it had had on creativity, but they did not actually use the word 'individuality' to describe possible solutions. The Nishioka memo was the foundation of the plans Nakasone launched during his election campaign in 1983. Significantly, the memo did not use the word individuality (*kosei*) but instead words like 'freedom/liberalisation' (*jiyuuka*) and 'diversification' (*tayooka*). The publications of the business world similarly avoided 'individuality' and instead chose 'diversification' and 'relaxation', 'flexibility' etc.

What made NCER use the expression 'individuality' was probably an attempt to get public and international consensus for their reform proposals, an assimilation of a popular term to pacify criticism. Many public statements on standardisation and lack of creativity, named *individuality* as the antonym, and presented it as a remedy, as indeed the majority of the opposition also did. This can be seen clearly from the above NKG quotation that *tayooka* and *koseika* are in fact opposites. Realising this, NCER presented plans in the guise of individuality for diversification and privatisation, as requested by the business world and LDP. Individuality (*kosei*) was mixed up not only with diversification (*tayooka*) but also with liberalisation (*jiyuuka*). Rightly, NCER was accused of presenting something that was not individuality, but then again, they had never really claimed that it should be such. It was the word itself combined with the interests of the opposition, which caused such confusion.

Additionally, NCER was most certainly aware of the academic debate on Japanese individuality and the arguments set forth by the literature of Nihonjinron. This gave them the word *kosei* and a uniquely Japanese brand of individuality, which was useful because it did not break with what was in the same literature perceived as traditional values. The opposition, however, chose an interpretation which was, by the same line of argument, more 'westernised', where the group had less importance and the individual was the protagonist. For the opposition individualising the institutions of education had no relation to true individuality.

4.2.5 On children's human rights

An issue which invariably came up in the discussions on individuality during the interviews with the teacher organisations' representatives and which frequently surfaced in both their written material and in that of WDCER was the issue of children's human rights. In NKG's material it was stated that 'education is a human right and as such should value people's individuality' (Horio, 1988b, 6). Very strong arguments and a lucid analysis of children's human rights have been produced by Professor Horio Teruhisa of Tokyo University. In numerous books on the state of children's rights in Japan he has expounded the ideological background for the argumentation of the teacher organisations as well.

He questioned whether education in Japan had really become the human right it ought to be, mentioning such violations of basic human rights as teachers physically punishing students, bullying and violence in the school yard, as well as the more hidden violations like the secret *naishinshoo* report card and career guidance. The following quotation pinpoints his opinion of freedom and human rights in Japanese education:

The enforcement of *Hinomaru* and *Kimigayo* removes the mood of freedom from the schools. The trials concerning freedom in the schools further exacerbates the problems with human rights and education. The current debate on 'liberalising education' is just placing a heavier financial burden on those using education and constitutes a commercialisation of education. (Horio, 1991, iii)

The importance of learning, in Horio's analysis, lies in the people's right to know the truth, to develop their basic human rights, realise themselves as individuals in society, culture and education. Learning was seen as *the* prerequisite for democracy. This right to learn was to be secured by firmly placing the authority over education with the people (Horio, 1991, 4-5). With this statement Professor Horio placed himself in the progressive camp which also worked against state authority over education.

A crucial blow to the people's direct authority over education came with the 1956 law for local educational administration (*Chihoo kyooiku gyoosei no soshiki oyobi unei ni kansuru hooritsu*) which was passed under unusual circumstances, because the government needed to call in 500 police officers to keep peace in the Diet while the voting was going on. The law provided that school boards, instead of being elective were to become appointive. The stratum above would appoint it — that is, a local school board would be appointed by the prefectural school board, the prefectural school board by the Ministry of Education. This meant a significant loss of popular influence on local schools. The potential for ministerial control over education became substantially greater as illustrated in an example given by a consultant from ATU: The school boards were to produce the necessary administrative regulations for the local schools. But with appointed boards the chance of new and progressive ideas gaining strength in the boards was zero. Further, the Ministry issued a set of 'model regulations for elementary and middle school administration' to all school boards. Not surprisingly, the school boards adopted the 'model regulations' (Zenkyoo, 1991, 180-82; Duke, 1973, 130-33).

Popular authority over education in this way was restricted legally. As Professor Horio proceeded to point out, education as a *right* of the people was not even explicitly stated in the Japanese Constitution, so that comments from Ministerial officials that it was futile to demand 'rights' that were not even acknowledged by the Constitution were in this narrow sense justified. However, in Professor Horio's interpretation, where education is seen as one of the basic human rights, this right is implicitly included in the general 'constitutional freedom' allotted to the people, and in the assurance that Japan will respect the basic human rights (Horio, 1991, 8; Roppoo, 1990, 4).

Now the issue of human rights has been well debated in most countries, but what has tended to be forgotten is that children have those rights too. As Professor Horio saw it, learning/development was the crucial factor for the growth of a dependent baby into an independent adult. Further, he said, children have the potential of surpassing their adult models. Education should stimulate the children's desire to learn, to discover. Education creates tomorrow's adults, so it would be vital, Professor Horio emphasised, that education should be as good and as perceptive as possible (Horio, 1991, 51-3). Obviously, in this analysis, disrespect for children's rights would entail the danger of educating adults with a general disrespect for human rights and with no urge to secure such rights for themselves. Horio enumerated three main aspects of children's rights:

1. Human rights and children's rights. When we speak of children's rights we must look upon children not as the property of parents, but as human beings with their own personalities.

2. 'Children's rights' are to be interpreted as 'children's rights as children'. Primarily, there is the problem of our patriarchal family relations in which children's rights are something determined by the father, it makes the 'rights of the parent' dominant.
   Secondarily, the tendency of regarding children as 'little adults', especially in milieus where children work, denies the children their right to be just children.

3. Education must be severed from the government if it is to be trustworthy. A person raised exclusively on the basis of a state ideology can never be a free person.
   (Horio, 1991, 58-61)

This call for respect for children's basic human rights has won much support especially in groupings with a left-wing orientation. The ATU chairman, Mikami Mitsuru, in a speech rounding up a two-day conference on the need to respect children's human rights spoke along the same lines as Horio when he said:

Basically, we must respect the children as human beings, because this is an essential prerequisite for ensuring *educational* activities in the true meaning of the word. (Zenkyoo, 1991, 161-2)

The conference had concentrated on a tragic accident where a high school girl in Kobe had been squeezed to death in the school gate because she had been late and had not made it through the gateway before it was closed. The fact that this could possibly happen, that a child could get killed because of inflexible school regulations, was taken by the ATU-sponsored conference as evidence of the extent of the disregard for children's rights as human beings. Many other examples of violations of children's rights were given, such as forcing elementary school children to eat their lunch alone in the corridors of the school because they had been noisy, corporal punishment and inflexible enforcement of dress codes, going to such extremes as teachers standing by the school gate in the morning armed with rulers in order to measure the length of skirts, hair, width of trousers etc. It has not been unknown for teachers to — then and there — cut hair which was found to violate regulations (Zenkyoo, 1991, 60; *East*, 1988, 48-50).

Not only the progressive camp was critical of the school regulations and their effect on children's human rights. Minakami Tadashi, the former NCER member, after referring to the tragic death of the girl in the school gate, continued:

Just the other day a newspaper wrote about a verdict saying that expelling a student from school for driving a motor bike, though indeed it was against school regulations, was going too far. Schools are to provide guidance for the students, so they create a lot of regulations. I suppose sometimes these regulations are too authoritarian and manipulative. (...) Many of these things are not for the school to interfere with but should be handled by the family. Hair, clothes and the like are really family affairs. (Interview with Minakami Tadashi, May 31, 1991)

School regulations are set by local school boards, not directly by the Ministry of Education, but with the use of administrative regulations, the Ministry naturally *can* influence this area should it so desire. But blaming the educational administration and the Ministry of Education solely for the inflexible regulations would be wrong. Higuchi Keiko, the WDCER representative, felt that part of the problem was that parents were no longer adequately equipped to deal with their children and take responsibility for persons other than themselves. Out of sheer fear parents prefer uniforms in school because it prevents discussions over clothes — parents are too afraid of conflict:

If everything is regulated by the school parents do not have to argue with their children about anything. So, many parents want harsh regulations. But some do not, of course, and their wishes are not accommodated. (Interview with Higuchi Keiko, June 27, 1991)

The extent of infringements on children's human rights which were felt to result from dress codes in particular, and school regulations in general, was such that in March 1988 a group of 124 Japanese lawyers formed an organisation to defend the human rights of minors. (*East*, 1988, 48-50)[7]

Dress codes and school regulations are areas where the violations of children's rights are particularly visible and they have received much public attention. These inflexible rules are no doubt responsible for many violations. ATU chairman Mikami's greatest fear was what result would be brought about by this lack of confidence in children:

I have also experienced this myself, but there is a tendency at the moment among children of feeling that they do not count, they lose their pride and are suspicious of other people. Their attitude to the future is nihilistic and at this point they become susceptible to fascism. (Zenkyoo, 1991, 147)

Children's conditions are described by ATU as 'lonely, with busy teachers, barren home environments and a cold disinterested society.' The responsibility of teachers and education was analysed as being that of giving children back their confidence in the future and in themselves (Zenkyoo, 1991, 146).

The motives which drove the Ministry of Education into allowing such blatant displays of disrespect for children's rights were, in ATU's admittedly tendentious analysis, the desire for a more militarist Japan:

For forty years we have been confident that Japan would never again send troops to other countries, but doing so is now being discussed in the Diet. The idea that the new curriculum guidelines have been designed to help create a country which could and would send troops overseas is tempting. And the *Daijoosai*, the coronation ceremony [for the Emperor], in one sweeping stroke destroys the principle of popular sovereignty. These are things we have to stand up against. (Zenkyoo, 1991, 163)

Evidently, the ATU saw the same tendency in everything the government did or condoned: a concerted effort towards authoritarian rule, ultra-nationalism and imperialism. By teaching the children to obey, the Ministry of Education, still in ATU's interpretation, would not only create an obedient people but also a people no longer interested in the future or in themselves as persons for that matter. Clearly, for ATU involvement, individual choice and confidence in children was what would ensure the perpetuation of pacifistic and democratic

7. A tiny indication of the budding desire for change towards less conformity in school uniforms is the 'small revolution' taking place in the area of school bags. Since the turn of the century is has been an unwritten rule that boys carry a black bag (randoseru) and girls a red, but lately around 10% sport bags in other colours such as beige, green, blue or even pink. (Rosario, 1993, 41)

values. For the progressive camp the human rights issue was closely linked to the issue of Japan's military status, and in the last resort, to democracy and world peace. To support individual choice and freedom ATU recommended the following:

We must not misunderstand the word 'freedom' and leave children to their own devices, but always offer them guidance and support. We must remind ourselves of the Osaka high school which endeavoured to teach its students about democracy and democratic habits by giving them real influence, encouraging public statements, teaching them to take notes of meetings etc.

We (teachers) must strive to achieve the five-day week in schools, as well as in work-places, in order to give back *yutori* (elbowroom) to the schools and allow us all to work in a satisfying way. We must try to create a high school education which leaves room for experiencing first loves, rich human relationships and for having dreams. (Zenkyoo, 1991, 152, 158, 160)

The tone of the proposals is one of creating more flexible circumstances in schools and putting relations between people at the centre of the efforts. The theme of school playing too large a part in children's lives was touched upon by both conservatives and progressives. Minakami Tadashi of NCER suggested that more responsibility should be entrusted to the family, quite in harmony with repeated NCER requests for strengthening the educating effect of homes and local communities.

Higuchi Keiko from WDCER used the following example to show how school's rights seemed to have gained the upper hand, thus violating individual rights:

One of my friends wanted to send her daughter overseas during a summer vacation but her school said no, even though the girl and both her parents thought it was a good idea. The school was afraid that if she had an accident or something bad happened it would reflect badly on the school. (Interview with Higuchi Keiko, June 27, 1991)

Since students are usually identified by school, the school was quite right that in the event of an accident its name was certain to be mentioned in the media. This was the reason for giving school's interests priority over the individual's.

As long as a school's identity is so closely linked to the students it will be difficult to allow the students individuality. If the school stands to lose face due to an individual's behaviour there can be no doubt that the school will try to curb this behaviour. And as long as students are identified by school, the school will stand to lose if a student acts badly or has an accident.

The issue of children's human rights was largely placed in the discourse of the progressive camp. The conservatives, in their worries over whether children would learn only about rights and not duties, did not emphasise children's rights in terms of global human rights, but more in terms of 'respect for the individual' as the expression in the NCER reports was.

4.2.6 How to produce more individuality

How to bring about more individuality in practice was a question which the NCER to a large extent left to the imagination of the policy makers. In most of its reform proposals NCER has been very vague on the subject of practical implementation. Of course, the matter of individuality requires extreme caution for, as Saitoo Taijun pointed out:

It is impossible for the government, through a policy, to enhance individuality. Individuality is something people have or nurture in themselves. When a government tries to implement it with a policy it ceases to be individuality. (Interview with Saitoo Taijun, May 17, 1991)

In the first NCER report the emphasis was on 'Diversification of Opportunities and Increase in Educational Routes'. Under this headline was a call for diversification and individualisation of higher education in order to produce diverse routes of access to higher education and to vitalise secondary education. To achieve this end NCER proposed that university entrance qualifications be made available as broadly as possible. In practice this meant granting entrance qualification to any student who had completed an upper secondary level course lasting three years or more (Rinkyooshin, 1988, 30).

The concern for the state of higher education in Japan was central to NCER's deliberations and was also voiced by General Director Satoo Jiroo from the Ministry of Education:

We have ensured that everybody gets basic education. But as for university, the level — in both teaching and research — should be higher, and graduate school in particular is a problem when we compare ourselves with other developed countries. Quantitatively, university is doing well, but the quality is not high enough. One in two of an age cohort gets tertiary education.[8] Nobody drops out. Once you are in you are certain to graduate. I suppose graduating is really too easy. (Interview with Satoo Jiroo, June 6, 1991)

In this he was supported by Minakami Tadashi who said:

---

8. Counting universities and special schools.

The number of universities has grown, but education-wise and research-wise they are not of an internationally comparable standard, they need more basic research and the individual university must be more distinguishable. (Interview with Minakami Tadashi, May 31, 1991)

Recognising that graduate school in particular needed drastic improvement, NCER proposed, for instance, that for some fields of study the length and function of a Master's or a Doctor's programme should be considered and that thought should be given to the introduction of a system under which excellent students may be allowed to enter graduate school after they had completed the third year of an undergraduate course (Rinkyooshin, 1988, 288). (See also section 2.2.5).

The tendency in the proposed reforms of higher education is liberalisation of admission, transfer and structure and shortening of the length of the studies. At the same time NCER called for promoting basic sciences so as to bring them to a level worthy of international recognition. Rather than letting graduate school students participate in basic research it would appear that the NCER wanted these activities to be undertaken by post-doctoral candidates as the expansion of post-doctoral fellowships was recommended (Rinkyooshin, 1988, 289).

The element of research in graduate studies was evidently not particularly cherished by NCER. Presumably, the result of these new proposals would be that Master's and Doctoral degree holders would not have conducted independent research, that these degrees would exclusively consist of *education*, and that the training of young researchers would take place at post-doctorate level and on location, that is, in the places where the young researchers find employment. This goes well with industrial demands for younger graduates from graduate schools, and it does not 'spoil' the young talent for the future employer by teaching them too many working habits and procedures that may not suit the future place of employment. It would also probably mean that the burden of financing university research could be shared. If university employees are to be mainly educators their time would be spent on teaching to a larger extent than now, and research could be carried out by post-graduate fellows, possibly financed by the Ministry of Education as well as other sources.

NCER also proposed the establishment of a national council on universities and colleges to deliberate on these new structures in graduate school. This council was established in September 1988 (Satoo, 1991).

Leaving the issue of the structure of higher education itself and turning to the much dreaded entrance, we find the proposal of another method (besides a general grant of entrance qualification to upper secondary graduates) to broaden the background of university applicants. This was the six-year secondary school, which was also requested by the business world. A six-year secondary school would be a new type of school combining the existing middle and high school, thus providing a consistent education suitable for adolescents.[9] As NCER saw it the advantages of such schools would be consistency and continuity. There would be continuous and planned programmes of instruction for six years and a continuity which would enable students to spend a more stable and composed school life by offering six years instead of three and three, divided by an anxiety provoking entrance examination. The disadvantage of such a system, NCER said, was that *no division* between middle and high school might create a rather monotonous school life and force the students to make choices for their future education at a very early time in their lives, that is, upon entering middle school.

NKG was positive to the idea of a six-year secondary school. They felt that the disruption after compulsory education was too big because entrance examinations would then become decisive. They envisaged a 'youth school' (*seinen gakkoo*) which hopefully would let the students think more about a future occupation to suit them than about advancing to the next level. NKG's reservations concerning NCER's proposal was that such a system would have to be a lot more flexible than the current, maybe using a credit system, and spend much more time on helping the students find out what to do with their lives (Oota, 1988a, 155-56).

The WDCER, though not opting for a unified six-year secondary school, was arguing along the same lines when recommending a free, comprehensive high school. Few children of fifteen knew what they wanted to be, they said, and further suggested more elaborate vocational counselling. However, they did not go so far as to move that high school be made compulsory — nobody should be sent to high school against their wishes, WDCER stated, at the same time deploring the current situation where high school education was all but compulsory in practice (WDCER, 1987, 106, 108, 111).

The business world on the whole supported the idea of deviating from the 6-3-3 system. *Keizai Dooyuukai* suggested a 6-6 system, in other words the six-year secondary school, to let the students 'devote themselves to study without anxiety' in a system without any entrance examinations. To avoid creating an overly standardised structure anew the *Keizai Dooyuukai* recommended that not all schools were converted to this new system and that admission to institutions of higher learning was left entirely to the accepting institution. In effect an

9. Many private schools are in effect six-year secondary schools, in the sense that they provide teaching for grades seven to twelve. However, as they maintain the division between middle school and high school curricula, they are not equivalent to the newly proposed model. One of the advantages of this new model was the relaxation of the division between middle and high school, making long-term planning possible. An example of a private 'six-year secondary school' is Nada in Osaka, which is famous for a very high rate of successful entrants into top-prestige universities.

abolition of common first stage tests (Keizai Dooyuukai, 1984, 39). The *Kyoto Group* and another business group, namely the *Group for Discussing Culture and Education* were also in favour of easing up on the 6-3-3 system (Kyoto Group, 1984, 34; GDCE, 1984, 22).

In the NCER proposal, six-year secondary schools were to be established at the discretion of those legally entitled to establish such institutions, provided they found 'such fields of secondary education, particular localities or feasible conditions as would justify the creation of a secondary school of this type'. NCER's ideas concerning the subjects to be emphasised in such schools did not introduce new subjects but rather concerned the opportunity of conducting long-term courses in the well-established subjects of secondary education. With the longer unbroken span of time, more specialised and integrated courses would become possible. This was in direct conflict with opposition views such as that of WDCER, who wanted a broad comprehensive school.

The structure of six-year secondary schools should allow for smooth transfers between different courses and schools, and above all use a selection method of entrants which would avoid fierce competition among the applicants. This was to be achieved by relying not only on a paper test, but also on interviews, practical skills tests, reports from the elementary schools etc. (Rinkyooshin, 1988, 31-32).[10] This structure coincided with WDCER's ideas for a more flexible high school.

The idea of a six-year secondary school was on the whole well received. The problem was that the opposition had serious doubts that the NCER version of secondary education would give the students enough individual choice. The opposition's vision was that secondary education could be a time of personal development while apparently the NCER was more in favour of taking it as a chance of earlier specialisation.

The section on enrichment and reform of elementary and secondary education placed emphasis on the individual, but not necessarily on individuality. Basic directions for improving the contents of instruction recommended that the following be emphasised: 'developing creativity (*soozooryoku*), mental abilities (*shikooryoku*), judgement (*handanryoku*) and the power of expression (*hyoogenryoku*)'. Earlier, individuality had been linked with creativity in the phrase 'creativity is closely related to individuality (*sozoosei wa kosei to missetsu na kankei o motsu*)'. It would be important to foster 'creativity,

10. This concern is probably prompted by the strong competition for entry into such famous private 'six-year secondary schools' as *Nada*. Recently a step was taken to counter the tendency for earlier selection, which carries the risk of making entrance into a prospective six-year secondary school quite as difficult as entrance into a prestigious high school at present. The Ministry of Education banned the use of placement tests which were prepared by private companies and used as a means of academic guidance in middle school. Instead, a new guidance system is now underway. (*East*, 1993, 38-39)

thinking ability and power of expression' since, NCER maintained, they would be required in all fields, such as the arts, science and technology:

In order to cope with the further development of scientific techniques and the changes in industrial production and employment structures, more human talent/resources with distinctive personality and creativity will be required. (Rinkyooshin, 1988, 278)

Subsequently it was noted that in the coming years there would be a need for 'not only abilities to acquire knowledge and information, but also to be able to make use of it properly, and the ability to think for oneself'. Though it had been said that 'creativity is closely related to individuality', 'creativity' rather than 'individuality' was used in the context of elementary education. It seems that individuality was not really meant for those attending elementary education, where basic skills were emphasised rather than skills of abstraction. This impression is strengthened by the subsequent sentence which said that teaching should endeavour to give 'children a deeper understanding of the tradition and culture of Japan, developing their awareness of themselves as Japanese citizens' (*Wagakuni no dentoo, bunka no rikai to nihonjin toshite no jikaku no kanyoo*) (Rinkyooshin, 1988, 292).

Particularly the last sentence became a target of attack from the opposition. They connected it with internationalisation and asked what kind of an internationalisation it was when children were taught to be Japanese citizens and the national flag and the emperor song (*Hinomaru* and *Kimigayo*) were re-introduced in the schools, as it was in 1990 (Kawai, 1991; Sakai, 1991). This concept of a culturally very aware Japanese existing in an international context was aired earlier in Nakasone's contributions to the education reform debate (Schoppa, 1991, 48). It is clear that NCER was voicing a conservative ideal of a 'traditional international Japanese' which is also found in the literature on Japanese uniqueness where internationalisation is all about spreading knowledge of Japan (see also 4.3).

Respect for the individual and creativity are words which were used several times in the section on enriching elementary and secondary education. But the scope of the respect for the individual and creativity was somewhat modified by the remedy the report proposed for enriching elementary and secondary education. This was moral education, a legacy of pre-war Japanese education, which was once used to disseminate nationalism and militarism. NCER emphasised the content of moral education as the teaching of basic manners and habits, development of self-control and a willingness to follow social norms in daily life and the development of a good attitude towards life. It was proposed that supplementary teaching materials be used and that teachers' training in this particular subject be improved (Rinkyooshin, 1988, 291).

Moral education and its content has been one of the great issues of the postwar educational debate. Those arguing for the strengthening of moral education usually list cultural reasons (the teaching of manners and habits, social norms). Apparently, the family is not seen as a suitable place for moral education for two reasons, as far as can be gleaned from the sources dealing with this. Firstly, because family ties are based upon feelings, a fact that does not go well with the enforcement of fixed moral codes (James & Benjamin, 1988, 43); and secondly, because with the replacement of the multi-generation family by the smaller nuclear family, the educating effect of the family has deteriorated, and thus the children often do not learn about basic manners and social norms (Rinkyooshin, 1988, 284; Monbushoo, 1987, 20, 56). Those opposing the strengthening of moral education fear a return to pre-war nationalistic indoctrination and prefer to have the family take care of this particular aspect of child rearing.

As for the contents of education, the most controversial issue by far in Japan has been modern history. The Ministry of Education, in textbooks for use in schools, wants a 'soft' presentation of Japan's role in the wars. During their screening of a history textbook, they required that some minute, but nevertheless significant, changes be made before giving their approval. For instance, Korea was 'entered' not 'invaded' (James & Benjamin, 1988, 44). In moral education itself it is argued by some observers that there are no overt practices to foster nationalism (James & Benjamin, 1988, 45), but to many, particularly the teacher organisations, the recently introduced flying of the national flag and the singing of the Emperor song in connection with revisions of textbooks like the above, is a clear step towards a more nationalistic school.

In any case, NCER's reports made it quite clear that the mission of compulsory education was to provide the pupils with the necessary basic skills. Luxuries such as individuality and creative thinking were the property of higher education and research. For elementary education there was 'respect for the individual' but not much space to exercise individuality. This division is reminiscent of the Meiji-period attitude that education and scholarship should be separated (see also section 2.1.1). Individuality was mainly to be a characteristic of the educational institutions and in a curious way individualising education became linked with national symbols and moral education.

4.2.7 Conclusions

The issue of individualisation in the Japanese educational debate is wrought with misunderstandings caused by different interpretations of the term. The two parties in the debate have different definitions and their goals are in conflict. While NCER, and with it the government and the business world, have their eyes fixed on manpower needs and liberalist ideals, the progressives are concerned with personal development, with upholding the ideals of the occupation reforms and with a crusade against central administration.

In Japan, the term individuality has become ambiguous and one of considerable opaqueness with conflicting interpretations flourishing. In the course of NCER's deliberations and the accompanying public debate it got mixed up with terms like liberalisation (*jiyuuka*), relative standing evaluation systems (*hensachi*) and diversification (*tayooka*). It is somewhat ironic that one would accuse the *hensachi*-system of rigid separation of people and then apparently proceed to separate people by ability in the name of individuality, and in the name of education suited to ability.

We here clearly see two different approaches to individuality. One is inspired by the traditionalist Japanese values of relational individuality, the other is based on a more 'Western' interpretation of the concept putting the person at the centre, the individual in its own right, an individual existing as an entity in a system of social relations.

The use of the seemingly familiar word 'individuality' in the debate on Japanese educational reform has led to accusations not only from the Japanese opposition, who are aware of the difference in interpretations of the concept, but also from the West, where the Japanese are accused of saying things they do not mean or 'back-pedalling' from initial emphasis on individuality, 'showing signs of hedging on the need to produce individual thinkers' (Wolferen, 118, 1989). Whether this is attributed to enigmatic oriental behaviour or to the deviousness of the yellow race is largely a question of temperament and both interpretations are equally wrong.

Closer to the truth is the observation that the concept is re-defined for its special purposes by the official parties. It has been assimilated by the official discourse so that it simply does not mean what we are accustomed to. This banal fact is muddled up because the opposition defines individuality much like we do it in Europe and the United States. What we *can* derive from this is the realisation that the concept of individuality in Japanese education is infinite, open to interpretation, and not a finite concept. This is necessary knowledge if we want to understand the logic of action in the efforts at individualisation in Japanese education.

4.3 Life-Long Learning

The concept of adult education as life-long learning was developed as an answer to the developments in demography and technology. The demographic trends showed that the number of young people was decreasing and the number of elderly people dramatically increasing. As it was aptly put by the NCER in its first report, the demographic trends necessitated a move from the 'fifty-year career to the eighty-year career', in other words a revision of the practice of retiring in your fifties. NCER foresaw that in order to maintain and enhance the vitality of Japan, society had to be transformed in order to let middle-aged and elderly people actively participate in and contribute to social and economic activities, which would also make the lives of such people more satisfying and worthwhile.

Another consideration prompting the interest for adult education was the increasing amount of information and new technologies employed in a highly industrialised society such as Japan. This would make it essential for people to engage constantly in acquiring new knowledge and new techniques. In-service training and retraining had become more important than ever before (Rinkyooshin, 1988, 15, 279).[11]

In NCER's terms the undertaking of life-long learning was to be in accordance with the 'differing abilities and spontaneous wills' of people, and hence the choice of ways and means of learning, in theory at least, was to be the responsibility of people themselves (Rinkyooshin, 1988, 170).

Apart from giving itself the task of developing a system suitable for the promotion of life-long learning, the NCER also touched upon the problem of the adverse effects of excessive emphasis on educational background. If the old mode of evaluation was maintained, the impetus for adults to learn would be low because such learning would not qualify them in practice. The means of evaluation in society should not be the traditional 'when and where did he learn' but 'what and to what extent did he learn', NCER stated. Over-emphasis on formal schooling had a harmful influence on education (*gakureki shakai no heigai ga ookiku natteiru*) because it contributed to the competition for entrance at prestigious institutions, NCER maintained.

The excessive value attributed to formal education was of great concern to NCER in connection with life-long learning. In order to make life-long learning desirable at all, there would have to be some financial and/or social gains associated with it. Just as people were generally able to assess the social and financial gains of formal education, so it should be with life-long learning, and this was what NCER was aiming at in its corrective efforts regarding educational credentialism — or the diploma disease, to use a term coined by Ronald Dore[12] (Rinkyooshin, 1988, 26, 279).

The expression 'community' (*chiiki*) was used a lot by NCER in describing

11. The term 'adult education' is used here to signify educational activities undertaken under the auspices of the Public Education Law, and 'life-long learning' is used for the activities envisaged by NCER.
12. The Diploma Disease, University of California Press, Berkeley 1976. The book elaborates on the relationship between education, qualification and development in seven countries, one of them being Japan.

the desirable structure of life-long learning. Expectations to its effects were extremely high and it would at times seem to be invoked almost like a mantra for its anticipated beneficial effect. Semantically 'community' is an entity placed between 'home' and 'society'. More public than the home and more homely than society in general. NCER clearly associated the expression with a neighbourhood with close human relations and tended in many passages to equal home and community. It was a very positive term in this sense, signalling something well-known and warm (home) as well as referring to a — perhaps nostalgic — longing for traditional close village relations. With the rapid urbanisation Japan has experienced since the end of World War II it is questionable whether it is not archaic to operate with this closely knit community-family model. Even many families today live polarised lives with the father — and maybe the mother — away for work most of the day and children occupied all day with school, homework and club activities.

4.3.1 NCER's ideas of life-long learning

In the second NCER report the headline was 'Transition to a life-long learning system'. Under this heading was a reiteration of the importance of discontinuing the practice of placing main emphasis on the school certificates, on formal education and educational background in the evaluation of individuals. It was also stated that people's desire for learning had increased and hence society had to live up to new learning demands. In addition, 'various changes' such as the shift to an information based society, internationalisation in many sectors and the maturing of the society, that is the ageing of the population, made countermeasures necessary, especially with regard to the excessive credentialism (Rinkyooshin, 1988, 71, 170, 279).

In order to get rid of the undue emphasis on formal schooling NCER underlined that:

Both industrial enterprises and government offices [must] improve their hiring practices and personnel management in order to revise the situation wherein people are evaluated on the basis of formal schooling. We must prompt a change in people's consciousness so that a person can be evaluated on the actual results of his learning regardless of when and where it was obtained — a more faceted evaluation. (Rinkyooshin, 1988, 71)

This meant that the doors to government and industrial employment should be more open to those with diverse talents, not just to new graduates. Thus talent, or skill, rather than credentials was to be emphasised if NCER had its way. The uniform criteria of evaluation were to be done away with. NCER emphasised that while the evaluation by society and others was indeed important, so was the self-evaluation and self-respect of people undertaking life-long learning. Without a change of the evaluation practice the incentive for people to under-take life-long learning would be insignificant. Diverse types of ability, and outstanding ability, should be given positive attention instead of disappearing in the prevailing evaluation method based on average marks, which invariably favours those able to obtain high marks in almost all subjects (Rinkyooshin, 1988, 71, 170-74, 283).

Further, NCER anticipated that industrial firms would come to depend more and more on mid-career hiring and transfers of workers, which would also require a new method for assessing diverse talents and abilities (Rinkyooshin, 1988, 174-75). NCER had the support of industry for this claim in the form of the Education Council's (Japan Committee for Economic Development) proposal in which a 'revision of personnel evaluation standards in business enterprises and government agencies' was recommended. Employees' individuality and special skills should be respected to a greater extent it was stated, and the industry would have to realise the great impact of their recruitment policy on the educational field. (Keizai Dooyuukai, 1984, 36)

In NCER's interpretation, a serious problem was generated by the uniform evaluation method, in that the use of this method resulted in outstanding abilities only being recognised with difficulty. They felt that Japan would have a problem in the future 'keeping up with other nations' in fields such as science and technology, education, culture, sports, politics, and economy. If Japan was to be able to make any contributions to the welfare of mankind, it would be essential to have creative people in the 21st century, that is, to cater especially for those showing outstanding abilities in a particular field (Rinkyooshin, 1988, 172).

It was not the value of evaluation as such which was questioned. It was the mission of evaluation which was interpreted in a new manner:

Evaluation is not just useful for bestowing credentials and qualifications. It becomes meaningful when its results are used in educational institutions, homes, communities and workplaces. As a result, we hope that people's urge to learn will increase, and that there will be improvements in space and time for such activities. (Rinkyooshin, 1988, 171)

NCER detected, as a result of the increase in income and leisure time, a new tendency for people to enjoy learning for its own sake. It was said that 'people's voluntary activities for learning are basic activities for life-long learning which lead to a fulfilling and worthwhile human life' (Rinkyooshin, 1988, 176, 285). NCER decidedly wanted to encourage the various learning activities in non-formal education that this had created, be it in special schools or nongovernmental cultural programmes, because those initiatives had shown an ability to cope flexibly with the needs and demands of the public.

In addition to supporting spontaneous initiatives, NCER also requested closer, organised interaction between educational and research organs and society, in order to cope with the learning demands created by the advancement of science and technology and the flow of information. This would, among other things, mean that institutions of higher learning should more readily accept working adults as students, and to this end they should develop new contents and methods of education as well as new scientific disciplines[13] (Rinkyooshin, 1988, 71, 17, 285).

Connected with accepting working adults into institutions of higher learning was the problem that some adults had previously had insufficient access to formal education. NCER deplored the 'vertical structure' of learning opportunities, which had resulted in each sector operating separately. There was a lack of cooperation between different sectors of education and between different government agencies and establishments, and the ensuing inadequacy of collaboration between formal and non-formal education caused limited access to educational facilities for individual learners.

The Kyoto Group had also touched upon this saying that it was 'worth considering a system whereby students without a high school diploma can still hope to acquire qualifications for higher education or employment', but this group's efforts at flexibility in education were mainly directed at children and young people, not so much at adults who were the target group of NCER's deliberations on life-long learning (Kyoto Group, 1984, 32).

NCER proposed more extensive use of the 'horizontal system' to replace the 'vertical system', in which the home and the community was included in the learning activities along with the schools. To support this, the introduction of the five-day week for workers was proposed — to give them time for learning activities — along with the upgrading of the social value of various occupational qualifications (Rinkyooshin, 1988, 72).

The perceived need for upgrading vocational qualifications indicated that there was a problem with the social status of manual workers. Industry wanted earlier specialisation of workers, but it was difficult to attract people to the vocational courses as long as higher status — and higher salaries — were attached to academic secondary education. The fact that this problem was very real and of concern to NCER was evident in numerous places in the reports. For example, the third report said that when it came to employment and treatment, graduates from special schools should be given equal status to graduates from secondary schools or institutions of higher learning with similar lengths of

---

13. NCER probably had in mind such subjects as 'information processing' which had been introduced at the University of Tsukuba in the 1970s.

schooling (Rinkyooshin, 1988, 174, 176, 284). In other words, the social status of vocational education was to be improved by eradicating differences in perceived status of secondary schools, high schools and vocational or special schools in the recruitment and employment situation.

Another measure for inspiring more people to undertake vocational training was a review of the system for granting official vocational qualifications, in essence it was a relaxation of the licensing system. Specific requirements for formal educational background were to be eliminated in order to duly evaluate those who may have the vocational capabilities but not the formal background. However, exceptions could be made, NCER suggested, for those types of qualifications requiring high-level specialized knowledge and skills. Though relaxing the requirements for formal background, NCER's proposal was not an overall loosening up. They proposed new measures for maintaining the proper level of knowledge and skills once the official qualifications had been recognised, particularly for jobs in which antiquated or insufficient knowledge could cause risks to human life or the human body (Rinkyooshin, 1988, 172-74, 284).

The role of home and community in education was allotted much importance by NCER. The home was to be the starting point of a 'lifetime of learning', it was to ensure the formation of a basic sound relationship of mutual trust between parents and children, as well as helping children acquire discipline and basic manners in daily life. With the nuclearisation of the family pattern, NCER felt that the opportunities for young people to gain the traditional life experiences needed for their own development and growth had decreased. Hence, more importance should be placed on children's games and the role of the neighbourhood in education. NCER hoped that invigorating the community's educational facilities, i.e., providing more opportunities of contact with nature and voluntary educational activities, would make it easier for younger generations to inherit the traditional culture (Rinkyooshin, 1988, 72-74, 284).

The references to home, neighbourhood and traditional culture carried various implicit statements with them. Emphasis on traditional culture and the transmission of it from generation to generation was a deeply felt conservative concern evident in Nakasone's opening remarks to NCER as well as in the proposals from the business groups. Nakasone talked about 'preserving and developing the traditional Japanese culture' and the business groups emphasised moral education and the need for a mastery of one's own culture in order to be able to understand other cultures (Kyoto Group, 1984, 34; Keizai Dooyuukai, 1984, 40; Rinkyooshin, 1988, 323).

The emphasis on the role of home and neighbourhood implicitly attacked women or more precisely, working women. An important factor in restoring the educational function of the home would undoubtedly have been to keep mothers at home, but this was never stated explicitly by NCER, presumably because it was realised that such suggestions would become targets of severe criticism from both native and foreign sources. Nevertheless, as NCER apparently did not anticipate great numbers of men being in the neighbourhood — they would either work or attend adult education courses — the task of enriching the neighbourhood and the family would fall on women. Given the male dominance in NCER it is perhaps not so surprising that this consequence of the proposal was not discussed.

Another interesting point in the NCER line of argumentation was faith in the community or neighbourhood (*chiiki*) as an institution capable of contributing to the education and raising of children. As there were no qualifying remarks to this term we are left with the impression that it means the modern urban neighbourhood inhabited by women and children. NCER's reference to the neighbourhood may be an example of the tradition of using hamlets or villages as administrative units, seeing them almost as extended families. Many anthropologists use villages as their objects of observation as well — they may even speak of 'my village' — but the question is, whether the average village or neighbourhood of today is actually a unit. Alienation and non-involvement is known in many Japanese urban areas as it is in cities all over the world, and this, paired with a lack of neighbourhood facilities which often accompanies urban settings, would make it extremely difficult for many neighbourhoods to function as NCER has suggested.

To enhance the influence of home and community and recover and utilise their educational potential, the limits of the school ought to be clarified, NCER maintained. It was felt that many of the tasks then assumed by the school should appropriately be performed in homes or communities. Again, NCER was not very clear about how the home and community should handle these tasks or what they were, and one can only assume that NCER had the housewife as well as the traditional idea of the neighbourhood as an extended family-like unit in mind, which, as mentioned above, is at best a very unclear reference.

Further NCER lamented the fact that an unduly large part of children's lives was taken up by formal schooling and intellectual training, and they considered relegation of tasks to other sectors of children's daily lives desirable. This theme of the unduly large part school played in children's lives was also often touched upon by the opposition. For instance, the interview with WDCER representative Higuchi Keiko, started off with her expressing regrets about this aspect of Japanese education. To support the home in assessing its role in relation to school and society, NCER proposed enrichment courses in the art of parenting. The content of the school subject 'home-making' was to be reviewed, counselling services and maternity/infant-care leave for women should be made more widely available, and women's discussion groups should be encouraged. Here at last it became clear that, in NCER's opinion, the task of restoring the educational function of the home fell on women.

The community — whoever this may be — was to participate by helping children develop sentiments such as reverence for life and nature, by providing them with direct experiences of nature and by establishing exchange programmes so that urban children could get an opportunity to live in rural areas and vice versa (Rinkyooshin, 1988, 284).

Clearly this required a well-functioning community with the degree of administration suited to take care of such programmes, but suggestions for actual procedures were not made by NCER. It remained unclear then, whether these tasks were to be taken care of by local government officials or whether they were to be performed on the initiative of community members.

Concretely, NCER proposed among other things the five-day school week. This brought about the need for reducing the work-load of schools and further re-adjusting the role of the home and the community in education, so that 'the educational functions as a whole in society may be maintained or improved' (Rinkyooshin, 1988, 75-76). Interpreting this last proposal, it seems clear enough that while the five-day week necessarily entails a reduction of the workload in school, it does not mean a reduction of the total workload of the children. The tasks given up by school were to be taken up by the home and the community, so that the 'educational functions as a whole may be maintained or improved'. Although this was to be done with the 'position of the children as a central concern', it does not strike one as an obvious solution to the problem of intellectual training taking up too much of the children's lives. In practice the curriculum has become more compressed as explained in section 4.1, so the idea apparently is to make children learn more in less time, or use more out-of-school time for learning.

Another concrete proposal for restoring the educational effect of home and community was opening further the functions and facilities of educational institutions to people and the community. In principle, such facilities had been open for some time to the public, but with the provision that public use did not 'hamper school activities' and this clause apparently was interpreted in a very narrow manner. NCER wanted to make schools adapt more to the community and to make unequivocal regulations for opening facilities to the public. NCER envisaged that activities such as cultural and sports activities and non-formal education for adults and out-of-school youths would take place in the schools, and further, schools ought to find ways of using community people as part-time school instructors to teach the culture and history of the community (Rinkyooshin, 1988, 76-77). In this manner the problem of lack of common facilities as experienced by many urban neighbourhoods could be solved.

Finally, the establishment of community centres within universities, to conduct training and research for the promotion of local industries, was proposed. This was not only to benefit local industry, but also to make sure that learning and study for adults would focus on problem-solving and relate to their own role in the community. To further inspire adults to learn more, NCER recommended that arrangements such as allotting certain university credits for extension courses should be considered. NCER acknowledged that by then some universities and junior colleges had already set up 'extension centres' to offer community members various services for learning, and felt that such initiatives should be encouraged and further developed in the future (Rinkyooshin, 1988, 77).

The role of elementary education in the concept of life-long learning was stated as being that of enabling children to acquire basic skills and knowledge as well as having them develop a capacity for independent learning — learning how to learn. Education should be adapted to the developmental stage of the child and the promotion of the vocational tracks in education was emphasised.

The perceived future manpower requirements prompted NCER to propose a new system in which children would be adequately versed in the basics of reading, writing and arithmetic to fulfil future occupations, on the one hand, while on the other, that the career guidance system in secondary schools was to be reviewed in order to help children choose a career suited to their own personalities and aptitudes. Vocational education was to be enriched and children should be better acquainted with the realities of production and work. The efforts were to be concentrated around promotion of the vocational tracks.

The task of higher education was defined as being that of helping students acquire specific skills and knowledge in specialised fields as well as developing broad powers of thinking. Also, NCER urged that efforts be made to invigorate the educational function of institutions of higher learning. Probably this last proposal was a result of the above mentioned widespread tendency of putting emphasis on the place of study rather than the nature of study (Rinkyooshin, 1988, 72-74, 285).

Another concern which apparently prodded the request for invigorating the educational function of institutions of higher learning was that those institutions had, according to NCER, often been criticised for being too isolated from the demands of society. As NCER explained it, part of the reason for this problem was in the way employers saw universities in particular, namely as nothing more than 'agencies for selecting human resources'. The usual policy of recruitment was to select employees from among new university graduates based on their university *entrance* examination marks (their 'deviation values' *hensachi*). NCER proposed to change this by requiring students to acquire specialised skills at university as well as problem-solving ability and thinking power, which would enable them to adapt to the demands of a society undergoing rapid changes. Thus the universities would have to make their structures of teaching and learning relevant to the development of society and the advance of science and technology (Rinkyooshin, 1988, 74).

One would think that in order for this to materialise it would be imperative to introduce a kind of graduation examination assessing the accomplishments of the graduates for use by future employers. This would at least have eliminated the need for 'recruitment examinations', which are common practice today, but NCER did not touch upon this problem. One can only assume, then, that NCER found it quite appropriate that the assessment of the special skills supposed to have been obtained through university studies should take place at the point of recruitment and be conducted by the employer rather than by the university.

However, a change of the recruitment procedures did form an integral part of the efforts to correct the adverse effects of over-emphasis on educational background. Traditional procedures like selection of recruits from among the graduates of a limited number of universities (the most prestigious ones in terms of desirable employment positions) should be abolished, as well as the illegal practice of approaching prospective graduates before the official date from which recruitment was allowed. All new recruits should be given equal status regardless of educational background, that is, in the recruitment procedures the graduates from special training schools should not be discriminated against by being unfavourably compared with graduates of secondary school or higher education (Rinkyooshin, 1988, 284).

But what was to make industry work in earnest for those goals? How were they to select the 'best' graduates with the largest potential if not by school certificates? By further developing their recruitment test?[14] The NCER provided no answers, and though there is more mobility in the workforce than ever (Kusaoi, 1988, 4), the race for hiring the most desirable graduates is also as fierce as ever. The problem is that there are three times more jobs than male graduates[15] from top-universities, and the race to recruit these attractive graduates (of Tokyo, Kyoto, Keioo, Meiji, Hoosei, Waseda etc.) is of great intensity.[16]

As long as there is no suitable substitute for the certificates as a sorting mechanism, particularly for recruits for middle and higher managerial posts,

14. Some conduct a written exam, which could easily be put to more use. Usually the personal interview and the school certificate is used as a basis for recruitment. (Ishikawa, 1991, 197)

15. Male graduates are still more attractive to Japanese firms than female graduates. Firstly, girls often go to junior college (*tanki daigaku*) instead of university and in that case presumably are not so well educated. Secondly, girls are expected to marry and stop working in their mid- or late twenties — which they in fact usually do — and therefore are not suitable for career tracks.

16. An article on the subject humorously entitled 'The Wooing of Yoohei' gives a vivid account of the amount of gifts, postal and telephone messages and personal encounters involved in this courtship. Note that it is the employer who does the courting! (Logan, 1990, 8)

desirable jobs will still be given to graduates who have proved their potential by being able to enter a top-university. Vague statements of intention like those of the NCER do not by themselves make a change. However, it seems that the employers on their own initiative have started to recruit employees with untraditional backgrounds for particular positions, so the picture is changing, though probably not as a direct consequence of any government initiative.

As for higher education it could be vitalised and play an important part in life-long learning if it would provide the opportunity for adults to learn. The strong focus on young people should be given up, NCER proposed, and institutions of higher education should make efforts to respond to the needs of technicians, engineers, researchers and others who wished to learn. With adults in mind, NCER recommended that they develop and improve their facilities. Further, employers should consider the option of using overseas universities for off-the-job training of workers, especially workers destined to take overseas positions.

Necessary changes in the university system to adjust for the admission of adults would include changing the entrance examinations, more flexible curricula, new teaching and evaluation methods, to name but a few. In fact, NCER recommended that institutions of higher education reserve a specific number of places for working adults, so that a 'substantial' proportion of the students would be adults (Rinkyooshin, 1988, 74-75, 172, 175, 285).

This was bound to create problems. Already there was a massive pressure on the prestigious universities and this would be further aggravated by reducing the number of places available for newly graduated high school students. Presumably, NCER hoped to direct a larger number of students towards the less sought after vocational institutions, thus alleviating the pressure on the universities.

Reflections on how to make it possible for part-timers to acquire university degrees ought to be included in deliberations on changes of course structure and duration of courses, NCER suggested. Also, to provide incentives to motivate working adults into joining university courses (other than the incentive of acquiring a university degree), NCER proposed that employers not only gave favourable consideration to employees enrolled in an educational institution, but also that the employers developed a means of evaluating and utilising such newly acquired knowledge, thereby ensuring the equal evaluation of *all* learning results, regardless of *when* they were obtained (Rinkyooshin, 1988, 74-5).

The fourth report made much of emphasising the importance of supporting the physical exercise activities of the population, both mass and elite sports under the headline of life-long learning activities. The efforts in this area apparently were designed to allow Japan to manifest itself more strongly in the international world of sports, judging by proposals such as the establishment of sports curricula, an appropriate coach system, better opportunities for active players and others to participate in international games, etc. (Rinkyooshin, 1988, 286).

The references to sport and to health (*kenkoo*), that is, to a healthy body and mind, were certain to elicit positive reactions in the public. Indeed the association of sport and health was also in some cases supplemented by the equally positive word richness/abundance (*yutakasa*) as can be seen in the subtitle of the 1992 Ministry of Education white paper: *Supootsu to Kenkoo — Yutaka na Mirai ni Mukete* (Sport and Health — Facing a Rich Future).

The last feature of the life-long learning concept was the development of life-long learning towns and centres. In order to provide all learners with facilities in which they could choose at their own discretion the ways and means of learning, the whole community should cooperate in creating adequate facilities, NCER stated. The responsibility aspect of the individual was strongly underlined. NCER recommended that the heavy-weight subjects in the life-long learning facilities should be information technology, internationalisation and measures to cope with the ageing of society, as well as activities based on personal interests and hobbies to give them a function in the social life of the individual.

Life-long learning centres and towns could be rooted in cooperation between educational, research, sports and cultural facilities, but efforts should also be made to develop towns where life-long learning activities were especially promoted. NCER urged local governments to select a certain number of distinctive municipalities, designating them as model municipalities (Rinkyooshin, 1988, 177, 286-87).

Such model projects should open their activities to all levels of society, including industrial firms — who in turn were expected to open their facilities to outsiders — and increase their activities for international cooperation, such as the exchange of scholars and students and cultural and sports exchanges. Also, life-long learning municipalities should consider such projects as: cooperation with school, experimenting with a five-day school week, developing data banks and networks, developing training programmes for volunteers, taking advantage of the teaching provided by the University of the Air, using satellites for developing international networks etc.

The University of the Air or *Hoosoo Daigaku* was established in 1983 as a new concept of university in order to adapt to the age of life-long learning. It provides higher education by utilising television and radio lessons and videos, supported by occasional classroom sessions and individual guidance from teachers. Initially its area of transmission was limited to the *Tokyo*-area (*Kantoo*), but plans have been made for it to become nationwide (Monbushoo, 1987, 55). NCER suggested that this University of the Air should endeavour to develop new modes of teaching and learning in order to expand the learning opportunities further.

NCER felt that facilities for life-long learning should also be very conscious of environment, in the sense that beautiful surroundings, well-developed transportation systems and the like would be important supporting structures for people's learning activities. Though essentially funded locally or privately, NCER suggested that life-long learning initiatives ought to receive assistance from the national government in the way of permission to use facilities which are owned by the national government, for example (Rinkyooshin, 1988, 178-79, 285-87).

A feature of life-long learning which was elaborated upon at length by NCER, was making facilities more 'intelligent' (*interigentoka*), meaning that modern technology should be used to a greater extent. In a rather detailed section of the third report NCER suggested that life-long learning facilities be equipped with advanced information and communication media, particularly in areas with limitations in space and time such as remote areas. The idea of the 'intelligent school' was also aired. This was a school into which was fused the functions of research institutes, public libraries, public halls, museums, art galleries, gymnasiums, cultural halls, conversation lobbies and dining rooms. In such a construction all the mentioned facilities could take advantage of the modern technology available and limitations of space and time would be diminished, NCER expected.

NCER proposed such constructions to enable communities to cope with more diversified and individualised learning activities and to improve the functions of education, including an important matter such as the development of information literacy. The guidelines for these 'intelligent' facilities were extremely detailed right down to the nature of the equipment, the lay-out of the surroundings and the possibility of lending part of the facilities to outside agencies or people. Being 'on the alert' was necessary with regard to the impact on human beings and the limitations of science and technology, especially what was called 'the dark side of the spread of information technology' such as the implications of information technology for nature and culture, and for people's practical and direct experiences (Rinkyooshin, 1988, 179-83, 286-87).

In the life-long learning project, the establishment of life-long learning centres and towns, and particularly the use of modern information technology, was apparently the prime concern of NCER, judging by the amount of detail with which this was treated. The other issues of new evaluation procedures, a strengthened role for neighbourhood and family in education, and the orientation of higher education towards vocational training and courses for working adults, was treated in less detail and caused much less opposition.

4.3.2 Views on life-long learning

The ATU mainly saw life-long learning as an expression of NCER's concern for industrial needs. As production would progressively shift from heavy to more refined industry, workers would have to be retrained. This would be a costly affair for industry to undertake on its own, so ATU believed that the government and NCER had come up with life-long learning as a hidden subsidy to industry. The public would supply the legal framework for the learning demands of industry, (organised independently of industry itself), and in most cases individuals would pay themselves for the received education.

In their argumentation against this particular type of life-long learning, ATU referred to the existing Public Education Law (*Shakai Kyooiku Rei*) which they felt was quite adequate for adult education but which operated with a type of adult education which was of a different nature than NCER's life-long learning. Life-long learning would be a more centralistic affair, the contents of it decided by the administration, whereas adult education under the Public Education Law was largely undertaken on local initiative. As the ATU representative put it:

One does try to create many places for [life-long learning] to take place, public and private, but the contents are decided by the state and the administration. The individual is not allowed many choices. NCER's life-long learning is of a very dangerous nature working against the adult education which is already existing. (Interview with Kawai Naoki, May 16, 1991)

The JTU representative recommended that the area of life-long learning was to be less controlled than formal schooling was, but feared a system in which people would have to pay more and get less influence. In JTU's opinion the most important aspect of life-long learning was the chance to return to formal schooling later in life since it would alleviate the pressure on children if they knew they could always come back, and also they emphasised that life-long learning should not only be formal education but also take care of hobbies and cultural activities (interview with Sakai Tomiko, May 7, 1991).

Apart form the fear that the government would attempt to gain control over life-long learning, the JTU was rather positive towards the concept, even to the extent of arousing the anger of ATU who, after the law for life-long learning had materialised in 1990, stated that:

This new law is a basic attack and an attempt to make changes shaking the foundations of FLE and the Constitution, and the organisations organising free workers and education labourers should fight against the implementation of this law. But organisations such as JTU have on the contrary associated themselves with a central organisation like *Rengoo* which calls for acceptance. (Zenkyoo, 1990b, 13)

A pamphlet issued by ATU stated that the effects of realising NCER's life-long learning would be:

1) The content would be decided centrally.
2) Adult education would no longer be autonomous.
3) Private education would take over from public institutions.
4) The whole system would be centralised and standardised.
(Zenkyoo, 1990b, 4)

This pamphlet was issued as a reaction to the passing of the law on life-long learning in June 1990, to be effective from July 1990. The law passed very smoothly through the Diet but in ATU's opinion would ruin current adult education which was based on the Public Education Law. Further, ATU also found the new law unconstitutional.

For ATU the following was the original democratic idea of adult education, an idea based on the 1985 UNESCO meeting in Paris on adult education:

Real life-long learning is a structure wherein anyone when and where he wishes can have access to the facilities he needs and can learn freely as he pleases ... (Zenkyoo, 1990b, 2)

ATU argued that since the law concerning life-long learning was a full implementation of the NCER proposals and the further elaborations on these proposals worked out by CCE, there were no explanations of the philosophy (*rinen*) behind life-long learning and more seriously, the references to the spirit of FLE and the Constitution which were so important in the Public Education Law were absent from this new law. This lead ATU to conclude that the NCER and government rhetoric on democracy was one of sheer appearances (*tatemae*) only. Further, the way the law was formulated and the lack of statements on the aims of life-long learning led — in ATU eyes — to grotesque claims by institutions such as the National Police Agency that they housed life-long learning facilities because they ran driving schools (Zenkyoo, 1990b, 5-6, 13).

Professor Amano Ikuo of Tokyo University suggested an ideal for life-long learning based on the *iemoto*-tradition. In the *iemoto*-tradition one would join a master practising the skill in question (flower arrangement, ceramics etc.) and learn from the master until eventually becoming a master oneself. Likewise, Professor Amano suggested an ideal of life-long learning in which the demarkation line between student and teacher was not so pronounced, an ideal of learning together and from each other (Amano, 1990, 36).

ATU also worried over the administrative structure of the new life-long learning. An office for life-long learning had been established in the Ministry of Education and the responsibility for promotion of life-long learning was delegated to the Minister of Education and the Minister of International Trade an Industry. The administration of the area was to be conducted by way of these offices, not the local and prefectural school boards. So, there would be no local participation in the official life-long learning commissions wherein the chairman would have the right to veto any proposal. ATU concluded that the law was undemocratic as well as unconstitutional and indeed poison to the adult education efforts which had taken place under the auspices of the old Public Education Law (Zenkyoo, 1990b, 6-7, 11).

As for the concrete contents of the law ATU criticised the following: The encouragement of private enterprises in life-long learning was pure NCER and *Rinchoo* policy, that is, a policy which would only benefit the business world and disregard the problems which might occur if profit interests took over education. In relation to the formal system of schooling, ATU maintained that this law could not help having an effect, primarily because the new life-long learning office in the Ministry of Education was to counsel and offer help in matters of formal education, but also because in effect the law was a guarantee that there would be a private system to cater for those who needed extra tutoring — something which would be needed even more badly with the further compression of the curriculum. This guarantee would serve as an excuse for not adapting the formal system to deal with problem students. Finally the NCER proposal that a five-day school week be considered was interpreted as having the covert aim of securing one more day for private education (Zenkyoo, 1990b, 8-9).

Professor Amano has pointed to the already strong bias towards private enterprise in life-long learning facilities. 'The problem is', he explained, 'that in our country the formal system of schooling is not geared to adults' learning activities' (Amano, 1990, 36).

Since the WDCER had stated that their main concern was education up to the age of eighteen, adult education naturally was out of their scope, but when directly asked, their representative naturally acknowledged the importance of the concept of life-long learning in a greying society and, focusing on the formal educational system, thought that adults should be admitted not only to universities but also to high schools because it was not an optimal situation with only people of the same age cohort attending high school (interview with Higuchi Keiko, June 27, 1991).[17]

---

17. It is curious how you tend to remain a 'child' (*kodomo*) until the end of your schooling in Japan. One may even find universities where the students are referred to as 'children', a practice which WDCER representative Higuchi Keiko found particularly insulting, and something that could hopefully change if larger numbers of 'acknowledged' adults attended formal education.

4.3.3 Facilities for life-long learning

In NCER's plans there were two providers of facilities for life-long learning. One was the formal system of schooling, higher education in particular, the other was private educational enterprises. Higher education was to open more of its courses and lectures to the public and accept more adults in regular courses. The University of the Air (*Hoosoo Daigaku*) was an important player in this as a supplier of correspondence courses and televised and radio lectures and instruction.

The private activities mainly took place in cram school and the so-called culture centres which were facilities established under the Public Education Law. The culture centres were very often sought by middle-aged housewives who would learn for fun, and cram schools, as mentioned in an earlier chapter, provided remedial and extra tutoring mainly for students but some also offered courses for adults. One may talk about a veritable craze for adult learning as a leisure activity. As Professor Amano noted:

In trains you may see office workers with white strands in their hair reading books on complicated matters, while university students read comic books. (Amano, 1990, 34-37)

4.3.4 Conclusions

Life-long learning as a key phrase of NCER was not discussed as extensively as some of the other key phrases. Perhaps because all parties acknowledged the need for extra training, particularly in the use of modern technology. The prime issue became the role of private education enterprises in life-long learning and in relation to this, control of the contents.

Whereas NCER saw a big role for private life-long learning centres, ATU for their part feared what consequences this would have for people's control of their own learning activities. The users of adult education who formerly were learners initiating their own learning activities, would become clients in a private system. With a craze for 'learning for fun' the potential for influencing people with particular ideas was huge.

The issue of private life-long learning was indeed complicated. Some — like the ATU — saw it as a means of disseminating conservative ideology and as the first step towards privatisation of the whole educational system. Others, like former NCER member Minakami Tadashi, were of the opinion that private institutions like cram schools would have no role to play in life-long learning because they were mainly geared for tutoring relating directly to examinations in school. Cram schools offering more hobby-oriented activities like piano lessons or lessons in the use of the Japanese abacus (*soroban*), should be part of life-long learning, he felt (interview with Minakami Tadashi, May 31, 1991). Culture and hobbies were expected to be a large part of the activities and probably in this area opposition like ATU had less fears. What loomed ominous in the discourse on life-long learning was the perspective of increased central control with the flow of information. This issue will be further treated in chapter 4. 5. on the adaptation to the information society.

In itself the law on life-long learning issued in 1990 was so much in accord with NCER's proposals that it offers further proof to the contestation that the NCER reports have been central documents in national educational policy since Nakasone. The proposals offered by NCER on life-long learning were accepted virtually unchanged and with the shortcomings they contained. The law on life-long learning was passed without a statement on the philosophical foundation of this kind of education. The effect of this lack of ideals is that life-long learning can be anything the life-long learning office and the government wants it to be, be it the police driving schools or courses in flower arranging, or engineering. There is no legal indication of direction or purposes, the issue is left open ended. It is of course dangerous to make conclusions based on what is *not* there, but it is entirely probable that the main inspiration for including the issue of life-long learning was the need for further manpower development combined with the international popularity the concept enjoyed after the 1985 UNESCO meeting.

4.4 Internationalisation

The third catchword of the NCER reform proposals was 'internationalisation' or *kokusaika* as it was termed in Japanese. The then Prime Minister Nakasone, in a speech delivered at the beginning of the NCER deliberations, requested that NCER give advice on how to make education compatible with the 'trends of internationalisation in various sectors' (Rinkyooshin, 1988, 5). Unlikely though it may seem, internationalisation became associated with nationalism in Japan. As a representative of the teacher organisation ATU deftly put it, using a pun: 'NCER's internationalisation is not *kokusaika* but *kokusuika* (ultranationalism)' (interview with Kawai Naoki, May 16, 1993).

Mouer and Sugimoto in their book 'Images of Japanese Society' (1986) devoted a chapter to the analysis of the meaning of internationalisation in Japanese terms. The term was an all-time favourite in advertising and the mass media and they found that to most Japanese it signified something positive. However, discussions of internationalisation tended to centre on *activities* rather than *ends*. Instrumental activities such as learning English, travelling overseas, teaching more about foreign cultures in Japanese schools etc, were steps towards an undefined goal, which it turned out to be impossible to make the Japanese define further.

Mouer and Sugimoto found two dominating goals for internationalisation reflected in the media. One was the goal of smooth promotion of Japan's national interests, mainly in economic terms. This was the view held by the establishment, LDP, business, in short, the conservative camp. It demanded understanding from the foreigners and tended to explain economic frictions in terms of cultural misunderstanding — unfortunate clashes in cultural style. Hence the establishment deemed it important for successful internationalisation to instruct foreigners in Japanese culture and language, while also ensuring that the Japanese themselves were well aware of their cultural heritage (Mouer & Sugimoto, 1986, 380-83).

Apparently, internationalisation in official terms was more about widening knowledge and understanding of Japan abroad, than teaching about foreign cultures and languages at home. As Peter Dale explained it, 'spreading knowledge of Japan abroad was seen as an indispensable device for bolstering Japan's national security', and arguments for larger investments in language programmes and culture centres abroad were buttressed by suggestions that 'the coming economic war will be a war of cultures in which the way foreigners interpret the Japanese mind will be decisive' (Dale, 1990, 19).

This projection of culture abroad constituted part of the 'internationalisation' efforts. Quite apart from the slightly ethnocentric aspect of this projection, it also served as a cover-up device. In Peter Dale's words:

Discussions on economic and diplomatic conflicts are entangled in dubious references to the decisive differences in mentality and culture, a tactic which often relies upon the outsider's ignorance, or his inability to verify such claims. Often the argument of culture is used astutely and consciously to deflect attention from the real problems at issue, or to rationalise a refusal to concede ground on issues that primarily involve economic interests. (Dale, 1990, 19)

A concrete example of this tendency in the establishment's opinion of internationalisation can be found in the second NCER report where it was said that:

Presently, Japan's economy is prosperous due to close economic relations with all countries in the world. With economic relations come human relations, and as direct personal contacts increase, the number of what may be termed 'cultural frictions' also increase. Such frictions should be considered normal in an international society and we envisage a new way of life which can change this into energy for vitalising Japanese society. (Rinkyooshin, 1988, 129)

Morita Toshio, formerly the director of the Citizens' Institute for Educational Research affiliated with JTU, found that NCER had uncritically accepted these ideas and thought that they failed to acknowledge that the 'clashes in cultural style' were not caused by erroneous or incomplete understanding of Japanese culture but by Japanese economic behaviour. Solving the problem by providing foreign countries with deep knowledge of the unique Japanese culture was in Morita's opinion sheer imperialism (Morita, 1988, 47-8).

Internationalisation in the establishment version had nationalistic ingredients in so far as it was used as a device in an economic war — or at least in economic relations, and this enculturation of politics — that is, making the strengthening of Japan's culture and economy the goal of internationalisation — made it difficult to argue with the concept of internationalisation for both Japanese and others.

Though Peter Dale presented his case very convincingly, picturing the Japanese efforts as being directed at self-enhancement and guided by nationalism, one must not forget that a much similar rhetoric can be found in other countries trying to define themselves in a global context. However, there is little doubt that Dale's interpretation was shared by the Japanese opposition.

This anti-establishment or progressive-camp interpretation, held true internationalisation to be a means of securing world peace through international brotherhood or, for the most radical, even a world government. This group was motivated by a perceived need for changing Japan's role in the world community, involving a change of Japanese government as well, the last aspect of course being the main source of disharmony with the establishment (Mouer & Sugimoto, 1986, 382).

Though not quite as radical as to demand a world government the teacher organisation ATU said about internationalisation that:

Genuine international understanding and consciousness is a necessity, not least for the sake of peace and the world environment. A country cannot take care of these things on its own, so it follows that a more international orientation is necessary to be successful in securing peace and a clean environment. (Interview with Kawai Naoki, May 16, 1991)

Though ATU and NCER agreed that Japan could not stand on its own in the world, their statements had different backgrounds. The ATU emphasis here was quite clearly placed on what might be termed 'human' values rather than on economy. This oppositional view of internationalisation was propagated in a proliferation of publications from the teacher organisation, bearing titles such as 'Listen to the Voice of Hiroshima' (*Hiroshima no Koe o Kikoo*), 'For the Children's Happy Future' (*Kodomotachi no shiawase na Ashita no tame ni*) and badges with inscriptions such as 'Children's greatest treasure is peace' (*Kodomotachi no saikoo no takara wa heiwa desu*).

Morita Toshio also found the motivations of the establishment dubious. He argued that NCER's version of internationalisation would rekindle Japanese militarism and imperialism and that the hidden ambition of the Japanese ruling class was a 'pax Japonica' hegemony over Asia and the Pacific. He emphasised that a scientific and balanced approach to the realities of world history, in which reform proposals based on theories of 'Japanese culture' were firmly rejected, was absolutely necessary to counter this movement towards nationalism (Morita, 1988, 12).

Morita was supported by his successor to the director post, Igasaki Akio, who, in an interview with Mark Lincicome in 1989, further emphasised the economic aspect by describing NCER's policy on internationalisation as economically inspired, Japan-centred and more nationalistic (*kokusuika*) than international in orientation. Igasaki also emphasised the proper goals of internationalisation as being those of securing world peace, opposing the proliferation of nuclear weapons, supporting environmental issues and contributing to the advancement of education in developing countries (Lincicome, 1993, 131).

As for the opinion of the ordinary Japanese citizen, Mouer and Sugimoto concluded from their findings that the ordinary citizen probably did not distinguish between these conflicting goals of internationalisation, but that he was spurred mostly by self interest and could swing in either direction, depending on what seemed to be the most promising (Mouer & Sugimoto, 1986, 380-83).

The two different interpretations of the nature of internationalisation stood out clearly in the debate on educational reform. The establishment needed internationalisation to ensure that Japan would not stop developing its economy and its share of the world market, while also maintaining its cultural integrity. The anti-establishment, in this case mainly the teacher organisations, were occupied with avoiding the horrors of war, with attaining world peace and understanding, and in the final analysis, perhaps even with overthrowing the government.

This conflict of goals quite naturally led to accusations that the internationalisation NCER was talking about was mainly a domestic or even a nationalistic concern.

4.4.1 Internationalisation in NCER terms

'Internationalisation' in Japan had meant 'catching up' with the industrialised world, but as Japan had in fact more than caught up, NCER declared that it was time for Japan to 'actively contribute in various fields to the peace and prosperity of mankind and to carry out relevant responsibilities as a member of the international community'. Again we see one of the five Nakasone ground rules reflected.

NCER described internationalisation as a concept which varied with the conditions:

Actually, the concrete contents of internationalisation change with the times. A policy based on today's conditions may be out of date tomorrow. Internationalisation is a *process* of accumulation of people's daily practices while constantly reflecting on the meaning of this concept. (Rinkyooshin, 1988, 234)

With a definition like this, one should clearly not expect any quick-acting medicine which would internationalise Japanese education overnight. NCER explicitly stated that it would be a process of repeated trial and error, groping to find the way and attempting to change the consciousness of the Japanese. Therefore one should not be afraid of failure but persist in the efforts, NCER stated (Rinkyooshin, 1988, 234).

The immediate reason for this emphasis on internationalisation apparently was to be found in problems at university level in particular. NCER in its description of the state of education at the time dealt, from the internationalisation point of view, primarily with the universities, saying that they had few educational and research activities of a high enough standard to earn them an international reputation. Also, NCER claimed that in respect to such areas as exchange of researchers and the teaching of foreign languages, Japanese universities had failed to respond to the need for internationalisation (Rinkyooshin, 1988, 7).

These ideas had also been aired by the business group the Education Council. Further, when NCER stated that the Japanese people ought to contribute internationally, to be tolerant of other cultures while not losing sight of their own, they were again handling issues which had also been requested by the Education Council. The Education Council had stated that:

There is no guarantee that man's mind will be further directed towards the outside with progress of economic internationalisation. In our country, the closed door trend deeply remains not only towards foreign nations but in many domestic areas also. (Keizai Dooyuukai, 1984, 40)

The theme of tolerance for other cultures, while maintaining affection for and mastery of one's own, was an area which the Education Council termed 'essential'. The themes taken up by NCER under the headline of internationalisation were remarkably similar to those noted by the Education Council. (Keizai Dooyuukai, 1984, 40)

Continuing the line of argument from the previous identification of the main source of problems, NCER saw as the main remedy an upgrading of education and research, especially at universities. The goal was to make these institutions more open to the international community. It was clear from NCER's initial statements on this subject that the target area was the universities, but there was also the already mentioned concern that too much internationalisation might make the Japanese lose their identity as Japanese. This was clear from the repeated provisions made in relation to internationalisation:

From now on the Japanese must have a deep understanding, respect and affection for Japanese culture as well as be tolerant towards other cultures. (...) It must be understood that a good world citizen (*yoki kokusaijin*) is also a good Japanese (*yoki nihonjin*), and our education must teach people love of country (*kuni o aisuru kokoro*) and a firm sense of the individuality of the Japanese culture as well as deepen the knowledge of the culture and traditions of all foreign countries. (Rinkyooshin, 1988, 15-16)

And further:

... people must strive to gain the ability of reviewing the situation in Japan relative to the values and traditions of other cultures. (Rinkyooshin, 1988, 240)

Profound knowledge of Japanese culture and a realisation of the relativity of Japanese values vis à vis other values was a prerequisite of international acceptance in NCER terms. The wording employed by NCER in this section was quite emotional as is clear from expressions such as 'have a deep understanding, respect and affection (*keiai*) for Japanese culture' and later: 'love of country' (Rinkyooshin, 1988, 15). The term *keiai* has been translated as simply 'love' in the English version of the report, but this fails to deliver the nuance of 'respect' which is also implied in the term. This particular term was the one used in connection with the Emperor in earlier more nationalistic days when one was to show *keiai* (respect and affection) towards the Emperor.

This particular emotional tone appealed to people's national feelings, to the eternal xenophobia so well-known in many countries, that the peculiarities of the culture would disappear in the contact with larger units of culture. Whether or not this fear is reasonable is not the issue. Here it is limited to an observation that fear of being swallowed up by an unidentified 'international community' apparently was one of the factors prompting NCER to emphasise Japanese culture and history in the context of internationalisation. Not only was this interpreted as nationalism by the opposition, it was also accused of backstabbing the whole plan of internationalisation and gave rise to the *kokusuika* rhetoric of the opposition. The opposition would argue that this emphasis on Japanese culture and 'Japaneseness' only made sense in the context of internationalisation if one saw the aim of internationalisation as being that of furthering one single country's international influence, namely that of Japan, and not that of creating a brotherhood of man. No allowances were given by the opposition for the idea that probably every existing country will try to define itself in an international context and define its international role. The latter is no doubt also part of the motivation, but at the same time there can be little doubt that the main emphasis was on what would further a conservative Japan and its economy. The three motivating factors for NCER then were: a) fear of losing national identity in a larger context, b) securing the economic position of Japan, and c) defining a role for Japan in the global context.

The reality of the need for Japan to assume responsibility in an international context has been demonstrated in the recent years. We only have to look back to the war in the Persian Gulf to find American misgivings about Japan not demonstrating its responsibility as a member of the international community. But hopes for stronger Japanese involvement in international affairs should not be too high. Even the NCER, which was indeed stating a policy that Nakasone was known to subscribe to, ended its section on internationalisation by saying that 'the main responsibility for realising new internationalisation rests with individual citizens', and as the 'buds of grass-root efforts' have to grow into a national movement before genuine internationalisation can be realised, 'no immediate solution should be expected' (Rinkyooshin, 1989, 281). This was said in 1987 and apparently still has value.

Internationalisation was treated as a long-term project. The first major demonstration of the policy initiated by Nakasone of taking responsibility came as late as in 1992 when in September 1992 the Japanese parliament, the Diet, decided to send 1,500 Peace Preservation Troops to Kampuchea under the UN flag. The law making such an activity possible was passed in the spring of the same year after heated debates and after a lot of opposition tactics for delaying the decision. This was the first time since the Second World War that Japan sent troops overseas.

In the council's agenda for further deliberations it set as the goal a re-examination of a wide range of subjects designed to make Japanese educational institutions more open to the international community. Again institutions of higher education received most attention. The subjects to be deliberated upon were the admission of foreign students to Japanese educational institutions, exchange programmes between Japanese and foreign institutions of higher education, international cooperation in the field of scientific research, education for international understanding, language teaching, education of Japanese children staying abroad and education of Japanese children who have come back from foreign countries after a long stay (Rinkyooshin, 1988, 22).

NCER's internationalisation centred on domestic needs. First the internationalisation was more or less left to an accumulation process which would enable the official Japan to do very little actively because inter-nationalisation was to be 'an accumulation of people's daily practices'. Then the issue of internationalisation was described as concerning higher education mainly as a device of raising the quality of research and education. Internationalisation was not for the compulsory and secondary levels, it would seem, where apparently time was to be spent on learning how to become a 'good Japanese' in order to later become a 'good world citizen'. The NCER rhetoric left no doubt that internationalisation was primarily a domestic matter and that international contacts where education was concerned were mainly to take place at higher levels.

4.4.2 How to internationalise

The five main concerns in NCER's internationalisation efforts were the universities, fostering a 'good' Japanese, the education of Japanese children abroad, how to receive Japanese children who had been abroad for some time and finally the admittance of more foreign students into Japanese educational institutions.

The first concern, which was also the one to receive most attention was that of the universities. The university's international role was described as follows:

The university is international by nature, and scientific research is basically undertaken by all mankind. If our country is to gain respect and trust in an international arena, and in order to make contributions to peace and progress in the world, we must — based on higher education of an international standard — further intensify international exchange in culture and science. (Rinkyooshin, 1988, 118)

NCER proceeded to propose methods for making the universities more international, concentrating on exchange. Exchange of researchers, especially the young, exchange programmes between Japanese and foreign universities, joint international research projects at university level with special consideration for developing countries, stimulation of international activities of learned societies and international exchange of scientific information were among the proposals.

NCER saw it as the task of the universities to develop international-minded citizens through strengthening their programmes related to international understanding and cooperation. This continued the trend from the emphasis on the exchange efforts in which it was repeated over and over again that existing efforts had to be strengthened and reactivated. Apparently, it was perceived that many of the already established programmes did not really work satisfactorily.

NCER called for immediate action in the field of post graduate education. Many students and young researchers had not been provided with the opportunity to study abroad, so in this respect the programmes had to be improved immediately in order to secure an international standard of future research. Also, NCER recommended that the complicated government formalities involved when teachers and researchers of national universities wanted to go abroad should be simplified and be made more flexible. Combined with an increase in the number of foreign researchers accepted at Japanese universities, particularly young researchers, and more favourable conditions for receiving foreign teachers, internationalisation of the university staff was envisaged to take place (Rinkyooshin, 1988, 118-19).

Individual exchange agreements between Japanese and foreign universities should be encouraged, NCER felt, and to help such steps NCER recommended that the Japanese universities should have more autonomy with respect to financial and personnel management. Also, the universities should set up independent funds for international exchange.

International cooperation on particular projects was also encouraged by the NCER, and it was emphasised that cooperation should be undertaken with both advanced and developing countries. With respect to the latter, NCER mentioned that such projects were already underway in the form of a 'core university system'. In this system a number of universities in Japan and a given developing country would cooperate on joint research projects, exchange of researchers and the like. The same system was to provide an opportunity for young researchers in developing countries to obtain a Doctor's degree from a Japanese university (Rinkyooshin, 1988, 119).

Though NCER would continually include the developing countries in its internationalisation proposals, the very fact that the exchange was to take place in advanced fields of education and ironically science would preclude the most underdeveloped nations from participating (Walter Edwards quoted in Lincicome, 1993, 133).

These efforts at internationalising the universities and their activities were to be supported by the provision of adequate human and financial resources. A close liaison was deemed necessary between the Ministry of Education and other bodies involved with the promotion of science in Japan and with international cooperation if the exchange programmes were to be effective. Establishing overseas offices for assisting Japanese researchers sent abroad was also suggested (Rinkyooshin, 1988, 119).

Apparently concerted efforts were to be made aiming at the internationalisation of the universities, but the university staff and students were not asked for their opinion. Of course some of the bodies involved in the coordination had university staff representation, but the universities were clearly not seen by NCER as autonomous bodies with their own opinions and wishes. The Ministry of Education was considered to be the representative of the universities and it would have much influence on university exchange efforts if NCER had its way. Obviously, the Ministry would always have to be involved to some extent since a substantial amount of money would be needed for realising the programmes, but the direct involvement of the universities as responsible for formulating the exchange programmes apparently had low priority.

After having dealt with the university issue in this manner, NCER turned to the question of how to cope with internationalisation more generally: 'We are entering an era of "new internationalisation" in which Japan cannot survive being isolated from today's international community' (Rinkyooshin, 1988, 129).

In the line of argument surrounding this quotation the economic aspect is again clear. The growth Japan had experienced was based on exchange with other countries and through this economic growth the exchange of persons had also become more frequent. This could cause the above mentioned 'cultural frictions' which were to be perceived as normal phenomena in an international community, to be used as energy for vitalising Japanese society. NCER envisaged increased exchanges of persons between countries and saw the resulting 'heart-to-heart' contacts (*kokoro no fureai*) as an insurance of international understanding.

Though the goal may have seemed to be determined by economic considerations, NCER emphasised that the efforts at internationalising should not only be economic but also educational, scientific and cultural. Not only the Japanese educational system but also the *minds* of the Japanese were to be opened to the international community, though as we have already seen, NCER at the same time found it important to foster a good Japanese (*yoki nihonjin*). First, students should be well informed about Japan and then they should be made aware of the different customs and values present in the world. In particular, the lack of knowledge about neighbouring Asian countries was regretted (Rinkyooshin, 1988, 129).

Cooperation and the acknowledgement of differences were the key words in the rhetoric of NCER. The differences between cultures rather than similarities were emphasised, and indeed this fact was much criticised by the opposition.

The responsibility for the realisation of this NCER type of internationalisation was seen as resting with the somewhat ambiguous 'people':

The main agent in the realisation of this new internationalisation is us, the people. One by one we must understand the problems and strive at solving them by letting grass roots efforts grow into a national movement. But no immediate realisation of reform should be expected. (Rinkyooshin, 1988, 130)

The quest of internationalising Japan was to be undertaken with a long-term perspective. The idea of an internationalisation growing from the grassroots level was acceptable to all parties in the debate, though the motivations for this differed. Igasaki Akio of the Citizens' Institute for Educational Research, and Suzuki Isao, director of the government-supported National Institute for

Educational Research (*Kokuritsu Kyooiku Kenkyuujo*) in interviews with Mark Lincicome in 1989 agreed on the necessity for internationalisation to be realised through grassroots efforts, but disagreed on the significance of this. For government-supported Suzuki, this meant working within the school system by strengthening the role of the teacher, while for JTU-affiliated Igasaki, it meant circumventing government interference and manipulation by turning to nongovernmental organisations (Lincicome, 1993, 131).

Clearly, the opposition wanted to separate internationalisation from government influence and use it to promote general human values rather than particular Japanese economic interests. But because the opposition is rather vague in its statements on the subject it is difficult to imagine a concrete version of their brand of internationalisation. It seemed to be used as a forum for flowery statements of intentions rather than a forum for concrete proposals. The biggest difference in the two positions in the debate lies in the fact that for the NCER-party internationalisation is an economically useful concept, while for the opposition it is more related to universal human values.

As for the concrete policy measures to implement internationalisation, the NCER suggested experiments with educational programmes and inter-nationalisation at different levels. National and local government authorities should take the lead in working out various innovations like 'resource centre services' for education in international understanding, exchange and dis-semination of information etc. Additionally, the government should prepare a 'White Paper on Internationalisation in Education' presenting the concrete attempts at internationalisation in education and indicating the government policy on this problem (Rinkyooshin, 1988, 296). This moved the responsibility for formulating a policy on internationalisation in education from NCER to the government. Perhaps the issue was too political for NCER to comfortably deal with on its own.

4.4.3 Returnee children and Japanese children overseas

A substantial number of pages in NCER's reports were devoted to treating the particular question of how to receive children returning to Japan after a long stay abroad and to the question of how to educate them while abroad.[18]

In future, Japan must think of the returnees (*kikokushijo*) as a valuable asset. Basic to the education of these children should be efforts by the Japanese schools to appreciate the particular advantages they have acquired abroad, both upon and after admission to a Japanese school (Rinkyooshin, 1988, 130).

18. See Roger Goodman: *Japan's 'International' Youth*, 1990, Clarendon Press, Oxford; and Merry White: *The Japanese Overseas: Can They Go Home Again?*, 1988, New York, Free Press, for studies on the topic of Japanese returnee children.

This was a reformulation of the policy concerning the returnees which had held sway until then. Until NCER redefined it, the policy had been one of 'de-internationalising' the returnees, reinforcing their Japanese consciousness and coping with the stigma of their foreign experience. The novelty of NCER's approach was the reformulation of the significance of foreign experience. It was no longer — officially at least — a stigma but a 'valuable asset' (Lincicome, 1993, 136). Returnees were considered useful in roles such as interpreters, international ambassadors of Japan, or consultants, functioning within the scope of jobs in which international contacts would be essential. Also, as the Education Council had pointed out, accepting those who had experienced foreign education would strengthen a company's ability to internationalise and, at the same time, internally resolve part of the worker problems accompanying overseas assignments (Keizai Dooyuukai, 1984, 36-37).

Despite the acclaimed high value of the foreign experiences of these children, it still seems that a disproportionately large part of the inter-nationalisation chapters in NCER's reports was devoted to returnees. In 1985 there were less than 40,000 Japanese children of school age living abroad — in 1991 the figure was slightly over 50,000 — and this was out of a total figure of more than 15 million children of school age in Japan (Statistics Bureau, 1992, 671; Monbushoo, 1989a, 23).

The reasons for the attention are various, but one is probably that the parents of the returnees have often been quite influential and active on their children's behalf. The parents are usually well-educated and hold, or have held, influential positions. Other reasons may be that the returnees are not only useful to the NCER as a tool in internationalisation and a demonstration of some activity in the area, but also they are of concern in NCER's attempts to maintain the cultural integrity of the Japanese. While being redefined as an asset they are also very often still looked upon as not entirely 'ordinary Japanese'.

NCER recommended that measures should be taken to facilitate the return of these children to Japanese schools, and that in high school and university special places and special admission procedures should be secured. Even non-Japanese students who did not speak or understand Japanese should in time be allowed to enter Japanese schools and universities, NCER suggested.

NCER further advised that schools accommodating returnee children or foreign children should have specialist teachers to facilitate counselling and Japanese language instruction. Also teachers with experience of foreign countries, as well as foreign teachers should be utilised. An opening for a special arrangement became possible with the proposal of establishing new schools for the purpose of mixing Japanese children, returnees and foreign children. This was to promote research and methodological and theoretical development of the area of internationalisation in education. Obviously such schools could also be used as a means of containing the impact of international contacts. NCER also felt that the Japanese educational system should take measures to accept high school attendance by a Japanese student in a foreign country as being equivalent to attending a high school in Japan. And finally, graduates from existing international schools in Japan were to be granted qualification for advancing to Japanese educational institutions of a senior level, provided they completed particular suitable courses (Rinkyooshin, 1988, 236-37).

For Japanese children staying overseas, NCER called the following to attention:

As for the education of Japanese children in foreign countries, emphasis on the basic training as a Japanese must continue and while taking into account the circumstances in the host country and the educational prospects for those children on returning to Japan, we recommend a basic policy of giving them as much experience of the host country as possible. (Rinkyooshin, 1988, 130, 297)

Given the heavy reliance on factual knowledge obtained through rote learning which is required for entrance examinations in Japan, there is probably not a single country in the world with an educational system that could be said to be other than detrimental to the chances of a Japanese child passing an entrance examination in Japan. For all practical purposes, NCER with its proviso that 'the educational prospects of those children returning to Japan' was to be taken into account, ruled out attendance at a local school. In practice, this provision meant that a Japanese child overseas would attend a Japanese school if possible. This school may add a few subjects relating to the host country, as for example extra language classes or excursions.

Though the passage could be interpreted as if NCER actually recommended that children attended local schools of their host country, the intensely competitive structure of Japanese schooling served as a brake on these ideas. NCER did try to remedy this situation by suggesting that the above mentioned special provisions for entrance be supplied, and by emphasising the desirability of making the most of the foreign experiences of such children, but in practice it is still often regarded as a liability in the examination competition to have been abroad for too long (Goodman, 1990, 2-3).

Another problem with these ideas, which was also acknowledged by NCER, was that the Japanese schools overseas tended to be very similar to the schools in Japan, focusing on high school entrance examinations and maintaining a very rigid policy of school management, as was evident in their reluctance to accept foreign (local) children, a fact that NCER greatly regretted. Rather, NCER said, Japanese schools overseas should cultivate in Japanese pupils a sense of international citizenship, be more open internationally by admitting foreign nationals and actively strive to improve their schools for the future (Rinkyooshin, 1988, 131).

4.4.4 Foreign students in Japan

Another measure for internationalising the Japanese system of education in NCER's plans was accepting more foreign students. This was expected to have the desirable effect of internationalising as well as upgrading the level of education and research, promoting international understanding and cooperation and increasing Japan's contribution to the development of qualified human resources for the world. To aid this, NCER suggested that teaching and advisory methods for foreign students at Japanese universities should be improved. Legal controls on foreigners in Japan, as well as entry and temporary residence in the country, ought to be made more flexible, and language teaching, arrangement of housing and procedures of awarding academic degrees should be improved, NCER recommended.

In very flowery terms the ideal situation was described. Japan's future image would be that of a country where:

... excellent foreign people will be pleased to come and study and work in science, art and other areas of Japanese society so that after their return home, they may contribute to the development of their own country. In other words, it is envisaged that Japan may be a country associated with the blooming of the talent of foreign people. (Rinkyooshin, 1988, 132)

The fact prompting NCER to suggest more foreign students in Japan was that the number of such students was actually smaller there than in many other advanced countries. The reasons for this in NCER's analysis were legion:

... the number of foreign students in Japan is small compared to that in the advanced countries due to an inadequate structure in universities and in other places for accepting foreign students, and due to limited opportunities for learning the Japanese language abroad. A basic prerequisite for Japan attracting more foreign students in the future is for our higher education and scientific research to become of an international standard, high enough to draw foreign students. (Rinkyooshin, 1988, 132)

This was a serious criticism,[19] particularly as nearly 40% of the foreign students in Japan at the time had come to study in a post-graduate programme. Graduate school in particular was the target of NCER criticism and was said to be lacking in quantity as well as in quality.

Other measures to be taken to facilitate the situation of foreign students in Japan were special courses at institutions of higher education for foreign

19. See also Amano Ikuo, 1988c. *Daigaku — Shiren no Jidai*, Tokyo Daigaku Shuppankai, ch. 3, for similar criticism.

students, enriched language teaching, new selection procedures for foreign students, preparatory courses, more flexible requirements for entrance into institutions of higher learning, home stays and 'aftercare' — sending former students Japanese academic publications, re-inviting them to Japan etc. Also, the level of information about Japanese education to students wishing to come to Japan should be improved, and NCER envisaged an increase of the number of foreign students in Japan to the level of 100,000 by the beginning of the 21st century. As there were slightly more than 33,000 foreign students enrolled in Japanese universities in 1989, this was a substantial increase (Statistics Bureau, 1992, 671). But exchange efforts should not be limited to university level, NCER said. As mentioned earlier, high schools should endeavour to make procedures for accepting foreign students and make sure that the performance of Japanese students at foreign high schools would be assessed properly, thus encouraging more mobility at high school level (Rinkyooshin, 1988, 132-33, 238).

In general, Japanese language instruction for foreigners received high priority. Methods, materials and Japanese language proficiency tests were to be improved and an examination for certifying teachers of Japanese as a foreign language was to be introduced. A close relation between Japanese language and Japanese culture was emphasised:

Needless to say, the Japanese language and Japanese culture are in balance with each other and the language is connected to esteem for the culture and other Japanese matters. So, it is conceivable that with the increased number of foreigners learning Japanese their understanding of Japanese culture will also increase. Therefore it is important, in accord with the structures and policies of the country in question, to strive for introducing Japanese culture in foreign countries in order to advance the teaching of Japanese. (Rinkyooshin, 1988, 135-36)

Culture was described as a necessary part of language studies and language studies were necessary for that real understanding of the Japanese culture needed to overcome cultural frictions. NCER pointed out the need for making a distinction between purposes of learning Japanese, namely between those learning Japanese as a tool of communication and those learning Japanese in order to study Japanese classics. This should be reflected in the teaching. Additionally NCER called for a more active promotion and involvement in the teaching of Japanese in foreign countries by providing teaching materials, sending Japanese teachers abroad upon request and establishing student exchange programmes for mutual benefit (Rinkyooshin, 1988, 239). To sum up, the existing efforts were to be intensified while graduate school in Japan was to be made more attractive by means of higher quality.

4.4.5 New requirements of Japanese education

In a more detailed analysis of the educational system, NCER vehemently criticised foreign language education in Japan for placing undue emphasis on grammatical knowledge and reading comprehension, while neglecting the acquisition of practical conversation skills. The level of foreign language proficiency was rather poor for a great many Japanese students despite the amount of time spent on language learning, NCER lamented. Emphasis should be placed on mastery of an international language as a tool for international *communication*.

To remedy this situation, NCER suggested the improvement of methods and materials along with a clarification of the objectives of language instruction — presumably a clarification entailing more emphasis on spoken language, but this is not clear from the context. Secondly, the English tests in university entrance examination should be improved so they may duly assess the abilities in listening, speaking, reading and writing. NCER also suggested that one might employ tests produced by bodies other than the university, of which TOEFL[20] is the most well-known (Rinkyooshin, 1988, 134-35, 238). Further NCER remarked that teaching English alone was not sufficient:

The need for learning languages other than English must be emphasised. That is, the second language in university should be chosen not only from among French, German and Spanish, but also from among Asian languages. (Rinkyooshin, 1988, 239)

There was — and is — a geographical imbalance between Japan's location and the language studies pursued in Japan. A further clear indication of the imbalance in the academic pursuit of knowledge was evident in statistics which NCER had found. These statistics showed that while the vast majority of Japanese students studying abroad were in Europe and North America, the majority of foreign students in Japan came from Asian countries. NCER concluded that Japanese students needed to be made aware of the fact that not only European countries and North America had valuable things to offer, but there were many other countries in which the Japanese ought to be interested. In this regard, NCER expressed its desire that the destinations of Japanese students become more diversified — a proposal which was also supported by Education Council recommendations (Rinkyooshin, 1988, 237-38; Keizai Doo-yuukai, 1984, 40).

Part of the suggested internationalisation efforts to be carried out by institutions of higher education in Japan, adding to the above suggestion of revised teaching methods and the acceptance of foreign students and staff, was

20. TOEFL stands for 'Teaching Of English as a Foreign Language'.

a revision of the content and curriculum of higher education. As NCER saw it, university students did not have sufficient knowledge about foreign history, culture, social environment and other subjects related to foreign countries, despite the fact that they had been given many lessons on the subjects. NCER instead recommended the strengthening of regional studies, comparative studies, international relations studies and the like as part of the general education courses. This would require inter-disciplinary research and education so a re-examination of the existing structures of university education and research would be necessary. Knowledge about foreign classics, Chinese and Indian classics as well as Western, was, in NCER's view, also an indispensable element of international awareness. It is questionable, however, how serious NCER was in its recommendation of more teaching of Asian languages. As Morita pointed out, NCER did not suggest any guidelines for teacher training in these subjects, they only called for knowledge of foreign history and society, for comparative research and studies of Chinese and Indian classics and this does not necessarily relate to the languages (Morita, 1988, 75).

A major element in NCER's efforts of internationalising the Japanese was the desire to be 'trusted and respected by other people' (*shinrai to sonkei o kachitoru koto ga dekiru*). This was to be achieved through understanding, international contributions in various fields and direct contacts between people (Rinkyooshin, 1988, 136-37).

NCER apparently saw its mission in upgrading the status of Asian countries in the process of internationalising Japan. But the exact purpose of this upgraded status and interest on the part of Japan was debatable, especially in light of the overall formulation of NCER's policy for internationalising Japanese education and in light of the strong concern for not only recovering and nurturing Japanese values but also for introducing Japanese culture abroad. Remembering Morita's earlier quoted warning that the ruling class of Japan was aiming at a 'Pax Japonica' in Asia, it would not at all be unreasonable if the targeted Asian countries were to be somewhat wary of the motives behind the interest the NCER professed to feel towards them.

In support of the policy of increasing scholarly exchange, NCER stated that more students should be sent abroad and that field studies and learning opportunities in developing countries should be encouraged (Rinkyooshin, 1988, 136-37).

The NCER requested that the education sector on its own initiative started activities of research and development related to the content and methods of educational programmes for coping with internationalisation without adhering to precedents. The opinions of parents and teachers who had experience of living abroad should also be fully reflected and utilised.

Non-government bodies were expected to play an important part in the internationalisation efforts as organisers of exchange projects, sister-city projects and other voluntary activities (Rinkyooshin, 1988, 235). That efforts of inter-nationalisation were necessary in all sectors of society was hardly a subject of debate, but the means and what was perceived by the opposition as the hidden agenda of furthering Japanese economic and nationalistic interests certainly were debated as will be seen in the following.

4.4.6 Views on internationalisation

No party in the debate disagreed with the statement that internationalisation was important. The ATU emphasised the necessity of international under-standing and international consciousness for securing world peace and a clean environment. NKG described the nature of internationalisation of education with five points:

1) Guarantee the right to education for those with foreign experience.
2) Provide globally oriented education for all citizens.
3) Educate people with appropriate skills for international society.
4) Guarantee international mobility of educational staff and material.
5) Internationalise the educational administration.
   (Kuwabara, 1988b, 50)

Characterising NCER's idea of internationalisation as that of every sovereign country having a national flag and anthem, ATU hit on the sensitive issue of *Hinomaru* and *Kimigayo*.[21] They complained that the use of the two would force people to honour the imperial system. The song was not mentioned in the Constitution and clearly was a prayer for the Emperor, not a celebration of constitutional democracy. As ATU saw it, the use of this song in the schools would be a crucial blow against political neutrality in education (interview with Kawai Naoki, May 16, 1991).

JTU, on the subject of *Hinomaru* and *Kimigayo*, as well as calling them nationalistic symbols, concluded that the promotion of them revealed that the official attempts at internationalising were a ruse. The Ministry of Education and the government's aim was interpreted as that of making Japan number one in international society, and in contrast JTU's own opinion was that all countries should be regarded equally essential to internationalisation (interview with Sakai Tomiko, May 7, 1991). NKG joined this line of argument stating that:

The national orientation is problematic because it fosters patriotism, militarism, low opinions of other countries etc. Without a revision of this hostile education,

---

21. The use of *Hinomaru* and *Kimigayo* at entrance and graduation ceremonies was made compulsory with the new curriculum guidelines in 1990.

a 'good Japanese' can never live in an international society as NCER wants him to. It will probably encourage anti-internationalism. (Kuwabara, 1988b, 48)

Evidently, the NCER efforts were seen as pulling in the opposite direction of internationalisation. Though NKG said that NCER 'wanted' a 'good Japanese' to live in the international society, their own analyses as well as those of the teacher organisations and WDCER pointed to the conclusion that NCER in fact did not want to internationalise but only to reinforce national identity and secure the economy.

Morita Toshio noted that the fourth and final NCER report of 1987 did not even attempt to conceal its recommendation of the use of nationalist symbols like *Kimigayo* and *Hinomaru* in the schools and stated that with this recommendation NCER had annexed the imperial ideology of the ruling class and the government and legitimated the claim that *Kimigayo* and *Hinomaru* were necessary for the internationalisation of Japan (Morita, 1988, 21).

The revision of the curriculum guidelines contained, for the first time since the war, directions on compulsory use of *Hinomaru* and *Kimigayo* and directions for the teachers on how to explain those symbols to the children:

(Social Sciences, grade 4) We must teach [them] that every country has a national anthem and that they must revere such a thing.

(Social Sciences, grade 6) The constitutional function of the Emperor must be explained to the pupils in a concrete and easily understandable manner, while they also learn to love and respect (*keiai*) the Emperor. (Zenkyoo, 1990, 20)

ATU saw this as creating great problems in teaching the children about the equality of all human beings. They would be told that they were all equal, but there would at the same time be someone above them, an august Emperor who was to be honoured. How was this to be explained? Part of internationalising, ATU stated, was to make the role of the Emperor clear, but on this issue NCER was silent.

The purpose of introducing national symbols was analysed by ATU in the following manner. When the Ministry of Education forced the use of *Hinomaru* and *Kimigayo* on the schools it was to have the effect of standardising and uniformising, functioning as a device to reinforce the 'good Japanese' identity (Zenkyoo, 1990, 20). This opinion was shared by JTU who saw *Hinomaru* and *Kimigayo* as part of the pressure to conform and declared that this was against the wishes of the people (interview with Sakai Tomiko, May 7, 1991). ATU pointed out the curious mixture of nationalism in the NCER concept of internationalisation quoting the above mentioned passages on 'fostering a good Japanese'. 'It is a strange kind of internationalisation', they said, 'that does not try to conform to international standards'. Here they were thinking of securing children's rights, teacher influence on educational methods and content and smaller class sizes. The point of departure for internationalisation, ATU felt, should be a revision of the contents of the text books, abandonment of censorship and abandonment of elements of Emperor worship in school admission ceremonies. With the rising number of Asian students in the Japanese schools, ATU pointed out that one was bound to experience problems with regard to the status of the Emperor and when teaching certain subjects like the history of the Pacific War (interview with Kawai Naoki, May 16, 1991).

In relation to foreign students in Japanese schools JTU, WDCER and NKG made a point of demanding lessons in the mother tongue for foreign nationals in Japanese schools. They saw this as an essential show of respect for foreigners in Japan and as an integral part of fostering an international outlook. As part of a larger scheme for internationalising, JTU called for a policy on how to deal with foreign residents in Japan, taking up problems like, for example, insurances, mother-tongue education, voting rights and assimilation into Japanese society etc. (interview with Sakai Tomiko, May 7, 1991). The problem of internationalisation was experienced in two contexts. One, the relation to other countries and their practices; two, the relation to foreign residents in Japan.

The last issue was given very little space in the NCER reports. In fact considerations were limited to noting that foreign nationals should be allowed to be active in various sectors of Japanese society and that favourable attention should be given to foreign nationals with permanent residence in Japan (Rinkyooshin, 1988, 398). The opposition, especially JTU and WDCER, saw the relation to foreign residents as a crucial component of internationalisation while NCER apparently did not place this issue within the scope of the term 'internationalisation'.

To a great extent WDCER and NKG shared opinions and issues in the matter of internationalisation. They both felt that the government was taking a militarist course and that too many guidelines and standardisation made children conform and encouraged discrimination. Because children with a different language or cultural background often were rejected or simply ignored, WDCER and NKG proposed the integration of these children in ordinary schools. These could be *kikokushijo*, repatriate Chinese, refugees and foreign immigrants (Kuwabara, 1988b, 48-9; WDCER, 1987, 121).

WDCER in particular deplored the fact that although many of these children already attended ordinary schools they were separated for training in the Japanese language and thus removed from the class group and the comradeship in it. Interaction was the code word:

Not only the foreign children suffer because of this. Japanese children suffer also.

Adults must understand that a warm and kind heart and understanding for others is developed in interaction with those who are different. (WDCER, 1987, 121)

WDCER and NKG felt that education in a Japanese school should be guaranteed for anyone who wanted it, and further WDCER requested that the existing international schools be acknowledged as regular schools and no longer be registered as *kakushuu gakkoo*.[22]

WDCER was not critical of all the NCER's internationalisation proposals and in fact supported the proposals regarding special openings for *kikokushijo* in high school and university, more effort to have local experiences when abroad, and transfer of credits earned in foreign schools (WDCER, 1987, 122).

The gravest oppositional criticism of NCER's brand of internationalisation concentrated on the lack of concern in NCER's reports for foreign children residing in Japan, and criticism of the lack of proposals for teaching the mother-tongue. Also the issue of nationalism as embodied in the introduction of *Kimigayo* and *Hinomaru* into the curriculum guidelines loomed large in the debate. The reports were attacked by NKG for not being specific about how education was to instill in children a global consciousness. All there was, at the elementary level at least, was emphasis on teaching English and Japanese language and culture. How the Japanese educational system was supposed to contribute to the international community was not specified and NKG felt that this was a misplaced kind of modesty.

Further, NKG was worried that NCER did not treat problems like how to present history and how to reform educational administration in order to make it more open and international. There can never be true internationalisation, they stated quoting NCER, when reforms in the area are carried out to solve 'the grave problem of our country's development and existence' (Kuwabara, 1988b, 50).

NKG felt that the NCER version of internationalisation, as something necessitated by the end of the catch-up phase and the need for international contributions, was too shallow and claimed that if the educational system was not fundamentally changed there was a danger that the Japanese might even turn against internationalisation. The Japanese educational system was characterised as being especially self-contained and introverted. To better the situation NKG recommended that all learners' rights were respected including those of students with foreign experience. With regard to international co-operation in the area of education and the available options, NKG pointed to Europe and the geographical proximity of the various countries and suggested that it was a good place from which to gain experience. Further, the educational

22. *Kakushuu gakkoo* means 'miscellaneous schools' and is the term for schools which do not conform to the standards set by the Ministry of Education.

system should adapt more to the fact that foreign school systems would establish branch schools in Japan and that Japanese schools would establish branch schools in other countries. NKG saw a big role for the educational media in internationalisation since such media would make international cooperation considerably more easy, and make possible international communication between schools and students (Kuwabara, 1988b, 47-8).

A further obstacle to internationalisation as seen by WDCER was the Japanese unwillingness to be different. If you are different you will be bullied, so efforts at internationalisation were in danger of concentrating only on 'safe' areas such as increased efforts in the teaching of English (interview with Higuchi Keiko, June 27, 1991).

4.4.7 Conclusions

The desire to be respected as an equal by other countries has been a driving motive in Japanese foreign relations ever since the opening of Japan in the middle of the nineteenth century. Initial treaties between Japan and other countries were very unequal as was a common feature at the time of treaties between the advancing West and other areas of the world. As one of its primary goals Japan wanted the U.S. and Europe to acknowledge its equal status, and also had the desire to earn their respect.

While Japan is undoubtedly now respected as an equal (or sometimes even as a superior) in economic and judicial terms, there are still matters in which Japan is accused internationally of not living up to its responsibilities. The United States expects Japan to shoulder more military responsibility, especially in UN operations. The Japanese contributions to the developing world are also a matter which receives much criticism internationally, particularly from Asian countries who feel that the Japanese as fellow Asians and former conquerors have a special moral responsibility towards them.

There is evidence that this criticism has been heard in NCER's emphasis on the place of Asian countries in Japanese education, as well as in the repeated references to developing countries, and there is no doubt that the opposition at least was greatly concerned with relations to the other Asian countries, so a more Asian outlook may be on its way, although perhaps mainly at grassroot level.

The basic message of NCER, with which one would have no hesitation agreeing, was that Japan in order to gain the respect of the international community must take up its social responsibility, as well as its responsibility for world peace and harmony. However, the *means* of internationalising and the *covert goals* as perceived by the opposition were the object of much discussion.

Of all the NCER concerns ranging from the standard of the universities, education of Japanese children abroad, *kikokushijo* and foreign students in Japan, the most problematic concern was that of fostering a 'good Japanese' and the issue of *Kimigayo* and *Hinomaru* which accompanied it. The opposition had — and still has — a hard time reconciling themselves with the idea of inter-nationalising Japan by first emphasising national(istic) values. Certainly Japan needs to define itself in relation to the international community but the problem is, rather than defining Japan in *relation* to other countries, the effect of NCER's reports and the government's policies has been to define Japan *in contrast* to other countries.

The emphasis on a peculiar Japanese culture, tradition and identity, as well as the notion of the Japanese assuming their world responsibility, has been traced back by Morita Toshio to terms such as 'the Yamato people of Amaterasu' and 'one country one people' used in the political rhetoric in the end of the sixties. Both terms were based on the assumption that Japanese culture and tradition had great contributions to make internationally, that Japanese culture was somehow universal (Morita, 1988, 19-20). Following this line of argumentation one can explain the emphasis on teaching other countries about Japanese culture. As a universal culture, Japanese culture would be universally applicable, and it then follows that teaching other countries about Japanese culture would be a valuable asset for the foreign culture itself rather than a manifestation of cultural imperialism.

The economic aspect of internationalisation in the NCER reports was strong. There was a basic notion that Japan could not remain an economic superpower without making the world 'understand' their need for imports as well as exports. The cultural information approach was one way of dealing with the problem. The other was strengthening Japanese national identity. Morita Toshio informs us that the expression 'a Japanese living in the global society' (*sekai no naka no nihonjin*) began to be popular after the G5 meeting in 1985 when Nakasone and LDP had felt the economic interests of Japan threatened by the controversy over the strong Yen versus the weak Dollar. The purpose of an expression like 'a Japanese living in the global society' Morita identified as being that of making people accept otherwise unacceptable consequences, such as expansion of armaments — because all other countries were well armed — rising rates of unemployment — because all other countries also experienced unemployment. Reference to world conditions could thus be used as a means of cajolement of the population to accept changes and ultimately to make them gladly resort to arms should this global society, or part of it, threaten Japan's interests (Morita, 1988, 49-52).

Though Morita may be pushing his point a bit too far there can be no doubt that the economic aspect had a lot of influence on the way internationalisation was defined. The emphasis on Japanese culture and national symbols all form part of the efforts to consolidate Japan as a strong unit in the world economy able to deal flexibly with changes.

The domestication of internationalisation and its relation to nationalism has made the term 'internationalisation' one of dubious meaning. As part of the NCER rhetoric it was an answer to international criticism of too little Japanese international engagement in areas other than trade. But, judging from an analysis of NCER's own explanations of the term, in practice it was mainly an internal Japanese matter of furthering economic development and creating national unity. Held up against the opposition's idea of internationalisation as a prerequisite for peace and a clean environment one can hardly be surprised that the two opposing parties found it hard to discuss the matter with one another. As the NCER and the Ministry of Education were — and are — not obliged to discuss this with any opposition like the teacher organisations, the chance of there ever being established a consensus on the meaning of the inter-nationalisation of Japanese education and the way to pursue it, is minimal. The teacher organisations will be the ones left unsatisfied because the Ministry of Education has every chance of realising its policy, if not directly through the Japanese parliament, then through the use of 'administrative guidance'.

4.5 The Information Society

NCER observed that Japan was facing the advent of the information society and therefore put it on its agenda, but the definition of the term 'information society' is unclear and therefore deserves a little explanation. Frank Webster, professor of sociology at the Oxford Brooks University, has identified at least five different definitions used as normal criteria, alone or in different combinations. The first and most used definition bases itself on the level of technological innovation. It simply reasons that when technology is as visible as it is today it must be a valid sign of the emergence of a new society. The problem is that there is no useful empirical method for measuring the distribution of technology. What should be the determining factors? Money spent on technology? Individual or institutional consumption? And what counts as relevant technology? Further, the definition does not distinguish clearly between 'information' and 'technology'.

The second definition is economic. There is a branch of economic studies looking into the size and growth of the information industry but the problem with this approach is that it homogenises all information activities in its need to price tag everything and thus has no way of differentiating between meaningless and truly valuable information.

The third definition focuses on changes in the employment structure. This definition states that when the work done in a society is primarily in the information sector a society can be said to be an information society. But this entails the subjective categorising of work as information related or not, and it also has no way of showing the different hierarchies in such work.

The fourth definition centres on the establishment of information networks. The key idea is that the networks are distributing lots of information, but there is no definition of how much information should be distributed to call it an information society and the term 'network' has not really been defined.

The fifth definition runs along cultural lines. This definition states that we are surrounded by signs and symbols and the explosion in the use of them has led many to assert that we are now living in an information society. But the very fact that we are now so entangled in signs and symbols has led to the post-modern idea that the signs and symbols are now losing their original meaning — their ability to signify is weakened. This definition is less traditional than the others, not least because it is very difficult to prove empirically!

What Frank Webster found problematic in all of those definitions was that they were all focused on quantitative measures rather than qualitative. One attempts to prove that just because the amount of information in circuit has grown the society has changed. Also, no distinction is made between data, knowledge, experience and wisdom, in other words, no differentiation is made between the tax bureau registers and research papers. One does not try to determine whether the information is useful, whether it is true or false. The semantic meaning of the word 'information' as something *meaningful*, as instruction about someone or something is ignored, the word has lost its meaning in many of these definitions and is reduced to a question of 'bits', which by the way was a measure created for engineers working with the storing of symbols having only the option 'on/off' at their disposal.

Webster, quoting Theodore Roszak, states that a society has certain overriding 'master ideas' which go before information. Notions of good and bad, of caring for other people are more basic than information and thus form the foundation of a qualitative involvement. He asks the important questions: 'Are we necessarily more enlightened because of a growing amount of information? What information should be stored? What kind of information work is increasing?' (Webster, 1993).

The term is thus in many ways problematic. In the context of Japanese educational reform one has to rely on the NCER definition of the term since they are setting the agenda, but as they do not really reflect on the dimensions of the term, dimensions as indicated by Webster's characterisations, it causes a lot of interpretative confusion. It is notable however that there was indeed general consensus about the fact that adapting to the information society was a reality with which one should be concerned.

4.5.1 The information society in NCER's interpretation

The adaptation to a new age of information which in NCER's view would be a reality in the 21st century, was the last of the four key phrases to be dealt with in the NCER reports. In order for Japan to flexibly adapt to the historical and social changes that this new age would entail, and if one was to build up a society which was both materially and spiritually affluent, it would be necessary to reform the educational system to make it adapt to the changes, NCER stated. They expected the advance of the information media to cause drastic changes in the whole social system as well as in people's vocational careers. In the coming years it would be imperative to create an information society in which a 'rich humanity' could be developed. It was reiterated that information technology should merge with the natural environment and traditional culture, and to elicit agreement, the term *yutaka* was used for 'rich'.

NCER suggested that the following principles be adhered to in the adaptation of the information media to education:

a) the educational functions of the various media should be utilised to invigorate and stimulate all educational institutions;

b) efforts should be made to determine how education should cope with the impact of the spread of the new technology;

c) the possible ill-effects of excessive dependence on information technology should be compensated by educational efforts. (Rinkyooshin, 1988, 16, 241)

In NCER's opinion information technology ideally should be employed to enhance the daily living of people, and so it would be essential for people to be trained in selecting and using information (Rinkyooshin, 1988, 22). In NCER's terms 'information media' covered radio, television, video, computers, advanced systems of information and communication, satellites etc. When NCER dealt with the information society in the reports, they strongly emphasised the danger of 'side effects', such as children's excessive preoccupation with game machines using computers, pseudo- experience taking over from real experience, and it was pointed out that 'undesirable influences' (*nozomashikunai eikyoo*) of the information technology could be the result unless immediate countermeasures were introduced.[23]

NCER described education as primarily a process of transmitting to the

23. One possible adverse effect of the new information technology is being investigated at the moment. Apparently a number of English and Japanese children have reacted to overindulgence in computer games by developing epileptic spasms (J. Kirkholm, 1993. Feature on Danish National Radio, Jan. 17). Also, a French report on such occurrences has been published. In Japan, 121 incidents were registered in January 1993, prompting the computer-game giant, Nintendoo, to print warnings on their cassettes. (Kurt Damsgård, 1993. Feature on Danish National Radio, March 4). If this is really a side effect of the new technology, there is all the more reason to comply with NCER's call for an assessment of both the positive and negative effects of this technology.

younger generation the information accumulated in human society, and in that respect emphasised the capacity of the information technology to reform the process of learning. With the development of two-way communication and the dramatic increase in the availability of information, NCER predicted that the unilateral character hitherto typical of the mass media, would gradually be mitigated. The new media would improve the capacity of human beings for information production by taking over part of the function of managing and processing information, in effect becoming a 'personal media'. The new developments would, with the possibility of two-way communication, greatly ease space and time limits imposed on learning (Rinkyooshin, 1988, 139, 281).

Two issues were deemed central in the deliberations on the information society: One was to determine the function of the educational system in order to ensure the spiritual and cultural enrichment of individual life in an information oriented society, and the other was to establish how the educational system was to utilise the outcomes of the spread of the information media. A number of important 'balances' which should be kept were listed:

[We should] seek the most appropriate balance in each aspect: the balance between 'sending' and 'receiving' information by learners; the balance between direct and indirect natural, human and social experiences of learners; the utilisation of technology and the dependence on manual skills and the balances between different patterns of instruction, such as individualised instruction and mass instruction. (Rinkyooshin, 1988, 140)

As NCER predicted that information media would gradually spread into every aspect of daily life, the importance of developing an 'information literacy' and an 'information morality' became apparent. This was to prevent users from becoming not only the victims of information but also from becoming wrongdoers who would misuse information technology. Information literacy meant that people had to be instructed in how to select and use information and to have equal opportunity to do so. Schools were asked not only to maintain a high level in the basics but also to make serious efforts to develop information literacy, since the level of proficiency in using and selecting information would — as NCER predicted — cause differences in the social and cultural activities of the individuals. In a highly information-oriented society, NCER foresaw that those who lack information literacy would experience great difficulty carrying out their vocational life as well as their daily life. Former NCER member, Minakami Tadashi, put it in the following terms:

Suddenly we can see, by one push of a button, what formerly was not to be seen. Children see a lot of things regardless of their age. This raises the question of how to choose between different information, the ability to choose. (Interview with Minakami Tadashi, May 31, 1991)

Information morality, on the other hand, would teach people to be 'aware of the impact the information they dispatch has on other people and on society'. The moral problems of information technology identified by NCER at the time were: The problem of 'hackers' invading the computers; the invasion of people's privacy by photo magazines and the infringement of copyrights due to the copying of material without the permission of copyright holders. Further, NCER stated that these were problems about which people were rarely aware, so such problems would have to be exposed more and, to guide the information oriented society, it would be necessary to create new social rules, an *information morality*. In concrete terms this would mean a set of objective criteria on the quality of information as well as a system for protecting personal data.

NCER saw a particularly great problem in people's lack of a basic sound awareness of the value of information, the fact that they tended to make too little of software as compared to hardware, and NCER felt that at the very least people should be made more aware of the actual cost of information. In a final remark NCER summed up the need for information morality in the following terms:

Just as traffic morality and well-functioning brakes are a prerequisite for driving safely at high speed, so information morality is a prerequisite for the full development of information functions. (Rinkyooshin, 1988, 241-43)

Referring back to the principle of utilising the educational functions of the new media, NCER talked about the potential for facilitating individualised instruction (*shidoo no kobetsuka*) and the possibility of implementing individualised instruction based on the different pace of learning and different characteristics of the individuals. NCER was very positive about the new opportunities these media could offer and further stated that creativity and power of expression could be developed by the possibility of meeting the diverse demands of learning and through experiences with simulation of phenomena otherwise not available to the individual (Rinkyooshin, 1988, 141, 242, 281). Education should be used as a means of presenting information to society and thus it should be a forerunner in the utilisation of the media. Printed matter should be transformed into systems more relevant to the information oriented society and such systems could make full use of the potentials of images, sounds and various other media (Rinkyooshin, 1988, 243).

The quality of transcending spatio-temporal limitations which the information technology possessed, NCER suggested should be put to use as a means to ensure true equal opportunity, particularly for 'those learners whose needs have not adequately been dealt with in traditional school instruction'. One saw in the new media an opportunity for more individualised teaching and also the opportunity of securing high quality teaching in all areas of the country.

However, the NCER also was on its guard against information technology, warning against, as well as praising, the 'transitory' qualities of information technology. This illustrated the principle of the need to compensate through education for the ill-effects of the new technology. It was said that many people were apt to absorb information in a superficial way, and others were excessively critical of it, and that mass media often brought about ill-effects on children's social norms. NCER further pointed to the danger that people may be seized with the 'illusion' (*sakkaku*) that everything could be done with the help of machines and that they would in that case be prone to give up manual work, and independent interpretations of things that happened. Pseudo-environments created by information technology should not take the place of real experience causing confusion between the real and the artificial, and lack of tranquillity of the mind, NCER warned (Rinkyooshin, 142, 246).

In effect, the information technology, which was first praised for offering the possibility of limitless and individualised learning and for taking over more routine processes of thinking and working, was now criticised for the adverse effects the same qualities might have:

There is also the danger that people's intellectual creativity will be dulled and that they will evade direct exchange with nature, people and society, relying only on indirect experience. (Rinkyooshin, 1988, 142)

The blessings of information technology were clearly viewed by NCER with caution — as a double-edged sword. In many passages the NCER seemed quite taken by the allure of technological development and the development it offered for education, but clearly, this was a mixed feeling as witnessed by the incessant warnings against 'side-effects', 'ill-effects' and the like. NCER attributed to modern rationalism the propensity of people to choose convenience over direct contact with nature, resulting in the degeneration of various human qualities, which indeed had provided an important impetus for the development of science, but had also tended to neglect the importance of human sentiments. Therefore, NCER's professed aim was harmony between science and technology and human sentiments and sensitivity (Rinkyooshin, 1988, 272-73).

Broadcasting stations should be aware of the impact of their activities and of their public responsibility, and NCER recommended the study of ways and means of introducing a system for ensuring quality information. The government should provide administrative support for ensuring favourable developments and central and local consultative committees on broadcast programmes should strengthen their activities by encouraging broadcast stations to feature such spots as reminders for children of the time to go to bed (sic!), and preparing guidelines for the users of mass media (Rinkyooshin, 1988, 246).

Though NCER emphasised the need for paying due regard to the initiatives of users and suppliers of information, measures such as the above clearly could be extended into something little short of censorship. Though some degree of censorship would always exist in any society — censorship such as attempts to prevent children from watching violent or pornographic movies — it was fiercely attacked by the opposition as being an improper attempt at political control of the media.

NCER underlined that in teaching, the information media should under no circumstances replace life-experience and object education but only support it by providing added possibilities. Teachers should strengthen personal contacts with students by concentrating their energy on areas in which tutorial teaching played a particularly large role, leaving memorisation and the like to the machines. Supported by new and better software suitable for the educational process as well as for the profiles of the media, teachers were encouraged to undergo in-service training in using the new tools, to create software themselves and further, the instruction in the use of information technology should be strengthened by teacher training courses. Also designs and functions of hardware should be standardised with a view to facilitate the adaptation of different software, and operation of hardware should be simplified (Rinkyooshin, 1988, 143-44, 244).

These proposals match very well the efforts requested by the Education Council in 1984 (Keizai Dooyuukai, 1984, 42).

NCER recommended that higher education should utilise information media in education as well as in scientific research, it should create expert personnel responsible in the future for leading the information-oriented society in a direction that would contribute to the spiritual and cultural development of human beings. Concretely, this meant the strengthening of university departments specialising in information sciences and technology and further, the introduction of information technology into library services should be promoted. Additionally, students who were enrolled in courses other than those specialising in information and technology should receive instruction in information science, which would then become part of general education. It was believed that the use of information media would upgrade the quality of activity while also making possible quick dissemination of scientific information.

To further the latter, a national centre for scientific information was proposed in order to make scientific material available immediately.

Finally, the universities were requested to make special efforts in educating people capable of exploring the most advanced areas of information technology and who were versed in other fields as well, so that a sound approach to the development of the information society could be ensured. Fields such as medicine, psychology and aesthetics were to be included, and further work for full cooperation between universities, industry and the government on the question of the most appropriate use of the information media in higher education.

In the future, NCER foresaw, teachers would no longer provide learners with information in a unilateral way. The teaching would become more active and flexible and teacher functions would concentrate more on assisting students in developing their spontaneity for learning (Rinkyooshin, 1988, 145-46, 243-44, 299).

To support the efforts of adaptation to the information oriented society, NCER recommended the development of a genuine information infrastructure. Society should not be information oriented in a uniform way, but be diverse while maintaining continuity with the existing culture and developing cooperation with other countries. Schools and other educational institutions were to function as information environments, open databases should be created and life long learning activities should utilise the new media to the full.

The notion of the 'intelligent school' was developed in connection with both life-long learning and the information society. It was envisaged that institutions related to education, culture or sports should be housed in such establishments, and that in financing these, one should 'utilise the energy of non-governmental bodies' (Rinkyooshin, 1988, 180). In the description of the information-oriented society NCER used rather flowery and somewhat unclear terms. It was said that:

In creating [an information-oriented society we should] strive for union with the natural environment and traditional culture, and we should establish sites for sports and sites for developing 'human nature/compassion' (*joo/nasake*) and 'will-power' (*i*)[24] taking advantage of the characteristics of the locality in which we live. (Rinkyooshin, 1988, 245, 300)

There was great concern for traditional culture which in itself was not a wrong thing to do, but problematic indeed because the associations to pre-war militarism of the term 'traditional culture' made it rather ambiguous and a target for much criticism.

The phrase 'adaptation to the information society' was closely intertwined with the other three key phrases. Information technology was expected to further individuality by making possible more individualised teaching methods, it was expected to further internationalisation because the new media would make international communication easier, and finally it was seen as forming an

---

24. This was the 'i' of *iryoku* or *ishi*.

integral part of the life-long learning efforts, not least because of the 'intelligent schools/buildings' which came to play a dominant role in the debate on both life-long learning and the information society.

The NCER was in no doubt that a change in society was underway, and that the sheer amount of information would change people's daily lives drastically. Though NCER did not define the concept of the information society it is clear from the proposed efforts to adapt, that they operate with a combination of the level-of-technological-innovation model and the network model. The information society was characterised by the number of computers in use and the flow of information through networks and data bases.

4.5.2 Views on the information society

Professor Amano Ikuo of Tokyo University has said of the information society that it would be a highly educated society, that the demands posed by the new technology and the use of it would force people to be better educated. Education would be emphasised even more, he predicted. In a society adapting to the information age knowledge and techniques would change ever faster, he pointed out, and further, the information society would also be a maturing society (*seijukuka shakai*) so adult education would become more necessary than ever. Concretely, professor Amano had the following criticism of the educational system's adaptation to the information society:

One can perhaps say that Japanese education is a type of education which teaches how to manage (*shori*) information. (...) An examination which forces you to manage problems you have never seen before has yet to materialise. (Amano, 1990, 144)

Without examinations to force students to apply their knowledge to new problems it would be hard to teach the students how to behave in, and respond to, an information society. Amano emphasised the need for developing the school system to enable it to offer adult education in the new computer-related disciplines, not least because as society matured, more importance would be placed on the retraining of older people than on the training of young students (Amano, 1990, 142-54).

Reacting to the NCER concept of adaptation to the information society, ATU and JTU opened by stating that these efforts were determined by the needs of the computer industry in particular. The adaptation to the information society would mean that all classrooms would have to be equipped with computers and so a stable home-market for hardware as well as a promising one for educational software would be established. ATU claimed that the reason for many people wanting more computers in the schools was that the future of

Japanese industry was seen as lying in the computer business (interview with Kawai Naoki, May 16, 1991; interview with Sakai Tomiko, May 7, 1991).

ATU could find support for this last claim in the writings of the Education Council where it was stated that 'the growth of manpower in the field of software as well as hardware is the primary task for the future' (Keizai Dooyuukai, 1984, 42). Given the influence of the business groups on the NCER agenda it was not surprising to find similar ideas in the publications of NCER and the business groups.

JTU's reservations ran more along the lines of how instruction was to take place. They seriously doubted that five to ten computers per school[25] and a fixed amount of computer lessons would prepare children for the information society. Besides, many of the teachers were not qualified to give such lessons. Therefore JTU, as an intermediary measure at least, preferred instruction to take place on a club-basis where the real experts (the children!) could learn from each other. Also, JTU suggested, one should work at raising money for more computers per school (interview with Sakai Tomiko, May 7, 1991).

Behind the NCER proposals for consultative committees, administrative support for 'favourable developments' and the emphasis on 'quality information' (however that was to be defined), ATU clearly saw the ghost of censorship:

Even in an information society we have no guarantee that we are told everything. We are told only what the administration agrees with, other information can be shut out — there is a real risk of censorship. (Interview with Kawai Naoki, May 16, 1991)

As an illustrative example of the dangers of censorship and of hiding information, the ATU representative related a case he had just heard of in the field of university research. As university research was not always made public (though the universities claimed to exist for the benefit of the people), military research could — and did, according to ATU — take place at the universities. Judging this to be against the interests of the Japanese people, ATU saw it as a dangerous example of an attempt to hide information from the public.

What ATU envisaged as beneficial effects of the development of the media was the chance children would get of broadening their minds and their knowledge about things like the universe, nature, other countries and events far away that become easier to relate to when they are presented on television. For example, ATU explained, during the war in the Persian Gulf children in first and second grades who had watched broadcasts from the Gulf were concerned

---

25. The average number of computers per school in 1991 was 3.3 in elementary school, 8. 3 in middle school and 35.3 in high school (Monbushoo, 1992, 533).

about the oil smudged birds, the fate of the captured pilots and the feelings of their families, among other things.

The last ATU objection was against the plans for 'intelligent schools'. As space was the eternal problem in Japan, ATU feared that the construction of intelligent schools based more or less on private financing would mean that schools currently housed in three to four storied buildings would be rebuilt as multi-storied high rises containing schools, libraries, city halls, cram schools, private special schools, restaurants, hotels or banks. As stated by NCER, anything that could possibly be said to relate to education, information, culture and sport could be included in such an 'intelligent building'. At the time such buildings did exist but no public schools were housed there. ATU feared such a construction, as they saw it as yet another step in the direction of privatisation of elementary education (interview with Kawai Naoki, May 16, 1991).

Similarly, the NKG was wary of what the construction of such 'intelligent schools' would entail. Particularly the economic set-up was attacked. In the third NCER report, trust companies were introduced. Such trusts were to function as supporting bodies for national universities in order to utilise the sites better (Rinkyooshin, 1988, 213-14). Quoting from a pamphlet issued by the deliberative body established to ponder on this NCER proposal, NKG explained how a trust company for a designated trust period (20 years for national establishments) would have the right, without charge, to use the facilities or site in question at their own discretion. The trust would then build or elaborate on facilities and let them to the users, schools, sports clubs, museums etc. The trustees would be responsible for financial losses, as well as benefit from profits. A bank would be the central organiser and source of funds for the trust. Such measures were expected to support local private enterprise — construction business, cram school owners etc. — and would, after the trust period when the site reverted to the (public) owner, supply the local authorities with new facilities without charge. The catch in the whole plan was that if the economy generally turned against such projects, the *deficit* as well as the facilities would revert to the owner at the end of the trust period. For the bank involved, the public authorities would then, in practice, be the most important trustees. Naturally, in relation to economy, what NKG was pointing out was that this construction could be vulnerable to fraud schemes which would then be publicly guaranteed. In educational terms, the end result could be privately run 'intelligent' schools/buildings over which public educational concerns may have little influence (Urano, 1987, 38).

4.5.3 How to adapt to the information society

The establishment of intelligent schools or buildings was one way of adapting to the information society. Another was for the regular schools to offer more training for adults in information related disciplines. Initially the special schools (*senshuu gakkoo*) had been expected to be able to fill out this role, but as Amano pointed out, the special schools were adapting more and more to young high school graduates who for various reasons did not go to a university, which meant that more and more teaching at these schools was taking place in the daytime, thereby excluding working adults from participating. In the past it was special schools that mainly offered night courses. It was felt that the regular schools should therefore take responsibility upon themselves for this kind of training and construct courses for adults where the contents were adapted to their special needs, and not just complacently sit back knowing that they will automatically have 'customers'/students, no matter what (Amano, 1990, 150-52). Probably, it will soon be impossible to rest on this comfortable knowledge since the age cohorts are progressively getting smaller and schools may have to close as a result of it.

NCER relied on computers for the adaptation to the information society with proposals for increased teaching in the subject in schools, establishment of networks and databases, use of CD-ROM and other new inventions of the information technology. Later, official White Papers on education also covered media such as educational films, videos and radio, but the main thrust towards the information society obviously was to be made by means of computers.

4.5.4 Conclusions

The topic of adaptation to the information society was heavily intertwined with life-long learning in particular. The facilities needed for adjusting to the information society such as computer bases, networks, libraries and teaching facilities were also necessary for establishing life-long learning.

What caused most dismay among the opposition was the concept of a privately financed intelligent building and the new possibilities of central control over the flow of information that the development of information technologies brought with it. The emphasis on traditional culture which was also made by the NCER in this area was not seized upon with the same zest as it had been where internationalisation was concerned, perhaps because it was felt that what was to be said about traditional culture had already been said once.

On the other hand, there were few objections to the idea that Japanese society should utilise the new media more and that re-training in the use of the new technology of adults was necessary. As Amano pointed out:

In the technical business the knowledge you acquire in university will be obsolete in five years ... things change very quickly nowadays ... therefore we must always be in a process of learning. (Amano, 1990, 147)

The concept of information literacy and the ability to choose seemed also to be accepted by the opposition. Here the JTU representative:

What is important is selecting and evaluating information — this is also useful for the study of other subjects. Education ought not to be passive receiving. (Interview with Sakai Tomiko, May 7, 1991)

Of course, real choice would only be possible if students had access to any information they wanted and developed the critical attitude necessary for information literacy. The agreement between conservatives and progressives may be based only on the fact that such literacy is necessary, but not on how to bring it about and how it should actually be defined. As the discussion was not that far advanced, and as issues such as central control of curriculum were dealt with in other connections, there is little material on this particular issue.

To the extent that this area was discussed, it was mainly in terms of the influence of private enterprise and the degree of central control, thus echoing the most important controversies found in the discussion of the other three key phrases, which meant that a discussion of the information society alone was rare. Many were inclined to think like Saitoo Taijun from the University of the Air who said that it was 'not really an area in need of reform', rather it was a question of how to utilise human resources better, the implication being that this would come naturally as the need presented itself (interview with Saitoo Taijun, May 17, 1991).

The meaning and the validity of the notion of the coming information society was not defined specifically in this debate. There was, with perhaps the exception of Saitoo Taijun, general consensus that the level of information would change society, and it was also generally agreed that such changes could be an advantage, provided the adaptation to them was carried out correctly. The NCER tended to lean on a quantitative technological definition of the information society and therefore the proposals were focused on the machinery and the dissemination of information.

CHAPTER 5

CONCLUSIONS

The Japanese reform efforts in the 1980s and onwards have been the topic of this study. The situation has been analysed as, in essence, a bi-polar discussion between those supporting government efforts and those critical of it. This is not to say that all parties in the two camps agreed on everything, of course they did not, but the fact that only those identifying with the conservative camp had access to the decision-making area certainly supports the case of viewing the debate as bi-polar in essence.

In the development of the agenda for educational reform before NCER started its deliberations there was a lot of cross-fertilising between business ideas and LDP ideas. A comparison of the Nishioka-memo of 1983 (Kurosaki, 1984) and the business world's proposals as voiced through the Kyoto Group and the Education Council (Kawamura, 1985) among others show that in general the same issues were dealt with, issues such as revision of the 6-3-3-4 system, revision of higher education, moral training, teacher training. Later, issues such as internationalisation and life-long learning joined in. The power of NCER's influence — and of those backing it — was evident in such an example as the law of 1990 on life-long learning, which was virtually a letter-by-letter copy of the NCER proposals on the subject.

Turning the focus towards the four NCER key phrases, it has been shown that in the NCER rhetoric the concept of individuality came to mean a relational self, a *self* defining *itself* in relation to a group, a workplace, a school. As *kosei*, the Japanese term used for 'individuality' was characterised as being totally disconnected from any notion of egotism — that was reserved for Western individualism! — and further, because it also had the connotation of 'individual characteristics' the efforts at individualising came to revolve around diversification of choice in terms of diversified curricula in higher education and institutions of higher education specialising in particular subjects, and around emphasis on the individual characteristics of families, the Japanese culture, the country. The rhetoric on individuality covered ideas related to what was traditionally believed to be Japanese identity, the group oriented identity, and efforts at strengthening national unity through emphasis on group relations and an ultimate common goal of supporting the nation's economic growth. This particular rhetoric was also designed to provide a response to the charges that the Japanese system of schooling lacked individuality, that the students were pressured into conformity and lacked creativity.

The opposition interpreted the term individuality as covering the free choice and development of personality of the individual, not as a matter of group relations and diversification of educational choice alone. The official brand of individuality was criticised for involving a strong element of 'liberalisation' (*jiyuuka*) of the educational system, which by all appearances was equal to allowing more private initiative gain access to compulsory education. Under the banner of 'teaching according to ability' streaming was introduced in middle school, thus adding to the pressure to perform. It is difficult to see how an individual can have much time for developing his or her personality in such a system. NCER's reaction to the charges that their proposals would pressure the individual further, and not release energy for development of personality, consisted in pointing out that they had never claimed to be especially concerned with the individual. As the opposition continually analysed the official moves in the area in the framework of individual individuality, so obviously no consensus could possibly be reached here, neither on the definition of individuality, nor on the method of enhancing it.

The effect of the re-definition by NCER of the concept of *individuality* was that the concept emerged infinite, was open for interpretation, and could mean almost anything. The NCER interpretation therefore rendered void the term *individuality* as used by the opposition, making it ambiguous, as it was often difficult to ascertain with which *meaning* it was used.

In life-long learning the NCER rhetoric claimed to be working for the rights of adults to freely learn what they pleased, when they pleased. As society was ageing it would also be more and more necessary to train people for new functions, especially in fields involving modern technology, rather than pensioning them off. Additionally, it was hoped that life-long learning would have the effect of discontinuing the practice of exclusive emphasis on school certificates, and that more value be placed on experience and learning obtained later in life.

The intentions of this rhetoric were severely criticised because simultaneously ideas were aired that private educational enterprises should play a greater role in life-long learning. This would mean, it was feared by the opposition, that money and private interests would be decisive in whether people could gain access to learning, and if they did, what they could learn. Further, it was feared that the proposed life-long learning centres would be vulnerable to censorship since with the proposed use of information technology they would be easy to control centrally. A serious problem pointed out by the opposition was that in the NCER reports, those sections about life-long learning did not elaborate on what the philosophy and ethics of such a system should be. There were no guidelines by which to determine what life-long learning was all about, how it should be conducted and how private institutions for life-long learning should operate. Perhaps this was because the real motivation was, as

ATU suggested, to finance retraining with user's fees rather than having work-places bear the burden of financing in-service training for their workers.

A change in evaluation procedures would be a *must* if life-long learning was ever to be successful as a provider of a 'second chance' for receiving useful education or training, rather than just being a forum for hobby fulfilment. Here the rhetoric is perhaps most glaringly at odds with practice, because while business groups actually proposed — and in many cases have implemented — changes in recruitment practices, Ministries are slow to change theirs.

Life-long learning was not discussed as extensively as individuality and internationalisation. Perhaps because the rhetoric was not so ideologically compromised by nationalistic ideas as that of the two other key phrases.

The issue of internationalisation was heavily loaded with rhetoric on the need for Japan to internationalise and live up to her international responsibility. Japan was to assert herself as a responsible nation and take a special interest in fellow Asian countries. But the analysis of the term 'internationalisation' showed a preoccupation with domestic matters, with widening the knowledge and understanding of Japan abroad and with fostering a 'good Japanese' who was knowledgeable about Japanese culture and tradition before he or she was sent out in an international environment.

The emphasis on the 'good Japanese' and the use of such words as *keiai* ('love and respect'), reminiscent of the *keiai* which before the war one was to feel towards the Emperor, and the focus on domestic problems, made the opposition call it not internationalisation (*kokusaika*) but 'ultra-nationalisation' (*kokusuika*), meaning that the rhetoric of internationalisation was a cover for ultra-nationalist aspirations for a centralised government and extended influence over the rest of Asia. Concrete changes with the new curriculum guidelines, such as the fact that the use of the flag *Hinomaru*, and the singing of the Emperor song *Kimigayo*, was made compulsory at school ceremonies, were taken by the opposition as proof of the nationalist intentions. Additionally, the NCER proposals were criticised for not attempting to deal adequately with resident foreigners in Japan and for neglecting to propose revisions of the history curriculum so that it could be tolerated by fellow-Asians in particular. It was criticised also that the teaching of foreign residents in Japan in their mother-tongue was not con-sidered.

The need for Japan to place herself as a cultural and political factor on the international arena was clearly of great concern to NCER, plus there was the concern that Japan would have to be strong internationally to keep its position as an economic superpower. The NCER reform efforts were not only accused of being nationalist, they were accused also of oversimplifying the matter with the proposals for practical application. These proposals, when not being directly nationalistic, were limited to a concern about more foreign language teaching, as well as greater knowledge of Asian and Western classics. NCER's internationalisation was domestically oriented with emphasis on national character and language proficiency. Granted there were — and are — active efforts at internationalisation in higher education, universities and university research in particular, where more international exchange of persons and materials was/is an aim, but in the wider context of the Japanese educational system this is a limited area. As in the *individuality* case, where the term was given a special NCER meaning, *internationalisation* seemed to have a special NCER meaning connecting it to nation-building rather than global concerns.

The information society was mostly discussed in connection with life-long learning because of its usefulness in this area and because of the need for life-long learning that the technology generated. It was not granted top priority in the debate on NCER issues. Though nobody doubted that in the future more advanced technology would be in use, NCER failed to define what was meant by the term 'information society' and how it was characterised, so the issue became very fixed on technology and the dissemination of information instead. Proposals concentrated on more computers in schools, on more teaching in computer science, information morality and the ability to choose. Questions such as the desirability of this development and its social consequences were rarely addressed in the debate.

The opposition primarily emphasised the need for the ability to choose between information, but also oscillated between a negative vision that the many proposed central networks and databases would be sources of censorship, and a positive vision that the new technology would further international contacts and understanding as well as be of immense help in teaching.

There were few discussions on the information society, again possibly because the rhetoric in this area was not as politically provocative as in individuality and internationalisation. Also, many felt that the development would more or less come about naturally and that if life-long learning offered a sufficient amount of training no further adaptations would be necessary.

It is clear that it has been difficult for oppositional views to bring any influence to bear on Japanese educational policy. However, some criticism was appeased slightly in the rhetoric of the NCER reports, but regrettably the reports concerned mainly those areas which were felt by Government and the business world to be most in need of reform, rather than the areas pointed out by parents and oppositional groups. The lack of useful proposals for revision of the entrance examinations is a case in point. Countless analyses have stated that examinations and recruitment procedures are at the root of the problem of the crammed Japanese education, but this area has yet to be dealt with. The problem of course is that a decision to change such procedures will create insecurity and necessitate new selection methods, and hence a decision to change the examination system could, politically speaking, be very costly.

In terms of the actor-model described on page 19-23 this 'freezing out' of divergent ideas was possible because the problem-regulating filter was functioning well from a power-holder's point of view, in other words, the arena of decision making was effectively monopolised by the conservatives.

The mood of the NCER reforms was conservative in the sense that good conservative values were emphasised, values such as family, nation, liberalism. Basically, the citizen had a *duty* towards the nation to educate himself. His *rights* were seen as concerned with choice of school and career. Some of the NCER proposals and the ensuing practices have been analysed as having nationalistic ends, and indeed the conservatives seemed intent on securing Japan's role as a superpower in all aspects, economically, politically and culturally. One wanted to foster a 'good Japanese', therefore Japanese culture and language was to be well-known in the world community. Perhaps this was caused by a realisation that the interjection of Japanese culture into other countries had not been as successful as its economic power may have warranted. In comparison, the Coca Cola culture of the United States has certainly had an infinitely greater impact on the world.[1] These efforts which are aimed at securing Japan's international position as a superpower are quite natural seen from the viewpoint that economic growth is *the* mode of survival. However, to most of the left-wing, traditionally more preoccupied with the position of the weak, the doctrine of growth as a universal remedy for all problems has outlived itself, and its application in connection with internationalisation is, at best, incomprehensible or, at worst, a sign of an egotistical nationalism taking no heed of the plight of others.

Economy has been mentioned as something which carried weight in the formation of the reform proposals. The need to secure Japan's economic position in the world prompted reform proposals for higher education and vocational education, in particular targeting computer technology and the natural sciences where Japan's future was seen to lie. One envisaged a Japan concentrating on software development and advanced technology rather than on heavy production. Through all the reform proposals, notions about 'the good of the nation', and 'retaining of the national Japanese household', were invoked to legitimise this kind of emphasis in the educational reform proposals.

Goals of strengthening the national economy and national unity naturally had an impact on the reform rhetoric. Internationalisation was more about being a good Japanese and teaching the world about Japan than about opening Japan to international influence and dealing with foreigners in Japan. Life-long learning and the adaptation to the information society concentrated on the supply of manpower and the dissemination of information, and individuality

1. See also the articles by Jean Pierre Lehmann in Lehmann & Henny (eds.), 1988. *Themes and Theories in Modern Japanese History*, Athlone Press, London, where the issues of trade friction and the lack of knowledge in other countries about Japanese culture and tradition are dealt with.

was a question of individualising institutions to provide more choice, and of securing for the future the small amount of creative researchers needed to keep Japan in the vanguard of economic development.

A necessary prerequisite for education to work satisfactorily, in terms of government ideology, was central control and centralised administration of education. It was here that the main friction with the business groups occurred. Business tended to hail such concepts as free competition and deregulation, which of course did not go well with the official insistence, particularly by the Ministry of Education, of a standardised curriculum and central bureaucracy and control with the educational institutions.

However, accusing the reforms of only being focused on economy and manpower needs, would clearly be wrong. The emphasis on the 'good Japanese' and references to having respect for 'that which is greater than ourselves' clearly show that there is another dimension. Apparently, Japan not only wished economic strength, but also respect and understanding.

NCER's references to transcendental beings and the respect for natural phenomena were analysed by the opposition as attempts to instill *Shintoo* values in children, the natural phenomena interpreted as meaning *kami* (deities), and for the opposition this was yet another example of an unconstitutional mixture of politics, education and religion. The opposition argued that this harked back to the way the *Meiji* government used education to cement the Emperor's status as a deity and thereby legitimate their own claim to power. They saw in this a further sign of the conservative notion of pre-war ideals being untainted, pure Japanese ideals — ideals which should substitute the American ideals in the FLE.

If we look at what has resulted from the NCER deliberations until now, only a few new laws have been enforced. In the period running from June 1987 to May 1991, fifteen reform proposals concerning education were presented to the Diet, thirteen of which were passed. One of the rejected proposals concerned the establishment of a body to deliberate on how to further the implementation of the NCER proposals, the other concerned the professionalisation of the principal job on the local school board. The rejection in 1989 of the first proposal naturally slowed down the implementation process. The second of the rejected proposals, if it had been passed, would probably have brought about a strengthening of the Ministry of Education's influence at local level, because the leading position on a local school board would have been related to the bureaucratic career structure.

Of the laws passed by the Diet, two related to life-long learning, two to the information society and four to the individualisation of institutions. These laws contained either minor changes such as making requirements for high school graduation more flexible or a relaxation of the strict faculty division between the studies of medicine and dentistry, or they were laws concerning particular cases such as the establishment of graduate schools for the study of advanced technology in Nara and Hokuriku.[2]

According to the actor-model, the available mode of influence for the opposition is either to get their interests accepted before they enter the arena of decision, or to influence the implementation process. The first option was rarely available, because the opposition was quite polarised, and was unable because of sheer numbers to unite and be heard. Massive popular demand would at least have a good chance of being accepted as valid interests, but not so the interests expressed by what could be perceived as narrow interest groups, such as teacher organisations or scholarly groups. But mutual suspicion between teacher organisations, between parent groups and organised teachers, made cooperation very difficult. The fact that not only the unions but also the grass roots had effectively been shut out of the political circuit meant that in practice, the implementation filter became their sole road to influence.

As for the business groups they were most active in the beginning of the NCER reform deliberations and participated to a great extent in the formulation of the problems to be dealt with. In terms of the actor-model they managed to get through the problem regulating filter. Their influence became less obvious later in the process but the fact that they had been so closely involved in setting the agenda meant that they were certain to have their interests considered. Also many of the members of the business groups ended up in the NCER, thereby able to exercise influence.

As stated in the introduction, a central assertion of this study has been that Japanese educational reform is not as immobilist as the list of laws passed by the Diet may suggest. The Ministry of Education can make use of the implementation filter to bring about reforms despite the Diets failure to legislate. Administrative guidelines are quite as effective as laws and sometimes even provoke the passing of legislation, as was the case with the Head Teacher system referred to in the Introduction where a Ministerial Order from 1957 was legislated in 1973. The new curriculum guidelines introduced in the beginning of the 1990s managed to introduce changes pertaining to the goals of the NCER reports. The introduction of the *Hinomaru* and *Kimigayo* was clearly a step towards strengthening of the national character, towards 'individualising' Japan, and 'internationalising' it by having the same type of national symbols as other countries. However, the problem with these specific national symbols is, that they remain the same as those used by the militarists during the war — no changes, like those made in Germany, have been made to the Japanese national symbols.

Systems for in-service training of teachers and Head Teacher systems are

---

2. This information was given to me by General Director in the Ministry of Education, Satoo Jiroo.

powerful devices for controlling teachers and the textbook authorization system severely limits the choice of viewpoints to be presented in the classrooms. Further, the subject of moral education, which was abolished by the Allied Occupation Authorities, is now included in the curriculum. The need for moral training was obvious to most of the involved educators, but the actual ends to which it was to be put are questionable. NCER proposed regulated textbooks for the subject and as the Ministry of Education authorises such textbooks they will necessarily follow the official line. The content of moral education is not only the teaching of manners and culture but also nourishes national pride. An example of a moral education test, referred to by ATU, teaches the child to be proud of Japan and to want to assist in its development. Its relation to 'morals' in the sense of an awareness of right and wrong is unclear, but it is evidently related to the nurturing of a national identity (Zenkyoo, 1990, 19).

Through this device of administrative guidance the Ministry has succeeded in orientating the educational system very much along the lines indicated by NCER and it is capable of making changes which are never debated in the Diet and in which it is all but impossible for the opposition to participate. Seen in this light I think it would be wrong to say that Japanese educational reform is an area of immobilist policies. Immobilism is only apparent where legal measures are concerned. But it is an oversimplification to assume that legal measures are the only indication of what is happening in Japanese education. The changes carried out administratively by the Ministry of Education testify to a very conscious policy and a very clear idea of how to realise educational reform.

The second central proposition of this study concerned the relation between rhetoric and political practice. Reading the NCER reports one will soon find what appears to be quite obvious discrepancies between the rhetoric of the reports, the proposals for reform, and the reforms that have been implemented inspired by the reports. The rhetoric does not match the political practice. A look at the calls for more individuality and the ever more crammed curriculum resulting from the latest revisions, and a comparison of the call for internationalisation with the emphasis on Japanese culture and national symbols like *Hinomaru* and *Kimigayo* can convince us of that. The way the two expressions were modified by NCER presented them in another rhetorical light. In this rhetoric individuality was about diversification of institutions and nurturing a few talented researchers, and internationalisation was about defining Japan's position in the world, about matching its power of cultural interjection and political influence to its economic power, about warding off American accusations of non-commitment to Japan's global responsibility. Internationally popular expressions were reinterpreted and changed to suit the ends of the NCER and the conservatives. The NCER rhetoric served both as an appeasement of criticism brought against Japanese education for being excessively standardised, focused on examinations, and against charges brought against Japan as a country for being xenophobic, racist and only interested in money. The very 'modern' rhetoric of the NCER was a defense, a call for agreement, and in this sense the key phrases of NCER *were* intended to be taken literally and understood as the opposition did.

The rhetoric clearly was based on conservative values. The modifications made on the key phrases by NCER demonstrated this. NCER's rhetoric covered a range of words with distinctively positive connotations to any Japanese, in this manner further eliciting agreement. These were words like *takumashii*, *chiiki*, *kenkoo*, *yutaka*, *handanryoku*, *hyoogenryoku*, *soozooryoku* and obviously also *kosei*, *kokusaika*, *shoogaigakushuu* and *joohooka*. All those words elicit agreement and recognition because they are used in public discourse and they indicate values one would hesitate to disagree with.

The confusing thing about the educational debate in Japan is that those termed 'conservatives' in this study are actually those working towards reform, and the 'progressives' hang on to the system initiated by the Allied Occupation Authorities. This has led to many accusations, particularly from officials in the Japanese bureaucracy, that the teachers who are generally critical of the government reform proposals for education, are actually the 'conservatives'. But this is confusing the issue and reducing the term 'conservative' to a semantic meaning without taking on the ideological connotations of the term. If we look at the rhetoric, there can be no doubt that the official proposals involving love for the nation, concern for manpower needs and liberalisation/privatisation as central concerns are indeed inspired by conservative values while the 'progressive' emphasis on democracy, peace and a global brotherhood are clearly not elements of the conservative rhetoric.

With the political turmoil going on at the moment it is difficult to make a prophesy about the position educational reform will hold in a new government, but the situation of political rupture is interestingly similar to the political situations when the previous great reform rounds took place, namely the *Meiji* Restoration and the Occupation period. Historically, one can make a case for saying that educational reform in Japan is possible only in situations of political instability, which is what we see now in Japan, so the conditions may become more favourable for reform in the coming years. But even if political changes are occurring, there seems to be no reason at the moment to suppose that the overall conservative policy will be given up. Other people will be in power perhaps, but they apparently are of much the same persuasion as the power-holders have been hitherto. We are certainly not looking at a left-wing take-over of power in Japan.

While political change is one important criterium for the realisation of educational reform, at the same time social instability would seem to have some influence. Instability of the social structure was certainly to be found during the two previous great reform periods, but what of now? There does not seem to be the kind of instability to make people reckless enough to be willing to risk the education of their children in order to get reform. The problem is, that any change may mean that a few age cohorts will, for example, be caught in a limbo between old and new practices, between old and new recruitment requirements, and no parents in their right minds would willingly take that risk (unless for other reasons, for example a child's unwillingness to walk the designated path). It must be noted, however, that until now this argument seems to have counted for little in political circles since parents are not asked directly for their opinions on educational reform. Their means of punishing the politicians is with their vote, but as LDP had been in a stable position for so long this could hardly have intimidated Prime Minister Nakasone in 1987. More probably, a revision of the educational system that would jeopardise its function as a social placement device was not on Nakasone's agenda and hence nothing fundamental was changed.

Surely, the system will change, but it will be a slow process and as it looks right now, it will be guided mainly by economic and manpower needs and the desire for national assertion. The surest path to a reform of the educational system would appear to be a revision of recruitment procedures. With new ways of recruiting and new means of evaluation, the risk faced by those who do not conform to the present standardised elite career structure will not be so great. A minimised risk may be another factor conditioning the likelihood of educational reform if social instability is not.

APPENDIX 1

INTERVIEW STRUCTURE AND ANALYSIS

In order to get further information on specific issues and make sure that all the parties I was dealing with were, at least at one point, answering the same questions, I decided from an early point in my project to use interviews as reference material to the publications I was going to use as central sources of information .

The emphasis was on written material because what is issued by an organisation in printed form is more certain to be an expression of policy and ideals than perhaps the utterances of an individual who, though asked to express organisational views, is bound to add a personal flavour. Written material may of course be just as individually coloured, but in the publishing process this has been accepted by the organisation responsible for the publication. Therefore the risk of mistaking one person's view for that of an organisation is considerably less.

As I wanted all parties to answer exactly the same questions — in so far as this is ever possible because we can interpret differently what we hear or read, I decided to use an interview guide. The questions were based on the five key areas which I had identified in the NCER reports. The interview also provided the opportunity for the interviewee to add his or her own opinion on what was of prime importance (the English version of the interview guide is shown in Appendix 2).

The qualitative interview was used because I was not interested in *how many* persons thought this or that, but in *what* particular individuals and organisations thought. Finally, it was not important whether what was said was 'true' or not, but rather it was important as a reflection of ideology and rhetoric.

Initially, I prepared a draft of the interview guide in English. In Japan I translated the guide into Japanese, and a Japanese teacher of Japanese for foreigners assisted me in comparing the intentions of the English and Japanese questions and we discussed the language at length. Finally, I persuaded Professor Fujita Hidenori of the Faculty of Education at Tokyo University to proofread the draft. On the advice of the Professor and the teacher of Japanese, I chose to use a handwritten guide. It would, as long as the writing was readable, be considered more polite towards the receiver if I submitted a handwritten copy of the guide, I was told.

The interview guide was mailed to the persons to be interviewed, and if they belonged to an organisation they were asked to present organisational views. The guide was mailed in advance for two reasons. One, it would be very difficult to get some of these people to agree to an interview if they did not know exactly what questions they would face. Not one of them failed to ask what the questions were like during initial phone conversations. However, due to delivery difficulties, the representative of JTU and Higuchi Keiko of the Women's Council on Education did the interviews without having previously seen the guide. The second reason for mailing the interview guide in advance was that by giving the interviewees a chance to prepare their answers the situation became less stressful for them. This proved particularly important with the teacher organisations where the persons interviewed were not accustomed to giving interviews, much less to a foreigner like myself. The JTU representative, deprived of the advantage of having seen the interview guide in advance, often found it difficult to answer, and the ATU representative was visibly nervous when I arrived but clearly found comfort in holding on to the guide and the prepared answers, though as the interview progressed, he spoke more and more freely.

Interviewees were selected from those whom I considered to be the main actors in the reform debate of the eighties, and on the advice of the professors at the Tokyo University Faculty of Education. The interviewees were first and foremost teacher organisations, the Ministry of Education and the National Council on Educational Reform. This meant dealing with rather important and busy people and I am very grateful to Professor Amano Ikuo of Tokyo University who counselled me in this. He introduced me to a colleague at the university, Professor Horio Teruhisa, who was known for his connections to the teacher organisations, and to Professor Saitoo Taijun of the University of the Air, a former official of the Ministry of Education, and both used their connections to help me obtain appointments.

Another important thing for even getting an appointment was language. The interviewees read English well enough, but very few would venture into an interview in English, let alone an interview in which they were to act as a representative of their organisation. Hence the interviews were conducted in Japanese and tape recorded. Later, they were transcribed and translated by myself into English.

The fact that I was a foreigner *and* a woman seemed to have some effect on the willingness of the prospective interviewees to accept a meeting. As one of the people helping me to establish contact said, 'those busy people will probably find the idea of meeting a Japanese-speaking foreign woman intriguing enough to find time for an interview'. Though all interviewees had been told that I was going to use the interviews for a PhD thesis, a few were very keen on being assured that the interview was not for the mass-media. This was the case for the Ministry of Education representative and the NCER representative in particular.

The form of the interview varied considerably. I usually negotiated the procedure with the interviewee before we began, and in one case the form ranged from my putting the questions one by one, to, in another case, the interviewee answering them in random order. The important thing was that all questions were in fact answered one way or the other and that all participants were comfortable with the situation.

The interviewees and the professors of Tokyo University were very helpful in recommending suitable material and I managed to collect a wide range.

Question 1: 'Present state of Japanese education'.

a) and b) aims at stating what the interviewee sees as particular problems in Japanese education, what are his or her special interest areas. Also, the questions are to determine to what degree interviewees agree on what exactly troubles education today.

c), d) and e) asks who influences education and who should influence it. These questions are to determine whether the interviewee feels that the system is centrally controlled or more 'democratic', whether all users have sufficient influence and whether they should or should not have influence.

f) asks if education is for the benefit of the state or for the individual and thus continues the line from the three previous questions. Education for the good of the state is a pre-war concept that the opposition often claims the government is still promoting. Nobody straight-forwardly said that education is for the good of the state, but there are several different ways of explaining who are the beneficiaries of education.

Question 2: 'Educational debate'.

a) asks for a list of topics that are the prime targets of argument for the individual or the organisation. This is again to find out what is most on their minds, and thus supports a) and b) of question 1. The term 'rigaikankei' ('interests') seemed to puzzle some of the interviewees somewhat, so it turned out to be valuable that there were two questions in the same line as it ensured that I got at least one answer to it.

b) also overlaps a) of question 1, but especially queries the particular strengths of Japanese education. It is a question that invites the well established tenets of Japanese education such as 'all children learn how to read and write' and 'Japanese children are the world's best when it comes to maths', 'there are no children who lag behind' etc.

c) To determine the main issues all interviewees were asked to name them. In this way not only the interviewees own opinion but also a wide range of subjects were expected to surface when the interviews were viewed as a whole.

Question 3: 'Government policy'.

a) requests an analysis of purposes, explanations of aims by both friends and adversaries. Issues of central control, standardisation etc. are likely to surface.

b) asks for the interviewee's own opinion on the previous question. Though it is usually quite clear whether they agree with the government or not, it was thought best to have the interviewee pinpoint this fact himself.

Question 4: 'Reform'.

a) is to find out whether the interviewee thinks that the system has for a long period — or always — been flawed, or if recent changes have resulted in a need to reform an, until then, well-functioning system. Ministry of Education publications often use the term 'due to rapid changes in society and technology' — do they agree with this?

The four main issues of educational reform, as I have deducted them from the NCER reports, follow as questions — are they truly areas that should be reformed, and if so in what way. b) is on individuality, *kosei*, c) on life long learning *shoogai gakushuu*, d) on internationalisation *kokusaika* and e) on the information society *joohoo shakai*. f) and g) ask if enough is being done and if not, why not. These questions are central in the interview as they deal concretely with the NCER reports. The answers cast light on the nature of the disagreement between government and opposition, and particularly on the motives attributed to the government by adversaries. Generally, those were the questions that took most time to answer but they were also most revealing as to the different interpretations of the NCER reports and the different ideals held.

Question 5: 'Participants in the educational debate'.

a) to d) are intended to cast light on *who* participates, *what* might be their goals, are the participants perceived to be ideologically involved and if so how? Also, the question aims at determining whether I should take other groups into account and who is seen to be important in the debate.

Question 6: 'The future'.

The questions here overlap some of the other questions, but the purpose of putting them is to make the interviewee share his or her ideals, dreams and visions with us and give a forecast on the future state of education. In this way ideas that the interviewee holds but which he/she has not found an outlet for in the interview, can hopefully be aired.

The interview usually ended with off-the-record chats on comparisons with Danish education, my project, and particular bits and pieces in Japanese education that the interviewee did not judge important enough to comment on in the actual interview. Those last remarks were not taped but I did take notes.

INTERVIEW GUIDE

The topic of this interview is educational reform, particularly the reforms contemplated by the *Rinji Kyooiku Shingikai* that Prime Minister Nakasone set up in 1984.

I would like to hear about your organisation's concept of education and educational purpose. Also, I am interested in your personal opinion on educational reform matters. I shall be very interested in hearing your opinion on what are important reform areas, how reforms should be carried out and what results have been obtained hitherto.

1. Present state of Japanese Education

   a)   What should Japanese education contain but doesn't?
   b)   What does it contain but shouldn't?
   c)   Do teachers have sufficient influence on education?
   d)   Should students have influence?
   f)   Education is for the good of whom? The State, the individual, both or something else?

2. Educational Debate

   a)   What is your organisation especially concerned with regarding educational reform?
   b)   What are the strong points of Japanese education?
   c)   What are the main issues in the public educational discussion?

3. Government Policy

   a)   What are the purposes of government policy on education?
   b)   Do you agree with this policy?

4. Reform

   a)   Is reform necessary and if so why is it/has it become necessary?
   b)   Enhancement of individuality. Is it necessary — how is it to be achieved?
   c)   Life-long learning. Necessary? Implemented how?

d)   Internationalisation. Necessary? How should it be done?
e)   Adaptation to the information society. Necessary? How is it best done?
f)   Are these areas being reformed by the government?
g)   If not, why not.

5. Participants in the Educational Debate

a)   Which groups or sectors of society etc. are concerned with educational reform?
b)   What are their respective purposes?
c)   Are there any 'schools of thought' in the educational debate?
d)   What or who are they?

6. The Future

a)   What are the three best things and the three worst things about Japanese education?
b)   What is the future for Japanese education — will it improve or will it deteriorate?
c)   If you were to describe ideal education what would it be like?

APPENDIX 3

LIST OF SPECIALIST MEMBERS OF NCER
(Appointed December 20, 1984)

Ishii Koichiroo | Chairman of the Board of Directors of Bridgestone Cycle Co. Ltd.

Ishino Seiji | Chairman, Social Welfare Judicial Person Imperial Gift Foundation Association for Maternal Child Health and Welfare; Chairman, Child Welfare Foundation of Japan; Executive Director, Shiseidoo Company, Ltd.

Kida Hiroshi | Director General, Japan Society for the Promotion of Science.

Kikuchi Sachiko | Professor, Bunkyoo University.

Koono Shigeo | Professor, Ochanomizu University.

Kumon Shumpei | Professor, Tokyo University.

Kuroha Ryooichi | Editorial Writer and Commentator, The Nihon Keizai Shimbun.

Onuma Sunao | Chairman of the Board of Trustees, Bunka Educational Institute; President, Bunka Women's University; Chairman, The National Association of Special Institutes of Japan.

Sakuma Tsutomu | Chairman, Chiba Keizai Gakuen; President, Chiba Keizai College.

Sengoku Tamotsu | Director, Japan Youth Research Institute; Lawyer.

Shimogawara Goroo | Principal, Koyamadai Upper Secondary School.

Takahashi Shiroo | Associate Professor, Meisei University.

Takanashi Akira | Professor, Shinshuu University.

Tawara Kootaroo | Critic; News Caster, Fuji Television Network Inc.

Toda Shuuzoo | Professor, Chuuoo University.

Tsubouchi Yoshio | Vice-President, National Recreation Association of Japan; Chairman, Diamond Inc.

Yaguchi Mitsuko | Representative Director, General Research Centre for Rural Life.

Yamamoto Shichihei | Critic; Owner of the Yamamoto Publishing House.

Yayama Taroo | Commentator and Editorial Writer, Jiji Press.

Watanabe Shooichi | Professor, Sophia University.

BIBLIOGRAPHY

Amano, Ikuo & Makoto Aso, 1972. *Education and Japan's Modernization*. Tokyo: Gaimushoo.

Amano, Ikuo 1984. 'Educational Reform in Historical Perspective' in *Japan Echo*, vol. xi, no. 3, p. 9-16.

Amano, Ikuo 1988a. 'The Dilemma of Japanese Education Today' in *The East*, vol. xxiv, no. 4, p. 42-7; no. 5, p. 42-5.

Amano, Ikuo 1988b. 'Educational Reforms in Modern Japan. Before and During the World War 2' in *Acta Asiatica — Bulletin of the Institute of Eastern Culture*, no. 54, p. 48-74, Tokyo: Toohoo Gakkai.

Amano, Ikuo 1988c. *Daigaku — Shiren no Jidai*. Tokyo: Tokyo Daigaku Shuppankai.

Amano, Ikuo 1990. *Kawaru Shakai, Kawaru Kyooiku*. Tokyo: Yuushindoo Koobunsha.

Amano, Ikuo 1990b. *Education and Examination in Modern Japan*. Tokyo: University of Tokyo Press.

Amano, Ikuo 1992. 'The Bright and Dark Sides of Japanese Education' in *The Japan Foundation Newsletter*, vol. xix, no. 5-6, May, p. 1-8.

Asahi, Shimbun 1987. 'Josei Minkyooshin. Kaikaku no Happyoo'. Sunday, June 14, p. 3.

Asahi, Shimbun 1987b. Articles from the year.

Ayuki, Machiko 1995. 'Ijime Hyakutooban kara no Hookoku' in *Shuukan Kinyoobi*, 6. 16, p. 44-5.

Beauchamp, Edward R. (ed.), 1978. *Learning to be Japanese*. Hamden, Conn.: Linnet Books.

Beauchamp, Edward R. 1984. 'Reform Traditions in the United States and Japan' in Cummings (ed.) *Educational Policies in Crisis — Japanese and American Perspectives*. London: Praeger, p. 3-22.

Benjamin, Gail R. 1991. 'Choices of Education in Japan' in *International Journal of Educational Research*, vol. 15, no. 3/4.

Bourdieu, Pierre 1990. *The Logic of Practice*. Oxford: Polity Press.

Bourdieu, Pierre 1992. *Language and Symbolic Power*. Oxford: Polity Press.

Christensen, S. & P.E. Daugård Jensen 1986. *Kontrol i det Stille — om magt og deltagelse* (Hidden Control — about Power and Participation). Copenhagen: Samfundslitteratur.

Conduit, Anne & Andy, 1996. *Educating Andy — The Experience of a Foreign Family in the Japanese Elementary School System*. Tokyo: Koodansha.

Croll, Elizabeth; Delia Davin, & Penny Kane (eds.), 1985. *China's One-Child Family Policy*. London: Macmillan.

Cummings, William K. 1978. 'The Conservatives Reform Higher Education', in Beauchamp (ed.), *Learning to be Japanese*, p. 216-328.

Cummings, William K. 1980. *Education and Equality in Japan*. Princeton, New Jersey: Princeton University Press.

Cummings, William K. (ed.), 1984. *Educational Policies in Crisis — Japanese and American Perspectives*. London: Praeger.

Dai Nihon Hyakka Jiten, 1967. Tokyo: Shoogakukan.

Dale, Peter 1990. *The Myth of Japanese Uniqueness*. London: Routledge. First published in 1986.

Defrancis, John 1984. *The Chinese Language, Fact and Fantasy*. Honolulu: University of Hawaii Press, p. 216-18.

Dore, Ronald 1965. *Education in Tokugawa Japan*. Berkeley: University of California Press.

Dore, Ronald 1978. 'The Legacy' in Beauchamp (ed.) *Learning to Be Japanese*, p. 13-41.

Duke, Benjamin C. 1973. *Japan's Militant Teachers*. Honolulu: University Press of Hawaii.

Duke, Benjamin C. 1978. 'The Textbook Controversy' in Beauchamp (ed.), *Learning to be Japanese*, p. 240-64.

Duke, Benjamin C. (ed.) 1989. *Ten Great Educators of Modern Japan*. Tokyo: University of Tokyo Press.

Eagleton, Terry 1991. *An Introduction to Ideology*. London: Verso.

East, The 1988. 'The Peculiar Dress Codes of Japanese Schools' in vol. xxiv, no. 4, Nov.-Dec., p. 48-51.

East, The 1993. 'The Rescue of Individuality — A Step Towards New Education' in vol. xxviii, no. 6, March-April, p. 38-9.

Education Council, 1985. 'A Proposition from Businessmen for Educational Reform' in Kawamura (ed.), *Discussions on Educational Reform in Japan*, p. 35-42.

Encyclopedia of Japan, 1983. vol. 2. Tokyo: Koodansha.

Fukuzawa, Yukichi 1969. *An Encouragement for Learning*. Tokyo: Sophia University.

GDCE (Group for Discussing Culture and Education), 1984. 'Main Points of the Report on Educational Reform' in Kawamura (ed.), *Discussions on Educational Reform in Japan*, p. 21-3.

Gill, Tom 1990. 'Nuts-and-Bolts Education' in *PHP Intersect*, March.

Goodman, Roger 1990. *Japan's 'International' Youth*. Oxford: Clarendon Press.

Goodman, Roger 1992. 'Japan — Pupil Turned Teacher?' in *Oxford Studies in Comparative Education*, vol. 1, Triangle Books, p. 155-73.

Goodman, R. & K. Refsing (eds.), 1992. *Ideology and Practice in Modern Japan*. London: Routledge.

Halpin, Keum Chu 1988. *Reform in University Governance in Japan: Case of the University of Tsukuba*. Michigan: U.M.I. Dissertation Information Service.

Hendry, Joy 1986. *Becoming Japanese*. Manchester: Manchester University Press.

Hendry, Joy 1989. 'An Interview with Chie Nakane' in *Current Anthropology*, vol. 30, no. 5, December, p. 643-9.

Hendry, Joy 1992. 'Individualism and Individuality: Entry into a Social World' in Goodman & Refsing (eds.), *Ideology and Practice in Modern Japan*, p. 55-71.

Hirabara, Haruko 1985. 'Rinji Kyooiku Shingikai "Shingi Keika no Gaiyoo (sono ni)" ni Tsurete' in Nihon Kyooiku Gakkai, *Kyooiku Kaikaku no Shomondai*, p. 32-45.

Hisatomi, Yoshiyuki 1987. 'Juku no Shinwa ga Kuzureru Hi' in Nihon Kyooiku Gakkai *Kyooiku Kaikaku to Kyooiku Jissen*, p. 39-47.

Horio, Teruhisa 1988. *Educational Thought and Ideology in Modern Japan*. Tokyo: University of Tokyo Press.

Horio, Teruhisa 1988b. 'Hendoo suru Gendai Shakai ni Okeru Kyooiku Kaikaku no Michisuji' in Nihon Kyooiku Gakkai, *Kyooiku Kaikaku no Kadai*, p. 3-9.

Horio, Teruhisa 1991. *Jinken toshite no Kyooiku*. Tokyo: Iwanami Shoten.

Hosogane, Tsuneo 1985. 'Daigaku Nyuushiki Seido Mondai to Jakkan no Kentoo Kadai' in Nihon Kyooiku Gakkai, *Kyooiku Kaikaku no Shomondai*, p. 46-52.

Ishikawa, Toshio 1991. 'Vocational Training' in the *Japanese Industrial Relations Series*. Tokyo: The Japan Institute of Labour.

James, Estelle & Gail Benjamin 1988. *Public Policy and Private Education in Japan*. London: Macmillan.

Japan Times Weekly, 1990. 'Nikkyooso Split Weakens Teachers' Unions', International Edition, May 21-27, p. 21.

Kavanagh, Dennis & Anthony Seldon, (eds.), 1989. *The Thatcher Effect: a Decade of Change*. Oxford: Clarendon.

Kawai, Akira 1986. 'Rinkyooshin no Ronri' in Nihon Kyooiku Gakkai, *Kyooiku Kaikaku to Kyooiku Kenkyuu*, p. 81-82.

Kawamura, Kinji (ed.), 1985. *Discussions on Educational Reform in Japan*. Tokyo: Foreign Press Centre.

Keizai Dooyuukai, 1984. 'A Proposition from Businessmen for Educational Reform' in Kawamura (ed.), *Discussions on Educational Reform in Japan*. Tokyo: Foreign Press Centre, p. 35-42.

Krauss, E.S., T.P. Rohlen, & P.C. Steinhoff, 1984. *Conflict in Japan*, Honolulu: University of Hawaii Press.

Kurosaki, Isao 1984. 'Jiyuuka Rinen no Kentoo — Kyooiku no Jijisei to Kookyoosei', in Nihon Kyooiku Gakkai, *Gendai Shakai to Gakkoo Seido*. Tokyo: Nihon Kyooiku Gakkai, p. 36-42.

Kusaoi, Akiko 1988. 'New Japanese Switch Jobs, Work Part-time' in *Japan Times Weekly*, International Edition, September 3, p. 4.

Kuwabara, Toshiaki 1988b. 'Kyooiku no Kokusaika to Kyooiku Kaikaku', in Nihon Kyooiku Gakkai, *Kyooiku Kaikaku no Kadai*. Tokyo: Nihon Kyooiku Gakkai, p. 47-54.

Kyoto Group, 1985. 'Seven Recommendations to Revitalise School Education' in Kawamura (ed.), *Discussions on Educational Reform in Japan*. Tokyo: Foreign Press Centre, p. 31-34.

Lebra, Takie Sugiyama 1992. 'Self in Japanese Culture', in Rosenberger (ed.), *Japanese Sense of Self*. Cambridge: Cambridge University Press, p. 105-20.

Lehmann, J.P. & Henny (eds.), 1988. *Themes and Theories in Modern Japanese History*. London: Athlone Press.

Lincicome, Mark 1993. 'Nationalism, Internationalism and the Dilemma of Educational Reform in Japan' in *Comparative Education Review*, vol. 37, no. 2, p. 123-51.

Livingston, Moor & Oldfather (eds.), 1973. *Postwar Japan, 1943 to the Present*. New York: Random House.

Logan, F.J. 1990. 'The Wooing of Yoohei' in *Intersect*, April, p. 8-12.

Lynn, Richard 1988. *Educational Achievement in Japan*. Basingstoke: Macmillan.

Mainichi, Shimbun, 1985. 'Josei Minkyooshin ni Kyooiku 110 Ban', May 2, p. 13.

Mainichi, Shimbun, 1985b. 'Rinkyooshin Tooshin — 42% ga "Shiranai"', July 17, p. 3.

Mainichi, Shimbun, 1985c. Articles from the year.

Marshall, Byron K. 1995. *Learning to Be Modern: Japanese Political Discourse on Education*. Boulder, Colorado: Westview Press.

Marsella, DeVos & Hsu (eds.), 1985. *Culture and Self*. London: Tavistock.

Mikami, Akiyoshi 1984. 'Kyooiku kaikaku rongi no zaikin no dookoo' in Nihon Kyooiku Gakkai, *Gendai Shakai to Gakkoo Seido*, p. 15-23.

Mikami, Mitsuru 1990. *Kyooiku ni Ai to Roman o*, Tokyo: Kamogawa Shuppan.

Minear, Richard H. 1980. 'Orientalising the Study of Japan' in *Journal of Asian Studies*, vol. xxxix, no. 3, May, p. 507-17.

Moeran, Brian 1989. *Language and Popular Culture in Japan*. Manchester: Manchester University Press.

Mogi, Chikako 1989. 'Hinomaru and Kimigayo Still Sensitive Symbols Here', in *Japan Times Weekly*, Overseas Edition, May 27, p. 6.

Monbushoo, 1987. 'Kyooiku Kaikaku no Suishin', in *Monbujihoo*, December issue. Tokyo: Gyoosei.

Monbushoo, 1989a. *Education in Japan. A Graphic Presentation*. Tokyo: Gyoosei.

Monbushoo, 1989b. *Nihon no Kyooiku*, Japan.

Monbushoo, 1989c. *Japanese Government Policies in Education, Science and Culture 1989*, Tokyo: Ookurasho Insatsukyoku.

Monbushoo, 1989d. *Waga Kuni no Bunkyoo Shisaku*, Tokyo: Ookurasho Insatsukyoku.

Monbushoo, 1990. *Waga Kuni no Bunkyoo Shisaku*, Tokyo: Ookurasho Insatsukyoku.

Monbushoo, 1992. *Waga Kuni no Bunkyoo Shisaku*, Tokyo: Ookurasho Insatsukyoku.

Monbushoo, 1993. *Gakushuujuku nado ni Kansuru Jittai Choosa*, Tokyo: Monbushoo.

Monbushoo, 1994. *Education in Japan. A Graphic Presentation*. Tokyo: Gyoosei.

Morikawa, Terumichi 1989. 'Mori Arinori' in Duke (ed.), *Ten Great Educators of Modern Japan*. Tokyo: University of Tokyo Press, p. 39-65.

Morita, Toshio 1988. *Rinkyooshin to Nihonjin — Nihon Bunka Ron*. Tokyo: Shin Nihon Shuppansha.

Morris-Suzuki, Tessa 1984. *Shoowa - an Inside Story of Hirohito's Japan*. London: Athlone Press.

Murakami, Yasusuke 1988. 'The Debt Comes Due for Mass Higher Education' in *Japan Echo*, vol. xv, no. 3, p. 71-84.

Mouer, R. & Y. Sugimoto 1986. *Images of Japanese Society*, London: Routledge.

Nakano, Akira 1989. 'Shimonaka Yasaburo (1878 — 1961)' in Duke, *Ten Great Educators of Japan*, p. 167-89.

Nakano, Akira 1989b. 'Moral Education in Modern Japan' from the series *Understanding Japan*. Tokyo: International Society for Educational Information Inc.

NCER, 1985. *First Report on Educational Reform*.

NCER, 1986. *Second Report on Educational Reform*.

NCER, 1987a. *Third Report on Educational Reform*.

NCER, 1987b. *Fourth and Final Report on Educational Reform*. Tokyo: Government of Japan.

Nihon Kyooiku Gakkai, Tokyo
1984. *Gendai Shakai to Gakkoo Seido*.
1985. *Kyooiku Kaikaku no Shomondai*.
1986. *Kyooiku Kaikaku to Kyooiku Kenkyuu*.
1987. *Kyooiku Kaikaku to Kyooku Jissen*.

1988a. *Gendai Shakai ni Okeru Kodomo no Hattatsu to Kyooiku Seido Kaikaku Genri no Kenkyuu.*

1988b. *Kyooiku Kaikaku no Kadai.*

Nikkyooso, 1991. *Kyooikukaikaku Toshite no Gakkoo Istukasei.* Tokyo: Nihon Kyooshokuin Kumiai.

Noguchi, Takuroo 1996. 'Shitsuke mo Bideomakase' in *AERA*, 11. 11, p. 12-13.

Oota,. Takashi 1987. 'Nihon Kyooiku Gakkai to Rinkyooshin e no Taioo', in Nihon Kyooiku Gakkai, *Kyooiku Kaikaku to Kyooiku Jissen*, p. 34-36.

Oota, Takashi 1988a. 'Matome', in Nihon Kyooiku Gakkai, *Gendai Shakai ni Okeru Kodomo no Hattatsu to Kyooiku Seido Kaikaku Genri no Kenkyuu*, p. 155-56.

Oota, Takashi 1988b. 'Hashigaki — Kyooiku Kaikaku to Kyooiku Gaku', in Nihon Kyooiku Gakkai, *Kyooiku Kaikaku no Kadai*, p. 1-2.

Oota, Haruo 1989. 'Political Teacher Unionism in Japan' in J.J. Shields (ed.), *Japanese Schooling*. University Park, Penn.: Pennsylvania State University, p. 243-59.

Ootsuki, Ken 1986. 'Kyooin no Jisshusei no Juujitsu ni Yotte Jisshuteki Ningen no Ikusei Suishin o', in Nihon Kyooiku Gakkai, *Kyooiku Kaikaku to kyooiku Kenkyuu*, p. 79-80.

Passin, Herbert 1982. *Society and Education in Japan*. Tokyo: Koodansha. First published in 1965.

Peak, Lois 1991. *Learning to Go to School in Japan*. Berkeley: University of California Press.

Pohl, Manfred 1988. *Japan 1987/88. Politik und Wirtschaft*. Hamburg: Institut für Asienkunde.

Reischauer, E.O. & A.M. Craig 1989. *Japan — Tradition and Transformation*. London: Allen & Unwin.

Reischauer, E.O. 1990. *The Japanese Today — Change and Continuity*. Tokyo: Tuttle.

Rinkyooshin, (Rinji Kyooiku Shingikai) 1988. *Kyooiku Kaikaku ni Kansuru Tooshin*. Tokyo: Ookurashoo Insatsukyoku.

Roesgaard, Marie H. 1991. 'Reform, Ideology and Practice — The Example of Tsukuba University'. Unpublished case-study, University of Aarhus.

Rohlen, Thomas P. 1983. *Japan's High Schools*. Berkeley: University of California Press.

Roppoo. (Kyooiku Shoroppoo) 1990. Gakuyoo Shoboo, Japan.

Rosario, Louise do, 1993. 'The Colours of Conformity' in *Far Eastern Economic Review*. June 17, p. 41.

Rosenberger, Nancy R. (ed.), 1992. *Japanese Sense of Self*. Cambridge: Cambridge University Press.

Sakata, Yoshio 1985. 'The Beginning of Modernization in Japan' in A.W. Burks (ed.), *The Modernizers*. Colorado: Westview Press.

Salaff, Janet W. 1985. 'The State and Fertility Motivation in Singapore and China' in Croll et al. (eds.), *China's One-Child Family Policy*. London: Macmillan, p. 162-89.

Schirokauer, Conrad 1978. *A Brief History of Chinese and Japanese Civilizations*. New York: Harcourt Brace Jovanovich.

Schoppa, Leonard J. 1991. *Education Reform in Japan: A Case of Immobilist Policies*. London: Routledge.

Shields, J.J. (ed.), 1989. *Japanese Schooling*. University Park, Penn.: Pennsylvania State University Press.

Shimizu, Kazuhiko (ed.), 1996. *Kyooiku Deetarando*. Tokyo: Jijitsuushinsha.

Shuukan Shinchoo, 1994. vol. 18, May 5-12, p. 56-8.

Soomuchoo, 1996. *Seishoonen Hakusho*, Tokyo: Ookurashoo Insatsukyoku. Statistics Bureau, 1992. *Japan Statistical Yearbook*. Tokyo.

Statistics Bureau, 1996. *Japan Statistical Yearbook*. Tokyo.

Steenstrup, Carl 1980. *Japans Idéhistorie*. Copenhagen: Berlingske Forlag.

Thelle, Notto R. 1991. *Hvem kan stoppe vinden?* Oslo: Universitetsforlaget.

Thurston, Donald R. 1973. *Teachers and Politics in Japan*. Princeton, N.J.: Princeton University Press.

Tobin, J.J.; D.Y.H. Wu; D.H. Davidson, 1989. *Pre-school in Three Cultures*. London: Yale University Press.

Tobin, J.J. 1992. 'A Dialogical Approach to the Probelem of Field-Site Typicality' in *City and Society*, Journal of the Society for Urban Anthropology, vol. 6, June, p. 46-57.

Tsukada, Mamoru 1984. 'A Factual Overview of Japanese and American Education' in W.K. Cummings (ed.), *Educational Policies in Crisis*. London: Praeger, p. 96-116.

Tsukuba, University of, 1988. *Tsukuba Daigaku no Jikohyooka to Kaikaku no Shihyoo*. Tsukuba.

Urano, Tooyooichi 1987. 'Rinkyooshin Daisanji Tooshin to Shintaku', in Nihon Kyooiku Gakkai, *Kyooiku Kaikaku to Kyooiku Jissen*, p. 37-8.

U.S. Department of Education, 1987. *Japanese Education Today*. Washington: USA.

WDCER, 1987. *Oya no Kyooiku Sekinin wa 18sai Made*, Tokyo.

Webster, Frank 1993. 'Misinformation' in *Times Higher*, October, 9.

Weisman, Steven R. 1992. 'For Japanese, Cramming for Exams Starts Where the Cradle Leaves Off' in *Herald Tribune* March 28, p. 1.

White, Merry 1987. *The Japanese Educational Challenge. A Commitment to Children*. New York: The Free Press.

White, Merry 1988. *The Japanese Overseas — Can They Go Home Again?* New York: The Free Press.

Wolferen, Karel van, 1989. *The Enigma of Japanese Power*. London: Macmillan.

Yasukawa, Jyuunosuke 1989. 'Fukuzawa Yukichi' in Duke (ed.), *Ten Great Educators of Modern Japan*, p. 17-37.

Yoyogi Seminaaru 1991. *Kaki Kooshuukai*. Tokyo: Yoyogi Seminaaru.

Zenkyoo, 1990. *Kodomo no Egao wa Watashi no Egao*, Tokyo: Zenkyoo Fujinbu Hakkoo.

Zenkyoo, 1990b. *Shoogai Gakushuu te Naani?*, Tokyo: Nihon Kyooshokuin Kumiai Kyoogikai.

Zenkyoo, 1991. *Kodomotachi e Ai to Shinrai no Suiro o*, Kyoto: Kamogawa Shuppan.

Other Sources

Damsgård, Kurt 1993. Feature on the National Danish Radio, March 4.

Higuchi, Keiko 1991. Critic, Professor at Tokyo Kasei Daigaku. Interview June 27, 1991.

Kawai, Naoki 1991. Head of Department of Education and Culture, ATU (Zen Nippon Kyooshokuin Kumiai). Interview May 16, 1991.

Kirkholm, Jørgen 1993. Feature on the National Danish Radio, January 17.

Kubo, Kaoru 1996. Personal communication.

Masuda, Takao, 1991. ATU Member. Interview, May 16, 1991.

Minakami, Tadashi 1991. Vice Managing Director, Edo-Tokyo Museum, and former member of NCER. Interview May 31, 1991.

Saitoo, Taijun 1991. Professor, University of the Air. Interview May 17, 1991.

Sakai, Tomiko 1991. Head of Department for Education and Culture, JTU (Nihon Kyooshokuin Kumiai). Interview May 7, 1991.

Satoo, Jiroo 1991. Director General, Ministry of Education. Interview June 6.

Index